# Deutsch 2000

# A Grammar
# of Contemporary
# German

## Max Hueber Verlag

DEUTSCH 2000
A Grammar of Contemporary German

by Renate Luscher and Roland Schäpers

adapted for English-speaking students
by Mary L. Apelt and Mary Snell

ISBN 3–19–02.1180–9
1. Auflage 1976
© 1976 Max Hueber Verlag München
Satz und Druck: Georg Appl, Wemding
Printed in Germany

# Preface

*A Grammar of Contemporary German* is a reference book of all grammatical forms commonly used in German today. It has been specially adapted for English-speaking students and can be used along with any modern German course. Those working with the course *Deutsch 2000* will find references to the text-book lessons of Books 1–3 where the grammar point under discussion is first introduced.

*A Grammar of Contemporary German* is a contrastive grammar based on examples. Hence rules are only given where they are really useful and the grammatical terminology has been reduced to a minimum; the grammatical tables have been explained in notes and illustrated by examples. Contrastive notes for English-speaking students can be found at the beginning of each main section and at relevant points throughout the book.

German as spoken and written today: this is both starting-point and goal of *A Grammar of Contemporary German.*

# Preface

# Contents

# The Verb

Verbs are unlikely to be the main problem for English-speaking students of German. Strong and weak verbs (*sing, sang, sung* as against *walk, walked),* regular and irregular verbs (*walk, walked* as against *go, went, gone*) and compound verbs (*to ring up, to put on*) all exist in English, while other features (variety of verb endings, different translations of *you,* verbs taking indirect objects, the existence of the subjunctive) will be familiar from other European languages. Real idiosyncrasies of German, which may present genuine difficulties for the English-speaking student, are the use of the subjunctive, some aspects of word order and the subtleties of the modal verbs.

## 1. Tenses

### A. Present (I, 1, 2, 3, 4, 11, 12)

**1 a. Forms**

| wohnen: | | arbeiten: | |
|---|---|---|---|
| ich | wohne | ich | arbeite |
| du | wohnst | du | arbeitest |
| er/sie | wohnt | er/sie | arbeitet |
| wir (sie, Sie) | wohnen | wir (sie, Sie) | arbeiten |
| ihr | wohnt | ihr | arbeitet |

**2** (1) The German infinitive ends in *-en* or *-n.*

> **wohnen, arbeiten, sammeln**   to live, to work, to collect

The same form is used for the 1st and 3rd Persons Plural (*wir, sie*) and for the formal mode of address (*Sie*) in singular and plural.

11

| | |
|---|---|
| **Wir wohnen** in Köln. | We live in Cologne. |
| **Die Kinder (sie) spielen** Fußball. | The children (they) are playing football. |
| Wo **arbeiten Sie**, Herr Meyer? | Where do you work, Mr Meyer? |
| Woher **kommen Sie**, meine Herren? | Where do you come from, gentlemen? |

The stem of the verb is the infinitive minus the *-en* or *-n* ending.

3  (2) Verbs whose stem ends in *-d-*, *-t-*, *-m-* or *-n-* (preceded by a consonant other than *l*, *r* or *h*) take an *-e-* between the stem and the ending. This enables the endings *-st* (*du*) and *-t* (*er/sie*) to be pronounced.

| | |
|---|---|
| arbeiten: | du arbeit**est**, er arbeit**et**, ihr arbeit**et** |
| finden: | du find**est**, er find**et**, ihr find**et** |
| atmen: | er atm**et** |
| rechnen: | du rechn**est**, er rechn**et**, ihr rechn**et** |
| but: | |
| lernen: | du lern**st**, er lern**t**, ihr lern**t** |

4  (3) Verbs ending in *-eln* drop the *-e-* of the stem in the 1st Person Singular (*ich*).

| | |
|---|---|
| klingeln: | ich kling**le** |
| sammeln: | ich samm**le** |

5  (4) Where the stem ends in *-s (ß)* or *-z-*, only *-t* is added in the 2nd Person Singular (*du*) instead of *-st*.

| | |
|---|---|
| reisen: | du reis**t** |
| heißen: | du heiß**t** |
| besitzen: | du besitz**t** |

6  **b. Irregular forms of modal verbs and „wissen"** (I, 8, 9, 19)

*Wissen* and the modal verbs *dürfen, können, müssen* and *wollen* have irregular forms in the singular.

| wissen: | ich | **weiß** |
|---|---|---|
| | du | **weißt** |
| | er/sie | **weiß** |
| | wir (sie, Sie) | wissen |
| | ihr | wißt |

| | dürfen: | können: | müssen: | wollen: |
|---|---|---|---|---|
| ich | **darf** | **kann** | **muß** | **will** |
| du | **darfst** | **kannst** | **mußt** | **willst** |
| er/sie | **darf** | **kann** | **muß** | **will** |
| wir (sie, Sie) | dürfen | können | müssen | wollen |
| ihr | dürft | könnt | müßt | wollt |

The modal verb *sollen* shows no change in the stem vowel: *ich (er/sie) soll, du sollst* etc. See p. 66.

## 7   c. The present tense of some irregular strong verbs (I, 8, 9, 10)

| geben: | ich | gebe | einladen: | ich | lade ein |
|---|---|---|---|---|---|
| | du | gibst | | du | lädst ein |
| | er/sie | gibt | | er/sie | lädt ein |
| | wir (sie, Sie) | geben | | wir (sie, Sie) | laden ein |
| | ihr | gebt | | ihr | ladet ein |
| essen: | ich | esse | fahren: | ich | fahre |
| | du | ißt | | du | fährst |
| | er/sie | ißt | | er/sie | fährt |
| | wir (sie, Sie) | essen | | wir (sie, Sie) | fahren |
| | ihr | eßt | | ihr | fahrt |
| nehmen: | ich | nehme | laufen: | ich | laufe |
| | du | nimmst | | du | läufst |
| | er/sie | nimmt | | er/sie | läuft |
| | wir (sie, Sie) | nehmen | | wir (sie, Sie) | laufen |
| | ihr | nehmt | | ihr | lauft |

Similarly:

| | |
|---|---|
| befehlen (befiehlt) | to command |
| besprechen (bespricht) | to discuss |
| betreffen (betrifft) | to concern |
| betreten (betritt) | to enter |
| sich bewerben (bewirbt sich) | to apply (for) |
| sich etw. brechen (bricht sich) | to break |
| erwerben (erwirbt) | to earn, acquire |
| gelten (gilt) | to be valid |
| helfen (hilft) | to help |
| lesen (liest) | to read |
| messen (mißt) | to measure |
| sehen (sieht) | to see |
| sprechen (spricht) | to speak |
| stehlen (stiehlt) | to steal |
| sterben (stirbt) | to die |
| treffen (trifft) | to meet |
| treten (tritt) | to tread |
| unterbrechen (unterbricht) | to interrupt |
| vergessen (vergißt) | to forget |
| vertreten (vertritt) | to represent |
| wegwerfen (wirft weg) | to throw away |
| zugeben (gibt zu) | to admit |
| anfangen (fängt an) | to begin |
| beitragen (trägt bei) | to contribute |
| beraten (berät) | to advise, debate |
| betragen (beträgt) | to amount to |
| empfangen (empfängt) | to receive, welcome |
| enthalten (enthält) | to contain |
| erhalten (erhält) | to receive, obtain |
| erlassen (erläßt) | to issue, enact |
| gefallen (gefällt) | to please |
| halten (hält) | to keep, hold |
| lassen (läßt) | to let |
| raten (rät) | to advise |

| | |
|---|---|
| schlafen (schläft) | to sleep |
| tragen (trägt) | to carry |
| sich unterhalten (unterhält sich) | to talk, enjoy oneself |
| sich verhalten (verhält sich) | to act, behave |
| verlassen (verläßt) | to leave |
| vorschlagen (schlägt vor) | to suggest |
| wachsen (wächst) | to grow |

Cf. List of Strong and Irregular Verbs, pp. 247 ff.

**8** German verbs are categorized as weak (see p. 11) and strong. The two groups differ basically in the preterite (see p. 23 ff.) and the past participle (see p. 17 ff.). In the present tense some strong verbs change the stem vowel in the 2nd and 3rd Persons Singular (*du* and *er/sie*):

$e \rightarrow i$ or *ie*
$a \rightarrow ä$
$au \rightarrow äu$

**9** Note:

(1) In all forms of the preterite and in the 2nd Pers. Sing. (*du*), the 2nd Pers. Pl. (*ihr*) and the 3rd Pers. Sing. (*er/sie*) of the present tense, *ß* appears instead of *ss*: *essen – du ißt, er ißt, ihr eßt; er aß.*

(2) *ß* appears after a long vowel, even when followed by a vowel or consonant: *er aß; er schließt; schließen.*
*ß* appears after a short vowel when in final position or when followed by a consonant: *iß!; er ißt.*
*ss* appears after a short vowel when followed by a vowel: *essen.*
NB. No *ß* in Swiss German!

#### d. The use of the present tense

The present tense denotes
**10** (1) the present state,

| | |
|---|---|
| Er **wohnt in Köln**. | He lives in Cologne. |
| Er **ist krank**. | He is sick. |

15

a present action (the -*ing* form in English),

| | |
|---|---|
| Er **arbeitet jetzt nicht**. | He's not working now. |
| Wo **gehst** du **hin**? | Where are you going? |

**11** (2) a present habit, frequently indicated by phrases such as *jede Woche*, *jeden Tag*, *zweimal im Jahr*,

| | |
|---|---|
| **Rauchen** Sie? | Do you smoke? |
| Ich **gehe jede Woche** ins Kino. | I go to the cinema every week. |
| Er **spielt jeden Tag** Klavier. | He plays the piano every day. |
| **Zweimal im Jahr mache** ich Urlaub. | I go on holiday twice a year. |

**12** (3) a continuous state or action beginning in the past (note: present perfect used in English),

| | |
|---|---|
| Er **ist seit einer Woche krank**. | He has been sick for a week. |
| Ich **warte schon zwei Stunden auf sie.** | I've been waiting for her for two hours. |

**13** (4) a future action, when used with adverbs of time like *nachher, morgen, in einer Stunde, nächsten Monat, nächstes Jahr* etc.,

| | |
|---|---|
| **Morgen fliege** ich nach Köln. | Tomorrow I'm flying to Cologne. |
| **Nächstes Jahr verbringe** ich meinen Urlaub in Griechenland. | Next year I'm spending my holiday in Greece. |
| **Heute abend gehe** ich ins Kino. | Tonight I'm going to the cinema. |

(5) a future action introduced by *wann* or *wenn*.

| | |
|---|---|
| **Wann besuchst** du uns? | When are you coming to see us? |
| **Wenn** du nach Deutschland **kommst**, **machen** wir eine Hafen-rundfahrt. | When you come to Germany, we'll go on a tour of the harbour. |

## B. Present Perfect (I, 10)

### a. Forms

### 14 Weak verbs

| spielen, arbeiten: | |
|---|---|
| ich | habe viel Klavier **gespielt** / viel **gearbeitet** |
| du | hast |
| er/sie | hat |
| wir (sie, Sie) | haben |
| ihr | habt |

| wandern: | |
|---|---|
| ich | bin früher viel **gewandert** |
| du | bist |
| er/sie | ist |
| wir (sie, Sie) | sind |
| ihr | seid |

### 15 Strong verbs

| lesen: | |
|---|---|
| ich | habe das Buch schon **gelesen** |
| du | hast |
| er/sie | hat |
| wir (sie, Sie) | haben |
| ihr | habt |

| bleiben: | |
|---|---|
| ich | bin gestern zu Hause **geblieben** |
| du | bist |
| er/sie | ist |
| wir (sie, Sie) | sind |
| ihr | seid |

Formation of the present perfect:

present tense forms of $\frac{haben}{sein}$ + past participle

For the past participles of the strong verbs, see pp. 247 ff.
NB. In normal German word order the past participle is placed at the end of the clause.

### b. „haben" or „sein"?

**16** In English, the present perfect is always formed with the auxiliary *to have*. Similarly, most German verbs form their present perfect with the auxiliary *haben*.

These include:

**17** (1) transitive verbs (i. e. verbs which can take a direct object)

| | |
|---|---|
| **lesen** | |
| *Hast* du das Buch schon *gelesen?* | Have you already read the book? |
| **vergessen** | |
| Ich *habe* die Einladung *vergessen.* | I forgot the invitation. |
| **anrufen** | |
| Er *hat* mich gestern *angerufen.* | He rang me up yesterday. |

**18** (2) reflexive verbs

| | |
|---|---|
| **sich ansehen** | |
| Wir *haben uns* den Film schon *angesehen.* | We have already seen the film. |
| **sich verabreden** | |
| Ich *habe mich* mit meinen Eltern zum Abendessen *verabredet.* | I'm going out with my parents for dinner. |
| **sich wünschen** | |
| Ich *habe mir* zum Geburtstag eine Uhr *gewünscht.* | I've asked for a watch for my birthday. |

**19** (3) impersonal verbs

> **regnen**
> Gestern *hat* es den ganzen Tag *geregnet*.
>
> **schneien**
> In den Alpen *hat* es schon *geschneit*.

| Yesterday it rained all day. |
| It has already snowed in the Alps. |

Some verbs, however, form their present perfect with *sein:*

**20** (1) intransitive verbs denoting a change in condition,

> **vergehen**
> Die Ferien *sind* schnell *vergangen*.
>
> **wachsen**
> Das Kind *ist* schnell *gewachsen*.
>
> **werden**
> Sie *ist* Lehrerin *geworden*.

| The holidays have gone quickly. |
| The child grew fast. |
| She became a teacher. |

**21** (2) verbs of motion denoting a change of place,

> **fahren**
> Er *ist* zu seinem Bruder *gefahren*.
>
> **gehen**
> Wir *sind* gestern ins Kino *gegangen*.
>
> **kommen**
> Meine Eltern *sind* heute *gekommen*.
>
> **laufen**
> Wir *sind* eine halbe Stunde zum Bahnhof *gelaufen*.

| He drove to his brother's. |
| We went to the cinema yesterday. |
| My parents came today. |
| We walked half an hour to the station. |

**22** (3) *sein* and *bleiben*,

| | |
|---|---|
| **sein** | |
| *Sind* Sie gestern im Büro *gewesen?* | Were you in the office yesterday? |
| **bleiben** | |
| Ich *bin* nur einen Tag in Berlin *geblieben.* | I only stayed in Berlin for a day. |

**23** (4) the following defective verbs (3rd Pers. Sing. only):

| | |
|---|---|
| **gelingen** | |
| Es *ist* mir *gelungen*, ihn zu überzeugen. | I managed to convince him. |
| **geschehen** | |
| Ihm *ist* nichts *geschehen.* | Nothing happened to him. |
| **passieren** | |
| *Ist* bei dem Unfall etwas *passiert?* | Was anyone hurt in the accident? |
| **vorkommen** | |
| Es *ist* schon häufig *vorgekommen*, daß das Telefon nicht funktioniert. | It's happened quite a lot that the telephone doesn't work. |

### c. Formation of the past participle

**24** (1) The past participle of regular weak verbs is formed by adding a *-t* to the stem. Most verbs also take the prefix *ge-*.

| | |
|---|---|
| wandern: | gewander**t** |
| spielen: | gespiel**t** |
| hören: | gehör**t** |

*-et* is added to verb stems ending in *-t* or *-d*.

| | |
|---|---|
| arbeiten: | gearbeit**et** |
| warten: | gewart**et** |
| beenden: | beend**et** |

**25** (2) The past participle of strong verbs is formed by adding *-en* to the stem and (sometimes) changing the vowel. Most verbs take the prefix *ge-*.

| | |
|---|---|
| lesen: | gel**es**en |
| gehen: | g**e**gang**en** |
| beschreiben: | beschr**ieben** |

**26** (3) *ge-* appears in the past participle of all verbs whose first syllable is stressed.

**árbeiten**

| | |
|---|---|
| Die Studenten haben in den Ferien *gearbeitet*. | The students worked during the vacation. |

**spréchen**

| | |
|---|---|
| Haben Sie Herrn Meier schon *gesprochen*? | Have you already spoken to Mr Meier? |

**fáhren**

| | |
|---|---|
| Er ist sehr schnell *gefahren*. | He drove very fast. |

**27** (4) In separable verbs, *-ge-* is placed between the prefix and the verb stem.

**sich ánsehen**

| | |
|---|---|
| Wir haben uns den Film schon *angesehen*. | We have already seen the film. |

**ábholen**

| | |
|---|---|
| Haben Sie die Tickets *abgeholt*? | Did you fetch the tickets? |

**zurúckkommen**

| | |
|---|---|
| Meiers sind gestern aus dem Urlaub *zurückgekommen*. | The Meiers came back from their holiday yesterday. |

**28** (5) Verbs with an unstressed first syllable form the past participle without the prefix *ge-*.

| | |
|---|---|
| verbs ending in *-ieren:* | |
| **studíeren** | |
| Er hat in Frankfurt *studiert.* | He studied in Frankfurt. |
| **passíeren** | |
| Bei dem Unfall ist nichts *passiert.* | Nobody was hurt in the accident. |
| **fotografíeren** | |
| Er hat im Urlaub viel *fotografiert.* | On holiday he took a lot of photos. |
| inseparable verbs: | |
| **bestéllen** | |
| Sie hat einen Kaffee *bestellt.* | She has ordered a coffee. |
| **bezáhlen** | |
| Wir haben die Rechnung schon *bezahlt.* | We have already paid the bill. |
| **entstéhen** | |
| Die neue Schule ist in einem Jahr *entstanden.* | The new school was built in one year. |
| **sich erhólen** | |
| Er hat sich gut *erholt.* | He ist well rested. |
| **intervíewen** | |
| Er hat die Passanten *interviewt.* | He interviewed the passers-by. |
| **überprüfen** | |
| Er hat die Maschine *überprüft.* | He checked the machine. |
| **sich unterhálten** | |
| Wir haben uns gut *unterhalten.* | We had a nice conversation. |
| **verbíeten** | |
| Rauchen *verboten.* | No smoking. |

## C. Preterite (I, 16)

### a. Forms

**29 Regular weak verbs**

| sagen: | | arbeiten: | |
|--------|--------|-----------|-----------|
| ich (er/sie) | sag**te** | ich (er/sie) | arbeit**ete** |
| du | sag**test** | du | arbeit**etest** |
| wir (sie, Sie) | sag**ten** | wir (sie, Sie) | arbeit**eten** |
| ihr | sag**tet** | ihr | arbeit**etet** |

**30 Strong verbs**

| geben: | | | |
|--------|--------|----------------|--------|
| ich (er/sie) | g**a**b | wir (sie, Sie) | g**a**ben |
| du | g**a**bst | ihr | g**a**bt |
| laufen: | | | |
| ich (er/sie) | l**ie**f | wir (sie, Sie) | l**ie**fen |
| du | l**ie**fst | ihr | l**ie**ft |
| fliegen: | | | |
| ich (er/sie) | fl**o**g | wir (sie, Sie) | fl**o**gen |
| du | fl**o**gst | ihr | fl**o**gt |
| fahren: | | | |
| ich (er/sie) | f**u**hr | wir (sie, Sie) | f**u**hren |
| du | f**u**hrst | ihr | f**u**hrt |

**31** (1) Regular weak verbs whose stem ends in -*d*-, -*t*-, -*m*- or -*n*- (preceded by a consonant other than *r*, *l* or *h*) take an -*e*- between the stem and the ending in all forms.

| arbeiten: | er arbeit**ete** |
|-----------|------------------|
| kosten: | es kost**ete** |
| sich verabreden: | sie verabred**eten** sich |

| | |
|---|---|
| atmen: | er atm**ete** |
| regnen: | es regn**ete** |
| rechnen | sie rechn**eten** |
| but: | |
| warnen: | er war**nte** |
| wohnen: | wir woh**nten** |

**32** (2) Strong verbs change their stem vowel in the preterite, sometimes even the whole stem.

| | | | |
|---|---|---|---|
| gehen: | er **ging** | sitzen: | sie sa**ß**en |
| kommen: | wir k**am**en | stehen: | ich st**and** |

The past tense forms (preterite and past participle) of the strong verbs are listed on pp. 247 ff.

**33** NB. The infinitive gives no clue as to whether a verb is strong or weak, regular or irregular. To conjugate a German verb correctly, it is best to learn the principal parts (infinitive, 3rd. Pers. Sing. Present, preterite and past participle). With some old Germanic verbs, especially those in common use and dealing with everyday matters, there is a distinct similarity in German and English:

| | | | | | |
|---|---|---|---|---|---|
| trinken | trank | getrunken | drink | drank | drunk |
| singen | sang | gesungen | sing | sang | sung |
| kommen | kam | gekommen | come | came | come |
| geben | gab | gegeben | give | gave | given |

**34 b. Irregular forms of some weak verbs** (III, 3, 19)

| | Present | Preterite | Present Perfect |
|---|---|---|---|
| kennen: | er kennt | kannte | hat gekannt |
| nennen: | er nennt | nannte | hat genannt |
| rennen: | er rennt | rannte | ist gerannt |

24

| bringen: | er bringt | brachte | hat gebracht |
|---|---|---|---|
| denken: | er denkt | dachte | hat gedacht |
| senden[1]: | er sendet | sandte | hat gesandt |
| sich wenden an: | er wendet sich | wandte sich | hat sich gewandt |

Modal verbs:

| dürfen: | er darf | durfte | |
|---|---|---|---|
| können: | er kann | konnte | (see Infinitive, |
| müssen: | er muß | mußte | p. 51) |
| wissen: | er weiß | wußte | hat gewußt |

Some regular verbs change their vowel in the preterite and present perfect.
The modal verbs *dürfen, müssen* and *können* lose the umlaut in these
tenses: *ich durfte, habe gedurft; ich konnte, habe gekonnt.*

**35**

| | Present | Preterite | Present Perfect |
|---|---|---|---|
| erschrecken: | er erschrickt | erschrak | ist erschrocken |
| sich erschrecken: | er erschreckt sich | erschrak sich | hat sich erschrocken |
| (jemand) erschrecken: | er erschreckt | erschreckte | hat erschreckt |
| schaffen: | er schafft | schuf | hat geschaffen |
| | er schafft | schaffte | hat geschafft |

Some verbs can be conjugated both regularly and irregularly. Note the
difference in meaning (III, 3, 19):

| | |
|---|---|
| Als plötzlich das Telefon klingelte, **erschrak** sie. | When suddenly the telephone rang, she got a fright. |
| Jetzt hast du mich aber **erschreckt!** | What a fright you gave me! |

---

[1] Note: *senden, er sendet, sendete, hat gesendet* (Das Fernsehen hat gestern einen interessanten Film *gesendet.* – There was an interesting film on television yesterday). But: Die Firma hat die Ware sofort *gesandt.* The firm sent the goods immediately.

| | |
|---|---|
| Beethoven **schuf** neun Sinfonien. | Beethoven composed nine symphonies. |
| Klaus hat das Examen nicht **ge-schafft**. | Klaus didn't pass the exam. |

**36  c. The use of the past tenses (present perfect and preterite)**

Both the present perfect and the preterite denote actions or events that took place in the past. There is no basic difference in meaning between the two tenses as there is in English, and in German both can often be used to express either of the English past tenses.

**37**  There are, however, some general rules governing the usage of the past tenses in German:

(1) The preterite is the past tense of historical narrative and is used in independent reports for matters in which the speaker or writer was not directly involved. In conversation, however, when someone is talking about himself or other people, the present perfect is used.

| | |
|---|---|
| Example 1: | |
| „Wo **haben** Sie denn Ihren Urlaub **verbracht**?" | "Where did you spend your holiday?" |
| „In Österreich." | "In Austria." |
| „Und was **haben** Sie **gemacht**? **Haben** Sie Sport **getrieben**?" | "And what did you do? Did you do any sport?" |
| „Nein, aber ich **bin** viel **gewandert** und **habe** auch viel **fotografiert**." | "No, but I did a lot of walking and I also took a lot of photos." |
| | |
| Example 2: | |
| „Gestern **habe** ich eine Karte von meinem Freund Hans Mayer aus Brasilien **bekommen**. Er **hat** dort vor zwei Jahren eine Firma **ge-gründet**. Vorige Woche **hat** er **ge-heiratet**." | "Yesterday I had a card from my friend Hans Mayer in Brazil. He started a company there two years ago. Last week he got married." |

26

In a newspaper report, however, the preterite would be used.

### Example 1:

| | |
|---|---|
| Auch in diesem Jahr **verbrachte** Herr X. seinen Urlaub in Österreich. Er **trieb** keinen Sport, aber er **widmete sich** seinem Hobby, der Fotografie. | This year Mr. X. again spent his holiday in Austria. He didn't go in for any sport, but devoted himself to his hobby, photography. |

### Example 2:

| | |
|---|---|
| In der vorigen Woche **heiratete** Hans Mayer. Er lebt seit langer Zeit in Brasilien, wo er vor zwei Jahren eine Firma **gründete**. | The wedding took place last week of Mr Hans Mayer. He has been living for some time in Brazil, where he started a company two years ago. |

### Example 3:

| | |
|---|---|
| Herr Müller, der Chef einer Automobilfabrik, sagt abends zu seiner Frau: „Heute **hat** mich ein französischer Wissenschaftler **besucht**. Nach dem Essen **sind** wir ins Deutsche Museum **gegangen**." | In the evening, Mr Müller, the manager of a motor-car factory, said to his wife: "Today a French scientist came to visit me. After lunch we went to the Deutsche Museum." |

The following day this appears in the newspaper:

| | |
|---|---|
| Der französische Wissenschaftler Professor Dupont **besuchte** gestern den Chef unserer Automobilfabrik. Nach dem Essen **gingen** die Herren ins Deutsche Museum. | Yesterday the French scientist Professor Dupont visited the manager of our motor-car factory. After lunch the two gentlemen went to the Deutsche Museum. |

(2) The preterite denotes habit or repeated action (English "used to" and "would") and simultaneous action (English past continuous tense).

| | |
|---|---|
| Damals **ging** ich jede Woche ins Theater. | In those days I used to go to the theatre every week. |

| Während ich in der Küche **arbeite-te**, las er Zeitung. | While I was working in the kitchen, he read the paper. |

Note also these special cases:

**38** (1) With *sein* and *haben* the present perfect is often preferred, even in direct speech, and especially when the sentence is introduced by an adverb of time.

| **Vorige Woche war** ich in Köln. (for: **Vorige Woche bin** ich in Köln **gewesen**.) | Last week I was in Cologne. |
|---|---|
| **Letztes Jahr war** ich in Afrika. (for: **Letztes Jahr bin** ich in Afrika **gewesen**.) | Last year I was in Africa. |
| **Gestern abend hatten** wir Besuch. (for: **Gestern abend haben** wir Besuch **gehabt**.) | Last night we had some visitors. |
| **Am Wochenende hatte** ich wenig Zeit. (for: **Am Wochenende habe** ich wenig Zeit **gehabt**.) | At the weekend I had little time. |

**39** (2) In questions, the present perfect and the preterite are used indiscriminately.

| **Waren** Sie schon mal in Italien? (= **Sind** Sie schon mal in Italien **gewesen**?) | Have you ever been to Italy? |
|---|---|
| **Hatten** Sie schönes Wetter? (= **Haben** Sie schönes Wetter **gehabt**?) | Did you have good weather? |

28

**40** (3) The present perfect form of the modal verbs is uncommon, even in direct speech.

| | |
|---|---|
| Gestern **mußte** er nach Köln **fliegen**. (for: Gestern **hat** er nach Köln **fliegen müssen**.) | Yesterday he had to fly to Cologne. |
| Letzten Sonntag **wollten** sie ihre Eltern **besuchen**. (for: Letzten Sonntag **haben** sie ihre Eltern **besuchen wollen**.) | Last Sunday they wanted to visit their parents. |

**D. Past Perfect** (I, 21; II, 9)

**a. Forms**

**41 Weak verbs**

spielen, arbeiten:

| | |
|---|---|
| ich (er/sie) | hatte viel Klavier **ge**spiel**t**/viel **ge**arbeit**et** |
| du | hattest |
| wir (sie, Sie) | hatten |
| ihr | hattet |

wandern:

| | |
|---|---|
| ich (er/sie) | war **ge**wander**t** |
| du | warst |
| wir (sie, Sie) | waren |
| ihr | wart |

29

| lesen: | |
|---|---|
| ich (er/sie) | hatte das Buch schon **gelesen** |
| du | hattest |
| wir (sie, Sie) | hatten |
| ihr | hattet |

| bleiben: | |
|---|---|
| ich (er/sie) | war zu Hause **geblieben** |
| du | warst |
| wir (sie, Sie) | waren |
| ihr | wart |

Formation of the past perfect:

preterite of $\begin{array}{c}\textit{haben}\\\textit{sein}\end{array}$ + past participle[1]

## 43  b. The use of the past perfect

The past perfect is mainly used in conjunction with the preterite. It refers to a point further back in time than the point of narrative in a text written in the preterite. This is very similar to the use of the past perfect in English.

> Example 1:
>
> Herr Fuchs wollte nach Frankfurt fliegen. Er nahm ein Taxi und fuhr zum Flughafen. Aber er konnte nicht fliegen, weil er sein Ticket **vergessen hatte**.
>
> Mr Fuchs wanted to fly to Frankfurt. He took a taxi and drove to the airport. But he couldn't get on the plane because he had forgotten his ticket.

---

[1] For the use of *haben* or *sein* to form the perfect tenses, see p. 18 ff.

**Example 2:**

| Zuerst sprach ein Vertreter der Gewerkschaft, dann ein Sprecher der Partei. Nachdem alle Redner **gesprochen hatten**, begann die Diskussion. | First a union representative spoke, then a speaker for the party. When all the speakers had finished, the discussion was thrown open to the floor. |
|---|---|

**Example 3:**

| Herr Fuchs fuhr mit dem Taxi zum Bahnhof. Aber er kam zu spät. Als er ankam, **war** der Zug schon **abgefahren**. | Mr Fuchs took a taxi to the station. But he was too late. When he arrived, the train had already left. |
|---|---|

**Example 4:**

| „Marion hat gestern auf dich gewartet!" | "Marion was waiting for you yesterday!" |
|---|---|
| „So? Das tut mir leid. Ich **hatte** ihr doch **gesagt**, daß ich nicht kommen könnte." | "Really? I'm sorry. But I had already told her I couldn't come." |

## E. Future and Future Perfect (II, 21, 22; III, 2)

**44 a. Forms**

| schreiben: | |
|---|---|
| ich | werde sofort schreiben |
| du | wirst |
| er/sie | wird |
| wir (sie, Sie) | werden |
| ihr | werdet |

Formation of the future: present of *werden* + infinitive
Note that the infinitive goes to the end of the clause.

### b. The use of the future and future perfect

**45** (1) The future tense corresponds in general to the English future (with *shall, will, going to* etc.). Like the present tense when used with adverbs of future time, it denotes an event that is to take place in the future.

| | |
|---|---|
| Nächste Woche **werde** ich in die Schweiz **fahren**. ( = Nächste Woche **fahre** ich in die Schweiz.) | Next week I'll be going to Switzerland. |

Whereas the present tense is used when the future action is absolutely certain, the future tense only indicates the speaker's intention to do something. It is therefore commonly used with inexact expressions of time.

| Example 1: | |
|---|---|
| Am Dienstag um 9 Uhr **fliegt** der Bundeskanzler in die USA. | The Chancellor will fly to the U.S.A. on Tuesday at 9 a. m. |
| But: Der Bundeskanzler **wird** noch in diesem Sommer in die USA **fliegen**. | The Chancellor is to fly to the U.S.A. before the summer is over. |

The second sentence, where the future tense is used, expresses the intention but does not indicate a specific time or date. (Something could still happen to prevent it.)

| Example 2: | |
|---|---|
| „Was machst du denn heute abend?" | "What are you doing tonight?" |
| „Das weiß ich noch nicht. Zuerst **werde** ich mal ein riesiges Schnitzel **essen**, dann lese ich Zeitung, und vielleicht gehe ich später ins Kino." | "I don't know yet. First I'm going to eat an enormous schnitzel, then I'll read the paper and maybe go to the cinema later on." |

**46** (2) *Werden* is also used to express an assumption; this has nothing to do with the future (III, 2).

| | |
|---|---|
| **Example 1:** | |
| Herr Schulz **wird** (sicher) 3000 Mark im Monat **verdienen**. (= Ich nehme an, daß Herr Schulz 3000 Mark im Monat **verdient**.) | Mr Schulz probably earns 3000 marks a month. (= I assume that Mr Schulz earns 3000 marks a month.) |
| **Example 2:** | |
| Er **wird** jetzt zu Hause **sein**. (= Vermutlich ist er jetzt zu Hause.) | He'll probably be at home now. |
| **Example 3:** | |
| Die Stadt, in der ich geboren bin, **werden** Sie nicht **kennen**. (= Ich nehme an, daß Sie sie nicht kennen, weil es eine kleine, ziemlich unbekannte Stadt ist.) | You won't know the town where I was born. (= I presume you don't know it, as it's a small town and not well known.) |

**47** Note:

A similar meaning is commonly expressed by the future perfect.

| | |
|---|---|
| **Example 1:** | |
| „Wissen Sie, wieviel Herr Mayer in Brasilien verdient hat?" „Nein, das weiß ich nicht. Aber er **wird** jedenfalls gut **verdient haben**, sonst wäre er nicht so lange geblieben." | "Do you know how much Mr Mayer earned in Brazil?" "No, I don't. But at any rate he must have earned well – otherwise he wouldn't have stayed so long." |

33

| Example 2: | |
|---|---|
| Sie **werden** Herrn Müller nicht mehr **gekannt haben.** Sie sind ja noch viel zu jung. (= Sie haben Herrn Müller sicher nicht mehr **gekannt**.) | You wouldn't have known Mr Müller. You're much too young. |

## 2. Subjunctive and Imperative

**48** There are two basic forms of the subjunctive in German: the present subjunctive and the past subjunctive.

**49  a. The present subjunctive** (II, 24)

Modern English only has a few relics of the subjunctive (e. g. If *I were* you . . .), and English-speaking students of foreign languages often have difficulty in making it out. In German the subjunctive is the mood of indirect statement and of supposed or unreal condition. It has two forms, the present subjunctive and the past subjunctive (see p. 36 ff).

| | |
|---|---|
| Er sagte, die Stadt **brauche** mehr Schulen. | He said the town needed more schools. |
| Er sagte, in dieser Stadt **gebe** es viele Theater. | He said there were a lot of theatres in that town. |
| Er glaubte, Herr Meier **habe** schon eine neue Stelle. | He thought Mr Meier already had a new job. |
| Sie meinte, die Ware **sei** zu teuer. | She thought the goods were too expensive. |

Where English indicates indirect speech by a change in tense, German uses the subjunctive. The tense of the original direct speech is retained, as long as the subjunctive and indicative forms of the verb are not identical (see (2) below). As indirect speech mainly reports the opinion or statement of a third person, the 3rd Person forms of the German present subjunctive are particularly important.

34

**50**  (1) In the present subjunctive, the 3rd Pers. Sing. always ends in *-e*.

| | | |
|---|---|---|
| brauchen: | er brauche | (Indicative: er braucht) |
| geben: | es gebe | (Indicative: es gibt) |
| haben: | er habe | (Indicative: er hat) |

**51**  (2) In spoken language the present and past subjunctive are often freely interchangeable.

| | |
|---|---|
| Sie sagte, die Ware **sei** zu teuer. (= Sie sagte, die Ware **wäre** zu teuer.) | She said the goods were too expensive. |

But when the present subjunctive form is identical with the indicative, the past subjunctive is used.

| | |
|---|---|
| Er glaubte, ich **hätte** schon eine Stelle. (for: habe) | He thought I'd already got a job. |
| Sie meinte, wir **hätten** genug Zeit. (for: haben) | She thought we had enough time. |

**52**  (3) The present subjunctive forms of *sein* are irregular. *Sein* is most commonly used in the 3rd Persons Singular and Plural.

| | |
|---|---|
| sein: | er sei |
| | sie seien |

**53**  (4) Examples:

| | |
|---|---|
| Inge sagte am Telefon: „Klaus ist für ein Jahr ins Ausland gegangen." | Inge said on the telephone, "Klaus has gone abroad for a year." |
| Inge sagte am Telefon, Klaus **sei** für ein Jahr ins Ausland gegangen. | Inge said on the telephone that Klaus had gone abroad for a year. |

| | |
|---|---|
| „Für ein neues Gesetz braucht die Regierung mehr Zeit", sagte der Minister. | "For a new law the government needs more time", said the minister. |
| Der Minister sagte, für ein neues Gesetz **brauche**[1] die Regierung mehr Zeit. | The Minister said the government needed more time for a new law. |
| „Das System ist nicht gerecht", meinte der Sprecher. | "The system isn't just", said the speaker. |
| Der Sprecher meinte, das System **sei** nicht gerecht. | The speaker said the system wasn't just. |
| Klaus schreibt: „Das ganze Wochenende habe ich auf euch gewartet." | Klaus writes, "I've been waiting for you the whole weekend." |
| Klaus schreibt, das ganze Wochenende **habe** er auf uns gewartet. | Klaus writes that he's been waiting for us the whole weekend. |

## b. The past subjunctive (II, 12, 14, 15)

**54 Regular weak verbs**

brauchen:

| | |
|---|---|
| ich (er/sie) | brauchte |
| du | brauchtest |
| wir (sie, Sie) | brauchten |
| ihr | brauchtet |

---

[1] In South German also *bräuchte*.

**55**  **Strong verbs**

| schreiben: | | geben: | haben: | sein: |
|---|---|---|---|---|
| ich (er/sie) | schriebe | gäbe | hätte | wäre |
| du | schriebest | gäbest | hättest | wärest |
| wir (sie, Sie) | schrieben | gäben | hätten | wären |
| ihr | schriebet | gäbet | hättet | wäret |

**56**  (1) The past subjunctive forms of regular weak verbs are identical with the forms of the preterite indicative.

| brauchen: | ich (er/sie) brauchte |
|---|---|

**57**  (2) The past subjunctive forms of strong verbs all take an -e- in their endings. An umlaut occurs if the stem vowel is *a, o* or *u*.

| schreiben: | ich (er/sie) schriebe | (Indicative: ich (er/sie) schrieb) |
|---|---|---|
| geben: | ich (er/sie) gäbe | (Indicative: ich (er/sie) gab) |

**58**  (3) The past subjunctive is also used in indirect speech wherever the present subjunctive is identical with the present indicative (see p. 35).

| Der Arzt sagte am Telefon: „Sie brauchen sich keine Sorgen zu machen." | The doctor said on the telephone, "You don't need to worry." |
|---|---|
| Der Arzt sagte, wir **brauchten** uns keine Sorgen zu machen. | The doctor said we didn't need to worry. |

The past subjunctive is also used to express the English conditional tense after *als ob* and in some conditional clauses with *wenn* (see p. 40).

| Wenn ich Zeit **gehabt hätte, hätte** ich das Buch schon gelesen. | If I had had time, I would have read the book by now. |
|---|---|

| | |
|---|---|
| Wir haben nicht genug Geld. Deshalb muß meine Frau arbeiten. | We don't have enough money. So my wife has to work. |
| Wenn wir genug Geld **hätten**, brauchte meine Frau nicht zu arbeiten. | If we had enough money, my wife wouldn't have to work. |
| Wenn mein Auto nicht kaputt **wäre**, **wäre** ich pünktlich **gekommen**. | If my car hadn't broken down, I'd have been punctual. |
| Er fährt so schnell, als ob er Rennfahrer **wäre**. | He drives as fast as if he were a racing driver. |

**59**  **c. würde + infinitive** (I, 24; II, 12)

This is an alternative for some forms of the past subjunctive, and also serves as an equivalent for the English conditional tense.

| | |
|---|---|
| Sie **würde** die Einladung gerne **annehmen**, wenn sie Zeit hätte. | She would gladly accept the invitation if she had time. |
| Es **würden** weniger Unfälle **passieren**, wenn die Geschwindigkeit begrenzt würde. | There would be fewer accidents if there were a speed limit. |
| Die Grenzen abschaffen? Nein, das **würde** ich nicht **tun**. | Abolish the frontiers? No, I wouldn't do that. |

**60**  (1) *würde* + infinitive is often used to avoid complicated or ambiguous sentences. In the following example, the first part of the sentence might be misunderstood because the subjunctive is not recognizable.

Es **passierten** weniger Unfälle, wenn man die Geschwindigkeit begrenzte.
→ Es **würden** weniger Unfälle **passieren**, wenn man die Geschwindigkeit begrenzte.

**61**  (2) In spoken German, the past subjunctive of *tun* is generally avoided.

| | |
|---|---|
| **Würden** Sie das tun? | Would you do that? |
| (instead of: **Täten** Sie das?) | |

**62**  (3) *würde* + infinitive can be a substitute for almost all forms of the subjunctive, though it is often stylistically clumsy.

| | |
|---|---|
| Er sagte, in der Bundesrepublik **würden** viele Ausländer **leben**. (instead of: Er sagte, in der Bundesrepublik **lebten** viele Ausländer.) | He said there were a lot of foreigners living in West Germany. |

In the above case, however, the use of *würde* helps to clarify the meaning, as *lebten* is also the preterite form of the indicative.

### d. The use of the subjunctive

**63**  (1) Indirect speech (II, 14, 15, 24)

| | |
|---|---|
| Er sagt, die jungen Leute **seien** in der Schweiz. | He says the young people are in Switzerland. |
| Sie sagte, sie **müßte** zu ihrer Mutter **fahren**. | She said she had to go and see her mother. |

Indirect statements may appear with or without the introductory conjunction *daß*.

| | |
|---|---|
| Sie sagte, sie **wäre** gern **gekommen**. ( = Sie sagte, **daß** sie gern **gekommen wäre**.) | She said she would have been happy to come. |

Note:

If the statement is not introduced by *daß*, the word order is the same as in a simple sentence; if it is introduced by *daß*, the verb is put at the end of the clause.

**64** (2) Indirect questions (II, 15)

| | |
|---|---|
| Es wird gefragt, **ob** nicht der Staat das Studium **bezahlen müßte**. | The question has arisen whether the state oughtn't to pay for University studies. |
| Es wird gefragt, **warum** das Stipendiensystem **ungerecht wäre**. | People are asking why the scholarship system would be unfair. |

**65** (3) Conditional sentences (II, 15)

In conditional sentences, the statements in the main clause and in the dependent clause correspond in tense (present, past or future).

| | |
|---|---|
| **Wenn** das Studium voll **finanziert würde, brauchten** die Studenten nicht nebenbei zu arbeiten. | If studies were fully financed, the students wouldn't need to take jobs. |
| **Wenn** er Zeit **gehabt hätte, wäre** er nach München **gekommen**. | If he had had time, he would have come to Munich. |
| Wenn die Geschwindigkeit **begrenzt würde**, **gäbe** es weniger Unfälle. | If there were a speed limit, there would be fewer accidents. |

**66** (4) Wishes

In this type of sentence, the past subjunctive is used, generally signalized by the particles *doch* and *nur*.

| | |
|---|---|
| Der Beckenbauer **müßte** man **sein**! | Beckenbauer's the man to be! |
| Wenn ich **nur** schon zu Hause **wäre**! | If only I were already at home! |
| **Hätte** ich **doch nur** die Tür **abgeschlossen**! | If only I'd locked the door! |

40

**67** (5) Comparisons using *als ob*

| | |
|---|---|
| Er tut so, **als ob** er uns nicht **kennen würde**. | He is pretending not to know us. |
| Er fährt so schnell, **als ob** er Rennfahrer **wäre**. | He drives as fast as if he were a racing driver. |

**68** **e. The imperative** (I, 7, 11, 12)

| | du | ihr | Sie |
|---|---|---|---|
| holen: | hol(e) | holt | holen Sie |
| bringen: | bring(e) | bringt | bringen Sie |
| bleiben: | bleib(e) | bleibt | bleiben Sie |

**69** (1) The imperative for the 2nd Pers. Sing. (*du*) is formed from the infinitive by omitting the *-en* or *-n* ending (I, 11).

| | |
|---|---|
| **holen** | |
| Hol(**e**) doch bitte die Zigaretten! | Do get the cigarettes, please. |
| **bringen** | |
| Bring(**e**) doch bitte den Brief zur Post! | Do please take the letter to the post. |
| **bleiben** | |
| Bleib(**e**) doch hier! | Do stay here. |

In colloquial language the *-e* ending is omitted (*hol, bring, bleib*), unless the verb stem ends in *-d-, -t-, -m-* or *-n-* (preceded by a consonant other than *r, l* or *h*), when the *-e* is always retained.

| | |
|---|---|
| **arbeiten** | |
| Arbeite nicht soviel! | Don't work so much. |
| **sich verabreden** | |
| Verabrede dich doch gleich! | Why don't you make a date right away? |

41

| **öffnen** | |
| Öffne doch bitte das Fenster! | Do open the window, please. |

With verbs ending in *-eln* and *-ern*, the *-e-* of the stem can be dropped.

| **klingeln** | |
| Klingle noch einmal! | Ring again. |
| **ändern** | |
| Ändre (ändere) deine Gewohn-heiten! | Change your habits. |

**70**  (2) The imperative for the 2nd Pers. Pl. (*ihr*) is the same as the 2nd Pers. Pl. of the present tense (I, 12) with the pronoun omitted.

| **kommen, ihr kommt** | |
| Kommt doch noch heute abend! | Do still come this evening! |
| **holen, ihr holt** | |
| Holt bitte die Gläser aus der Küche! | Please get the glasses from the kitchen. |
| **gehen, ihr geht** | |
| Geht doch mal ins Museum! | Why don't you go to the museum? |

**71**  (3) The formal imperative (*Sie*) is the same as the conjugated form of the present tense, whereby the personal pronoun *Sie* always follows the verb (I, 7).

| **anrufen** | |
| Rufen Sie bitte die Werkstatt an! | Please ring the workshop. |
| **sprechen** | |
| Sprechen Sie bitte mit Herrn Zinn! | Please speak to Mr Zinn. |
| **fahren** | |
| Fahren Sie doch mit mir nach Genf! | Why don't you come to Geneva with me? |

**72** (4) The e → i (e) vowel change found in the present tense of some irregular verbs (see p. 13 ff.) also occurs in the imperative singular (*du*).

| | |
|---|---|
| **Iß** doch nicht so schnell! | Don't eat so fast. |
| **Gib** mir bitte die Zeitung! | Give me the paper please. |
| **Lies** das mal! | Just read that! |

**73** (5) The imperative forms of the verb *sein* are irregular.

| | |
|---|---|
| **Sei/seid/seien** Sie pünktlich! | Be punctual. |

### 3. The Passive

**a. Forms** (II, 2, 11)

**74 Present** (II, 2)

| | |
|---|---|
| Die Schnellbahn **wird** jetzt **gebaut**. | The super-speed railway is now being built. |
| Die Schnellbahnen **werden** von Elektromotoren **angetrieben**. | The express trains are powered by electric motors. |

Formation of the present passive:
present of *werden* + past participle
The past participle goes to the end of the clause.

**75 Preterite** (II, 2)

| | |
|---|---|
| Das Projekt **wurde** von Fachleuten **geplant**. | The project was planned by experts. |
| Die Projekte **wurden** von Fachleuten **vorgeschlagen**. | The projects were suggested by experts. |

Formation of the preterite passive:
preterite of *werden* + past participle
The past participle goes to the end of the clause.

## 76 Present perfect (II, 11)

| | |
|---|---|
| Das Gesetz **ist verabschiedet worden**. | The law has been passed. |
| Die Gesetze **sind bekanntgegeben worden**. | The laws have been announced. |

In the present perfect (and past perfect) passive, *worden* is used instead of the past participle of *werden* (= *geworden*) and follows the other past participle at the end of the clause.

Compare:

| | |
|---|---|
| Das Ergebnis ist gestern veröffentlicht **worden**. (= Passive) | The result was published yesterday. |
| Er ist Lehrer **geworden**. | He became a teacher. |

## 77 b. The passive with modal verbs

| | |
|---|---|
| Luftbildaufnahmen **müssen freigegeben werden**. | Aerial photographs must be released to the public. |
| Das Gesetz **muß geändert werden**. | The law must be changed. |
| Die Geschwindigkeit **muß begrenzt werden**. | A speed limit must be enforced. |

Note the word order: *werden* follows the past participle at the end of the clause.

### c. The use of the passive

78 (1) Active and passive can express the same idea. But whereas in an active sentence the agent performing the action is named, he (or it) remains unnamed in a passive sentence. The passive is therefore used when the agent is unknown or unimportant.

44

| | |
|---|---|
| Die Arbeitsgruppe hat die Ergebnisse der Planung veröffentlicht. | The work group has published the results of the plan. |
| Die Ergebnisse der Planung **wurden veröffentlicht**. | The results of the plan were published. |
| Die Gemeinde baut eine neue Schule. | The local authority is building a new school. |
| Es **wird** jetzt eine neue Schule **gebaut**.[1] | A new school is now being built. |
| Drei Firmen arbeiten schon lange an dem Projekt. | Three firms have been working on this project for a long time now. |
| An diesem Projekt **wird** schon lange **gearbeitet**. | Work on this project has been going on for a long time now. |

Note: In the sentence *Die Ergebnisse der Planung wurden veröffentlicht,* the work group may have produced the results – but was not necessarily the agent of their publication. (They might have been published by the state or by an official board.)

**79** (2) The passive formed with *werden* denotes an action taking place, whether habitually, at the present moment or at a given point in time. The passive formed with *(worden) sein* – whereby *worden* can be omitted – indicates a state or a completed action.

| | |
|---|---|
| Das Gerät **wird** (jetzt gerade) **umgebaut**. | The instrument is being modified. |
| Das Gerät **ist umgebaut (worden)**. | The instrument is (has been) modified. |
| In einem Computer **werden** Informationen **gespeichert**. | Information is stored in a computer. |
| Informationen, die in einem Computer **gespeichert (worden) sind**, heißen Datei. | Information which is (has been) stored in a computer is called data. |

---

[1] *Es* often introduces a passive sentence, sometimes as the subject (see p. 164), but often only as a filler. The subject of this sentence is *eine neue Schule.*

**80** (3) As the passive emphasizes the event or action rather than the agent, it is most commonly found in the 3rd Persons Singular and Plural.

| | |
|---|---|
| In München **wird** ein neues Stadion **gebaut**. | A new stadium is being built in Munich. |
| Die Ergebnisse **wurden** gestern **veröffentlicht**. | The results were published yesterday. |
| Überall **werden** jetzt Supermärkte **gebaut**. | Supermarkets are being built everywhere now. |

**81** (4) The passive can, of course, be formed in the 1st and 2nd Persons too.

| | **Present** | **Preterite** |
|---|---|---|
| ich | werde gefragt | wurde gefragt |
| du | wirst | wurdest |
| er/sie | wird | wurde |
| wir (sie, Sie) | werden | wurden |
| ihr | werdet | wurdet |

| | **Present Perfect** | **Past Perfect** |
|---|---|---|
| ich | bin gefragt worden | war gefragt worden |
| du | bist | warst |
| er/sie | ist | war |
| wir (sie, Sie) | sind | waren |
| ihr | seid | wart |

| | |
|---|---|
| Ich **bin** (von dem Reporter) **gefragt worden**, ob ich viel fernsehe. | I was asked (by the reporter) if I often watch television. |
| Wir **sind** für den Unfall verantwortlich **gemacht worden**. | We were held responsible for the accident. |
| Ich **wurde** als Kind immer auf Reisen **mitgenommen**. | As a child I was always taken along when the family travelled. |

**82** (5) If the agent is specified in a passive sentence, it appears with the prepositions *von, durch* or *mit* (English *by*). *Von* is used mainly with a personal agent, *durch* expresses means, and *mit* expresses the instrument.

| | |
|---|---|
| Erst als er **von einem anderen Autofahrer** auf das Hinweisschild **aufmerksam gemacht wurde**, stellte er seinen Motor ab. | Not until he was made aware of the sign by another driver did he switch off his engine. |
| (= Erst als ein anderer Autofahrer ihn auf das Hinweisschild aufmerksam machte, stellte er seinen Motor ab.) | (= Not until another driver drew his attention to the sign did he switch off his engine.) |
| Die Schäden am Kölner Dom **werden durch die Luftverschmutzung verursacht**. | The damage done to Cologne Cathedral is caused by air pollution. |
| (= Die Luftverschmutzung verursacht Schäden am Kölner Dom.) | (= Air pollution causes damage to Cologne Cathedral.) |
| Der ganze Bericht **wurde mit der Hand geschrieben**. | The entire report was written by hand. |

(6) As the subject of a passive verb would be the direct object of the active form, only transitive verbs have a true passive. In German, however, intransitive verbs can be made passive in the impersonal form only.

| | |
|---|---|
| Es **wurde** viel **getrunken**. | A lot of drinking went on. |
| Samstags **wird** nicht **gearbeitet**. | No work is done on Saturdays. |

In English the subject of the passive verb can also be the indirect object of the active form (e. g. *I was given a pair of binoculars and told to keep track of the two men.*). This construction is not possible in German, where the indirect object is always expressed in the dative.

| | |
|---|---|
| **Den Damen wurde** Tee mit Zitrone **gebracht**. | The ladies were brought tea with lemon. |
| **Mir wurde gesagt**, ich soll morgen kommen. | I was told to come tomorrow. |

47

The same construction is used for the passive of verbs taking the dative (see p. 85 ff.) – take care when the corresponding verb is transitive in English!

| | |
|---|---|
| Was raten Sie mir? | What do you advise me to do? |
| **Mir wurde geraten**, das Land zu verlassen. | I was advised to leave the country. |
| Es hat mir sehr geholfen. | It helped me a lot. |
| **Mir wurde** viel **geholfen**. | I was helped a lot. |

(7) The passive is used much less in German than it is in English. It is frequently replaced by a construction with *man* (see p. 210) or by a reflexive verb, particularly in combination with *lassen*.

| | |
|---|---|
| Wie macht man das? | How is it done? |
| Beim Essen rauchen? Das tut man einfach nicht! | Smoke when you eat? That just isn't done. |
| Es findet sich immer ein Weg. | A way can always be found. |
| Das läßt sich schon machen. | That can certainly be done. |

The passive infinitive can sometimes be expressed more elegantly by the (active) infinitive with *sein* + *zu*.

| | |
|---|---|
| Es war niemand zu sehen. | There was no one to be seen. |
| Das ist sehr zu bedauern. | That is most regrettable. |
| Es ist mit Entlassungen zu rechnen. (Instead of: Es muß mit Entlassungen gerechnet werden.) | We must expect dismissals. |

## 4. The Infinitive (II, 8, 9)

### a. Forms
(see p. 11)

### b. The use of the infinitive

**83** The infinitive can appear with or without *zu*. It is placed at the end of its clause.

**84** (1) It appears without *zu*:

with modal verbs (*dürfen, können, müssen, sollen, wollen, möchte*) (II, 8, 9),

| | |
|---|---|
| Fräulein Heim **muß** die Werkstatt **anrufen**. | Miss Heim must ring up the workshop. |

with *bleiben* and *lassen* (II, 10; III, 4),

| | |
|---|---|
| Bitte, **bleiben** Sie doch **sitzen**. | Please don't get up. |
| Immer wieder **bleiben** in den öffentlichen Verkehrsmitteln wertvolle Sachen **liegen**. | Valuables are constantly being left behind in public transport. |
| Die Gemeinden **lassen** Schulen **bauen**. | The local authorities are having schools built. |

with *gehen* and *fahren* (verbs of motion),

| | |
|---|---|
| Er **geht** mit seinem Freund **schwimmen**. | He goes swimming with his friend. |
| Sie **fährt einkaufen**. | She's going shopping. |

with *sehen* and *hören*.

| | |
|---|---|
| Er **sieht** das Taxi **wegfahren**. | He sees the taxi drive away. |
| Er **hört** sie **kommen**. | He hears her coming. |

**85** (2) In conjunction with a second verb (finite form), the infinitive otherwise usually appears with *zu* (II, 8).

| | |
|---|---|
| Er **hat versprochen zu kommen**. | He has promised to come. |
| Politiker **schlugen vor**, das Ladenschlußgesetz **zu ändern**. | Politicians suggested changing the closing-time law. |
| Der Sprecher **versuchte**, den Standpunkt seiner Partei **zu erläutern**. | The speaker tried to explain his party's point of view. |

**86** (3) The infinitive also appears with *zu* in the following combinations (II, 8, 11, 18; III, 8):

| | |
|---|---|
| Er hat jetzt **angefangen zu rauchen**. | Now he has started to smoke. |
| Wir **brauchen** nicht länger **zu arbeiten**. | We don't need to work any longer. |
| Die Redner **waren** kaum **zu verstehen**. (= Man konnte die Redner kaum verstehen.) | The speakers were barely comprehensible. |
| Die Arbeit **war** in einem Tag **zu schaffen**. (= Die Arbeit mußte (konnte) in einem Tag geschafft werden.) | The work had to (could) be done in a day. |
| Er **hat** viel **zu erzählen**. | He has a lot to tell. |
| Die Kinder **haben** ihre Hausaufgaben noch **zu machen**. (= müssen . . .) | The children have still got to do their homework. |
| Es **scheint** nicht möglich **zu sein**, alle Arbeit zu rationalisieren. | It doesn't seem (to be) possible to rationalize all kinds of work. |

| | |
|---|---|
| Mit dieser Umfrage **scheint** ein altes Vorurteil **widerlegt zu werden**. (= Es scheint, daß mit dieser Umfrage ein altes Vorurteil widerlegt wird.) | With this poll, an old prejudice seems to be refuted. |

**87** (4) With separable verbs, *zu* is placed between the prefix and stem.

| | |
|---|---|
| Er **braucht** nicht **mitzukommen**. | There is no need for him to come along too. |

**88** (5) The infinitive with *zu* can be expanded as follows:

| | |
|---|---|
| Er hat jetzt angefangen **zu rauchen**. | Now he has started to smoke. |
| Er hat jetzt angefangen, **Pfeife zu rauchen**. | Now he has started to smoke a pipe. |
| Er hat versprochen **zu kommen**. | He has promised to come. |
| Er hat versprochen, **nächste Woche zu kommen**. | He has promised to come next week. |

**89** (6) The following verbs appear in the infinitive and not the past participle form when used with another infinitive in either of the perfect tenses.

| | |
|---|---|
| **müssen** (and the other modals) Fräulein Heim *hat* die Werkstatt *anrufen müssen*. | Miss Heim had to phone the workshop. |
| **brauchen** Er *hat* nicht *zu arbeiten brauchen*. | He didn't need to work. |
| **lassen** Die Gemeinde *hat* eine Schule *bauen lassen*. | The local authorities had a school built. |

| | |
|---|---|
| **sehen** | |
| Wir *haben* das Auto *wegfahren sehen*. | We saw the car drive away. |
| **hören** | |
| Ich *habe* dich nicht *kommen hören*. | I didn't hear you coming. |
| but, for example: | |
| **bleiben** | |
| Er *ist sitzen geblieben*. | He remained seated. |

However, the simpler form – the preterite – is usually preferred here.

| | |
|---|---|
| **müssen** | |
| Fräulein Heim *mußte* die Werkstatt *anrufen*. | Miss Heim had to phone the workshop. |
| **brauchen** | |
| Er *brauchte* nicht *zu arbeiten*. | He didn't need to work. |
| **lassen** | |
| Die Gemeinde *ließ* eine Schule *bauen*. | The local authorities had a school built. |

**90**   (7) *um . . . zu; ohne . . . zu; anstatt . . . zu* (II, 10; III, 2)
All verbs can be used in conjunction with *um . . . zu, ohne . . . zu* and *anstatt . . . zu*.

| | |
|---|---|
| Er fuhr in die Ferien, **um sich zu erholen.** | He went on holiday to get a good rest. |
| Sie fuhren in die Stadt, **um einkaufen zu gehen.** | They drove into town to do some shopping. |
| Er verließ das Restaurant, **ohne zu bezahlen.** | He left the restaurant without paying. |

| **Ohne** ein Wort **zu sagen**, ging sie nach Hause. | Without saying a word, she went home. |
| **Er ist in die Stadt gefahren, anstatt zu arbeiten.** | He drove into town instead of working. |

## 91  c. Word order

| Er  |         | **hilft** | in der Küche      |             |
| Er  | soll    |           | in der Küche      | **helfen.** |
| Er  | braucht |           | nicht in der Küche | **zu helfen.** |

| Ich |         | **fahre** | jetzt ins Büro.   |             |
| Ich | muß     |           | ins Büro          | **fahren.**  |
| Ich | brauche |           | nicht ins Büro    | **zu fahren.** |

| Er  |         | **bringt** | Wein            | **mit.**    |
| Er  | soll    |           | Wein             | **mitbringen.** |
| Er  | braucht |           | keinen Wein      | **mitzubringen.** |

## 5. Present and Past Participles

## 92  a. Forms (II, 13)

The present participle is formed by adding -*d* to the infinitive.

| wachsen – wachsen**d**; zunehmen – zunehmen**d** | |
| **Der zunehmende** Verkehr ist ein **wachsendes** Problem. | The increase in traffic presents mounting problems. |
| Er ließ seinen Wagen mit **laufendem** Motor stehen. | He left his car with the engine running. |

For the formation of the past participle, see p. 20 ff.

## b. The use of the present and past participles

**93** (1) The present participle is often used as an adjective before a noun. It then takes the normal adjectival endings (II, 13).

| | |
|---|---|
| Die **zunehmende** Verschmutzung der Weltmeere ist eine gefährliche Entwicklung. (Die Verschmutzung der Weltmeere nimmt zu.) | The increasing pollution of the oceans is a dangerous development. (The pollution of the oceans is increasing.) |
| Sie hat ihre Abschlußprüfung gemacht. Jetzt sucht sie eine **entsprechende** Stelle. (Sie sucht eine Stelle, die ihren Qualifikationen entspricht.) | She has passed her final exams. Now she is looking for a suitable job. (She is looking for a job to match her qualifications.) |

The same applies to the past participle.

| | |
|---|---|
| Die Luftbildfotografin fotografiert bei **geöffneter** Kabine. (Die Kabine ist **geöffnet**.) | The aerial photographer takes her photographs from an open cabin. |
| Er kann bei **geschlossenem** Fenster nicht schlafen. (Das Fenster ist **geschlossen**.) | He can't sleep with the window open. |

**94** (2) When used adverbially, the participle is not inflected.

| | |
|---|---|
| Sie verließen **protestierend** den Saal. | Protesting, they left the hall. |
| Er hörte **interessiert** zu. | He listened with interest. |

**95** (3) Many participles are used predicatively like adjectives after the verb *sein*.

| | |
|---|---|
| Die Meinung der Autofahrer über die Geschwindigkeitsbegrenzung **ist geteilt**. | Among motorists opinions on the speed limit are divided. |

54

| Die Alpen **sind** 100 km von München **entfernt**. | The Alps are 100 km away from Munich. |

Compare (II, 5):

| Das Ergebnis **überrascht** die Öffentlichkeit. | The result surprises the general public. |
| Das ist ein **überraschendes** Ergebnis. | That is a surprising result. |
| Das Ergebnis ist **überraschend**. | The result is surprising. |
| Die Öffentlichkeit ist **überrascht**. | The general public is surprised. |

Sometimes participles have comparative and superlative forms like adjectives.

| Das ist das **faszinierendste** Theaterstück, das ich kenne. | That is the most fascinating play I know. |
| Dieses Stück ist das **bedeutendste**, das er komponiert hat. | This piece is the most significant one he composed. |

**96** (4) Like the infinitive, participles can be expanded into phrases (III, 19).

| Ein Lied **pfeifend**, packte er seinen Koffer. | Singing a song, he packed his suitcase. |
| Die Schule **vergessend**, rannten die Kinder auf die Straßen. | Forgetting school, the children ran on to the streets. |
| In Hamburg **angekommen**, fuhr er zuerst zum Hafen. | On arrival in Hamburg, he first drove to the harbour. |

Note: The German present participle is much more limited in use and function than the English *-ing* form. There is nothing to compare with the English continuous tenses, and the English gerund is usually rendered by an infinitive or by a finite verb in a dependent clause.

55

## 6. The Auxiliary Verbs

**97**  **a. sein** (I, 1, 2, 9, 10, 11, 12; II, 24; III, 14)

**Present** (I, 1, 2, 9, 11, 12)          **Preterite** (I, 10)

| ich | bin | ich | war |
|---|---|---|---|
| du | bist | du | warst |
| er/sie | ist | er/sie | war |
| wir (sie, Sie) | sind | wir (sie, Sie) | waren |
| ihr | seid | ihr | wart |

| | |
|---|---|
| Er **ist** Student. | Ich habe ihn gestern angerufen, aber er **war** nicht zu Hause. |
| He is a student. | I phoned him yesterday, but he wasn't at home. |
| Was **sind** Sie von Beruf, Herr Braun? | **Waren** Sie schon einmal in England? – Ja, da **war** ich Anfang Mai. |
| What are you by profession, Mr Braun? | Have you ever been to England? Yes, I was there at the beginning of May. |

**Present perfect**          **Past perfect**

| ich | bin . . . gewesen | ich | war . . . gewesen |
|---|---|---|---|
| du | bist | du | warst |
| er/sie | ist | er/sie | war |
| wir (sie, Sie) | sind | wir (sie, Sie) | waren |
| ihr | seid | ihr | wart |

| | |
|---|---|
| Sie waren in Teheran? Wie lange **sind** Sie denn da unterwegs **gewesen**? | Er **war** krank (**gewesen**). Deshalb konnte er lange keinen Sport treiben. |
| You were in Teheran? How ever long were you travelling? | He had been sick. So he couldn't go in for any sport for a long time. |

| | |
|---|---|
| Warum seid ihr nicht gekommen? Wir **sind** den ganzen Abend zu Hause **gewesen**.<br>Why didn't you come? We have been at home all evening. | Es waren viele gekommen, die seine Schüler **gewesen waren**.<br>Many had come who had been his pupils. |

The form . . . *war (+ adjective)* . . . *gewesen* is rare.
More common is . . . *ist gewesen*.

**Future**

| | | |
|---|---|---|
| ich | werde . . . sein | Future perfect: wird . . . gewesen |
| du | wirst | sein (see note p. 33) |
| er/sie | wird | |
| wir (sie, Sie) | werden | |
| ihr | werdet | |

| | |
|---|---|
| Kommt ihr morgen abend? – Ja, wir **werden** gegen 6 Uhr bei euch **sein**. | Are you coming tomorrow evening? Yes, we'll be with you at about six. |
| Sie wollen die Arbeit in einer Woche schaffen? Das **wird** schwierig **sein**. | You want to get the work done in a week? That'll be difficult. |

**Present subjunctive** (II, 24)      **Past subjunctive** (I, 24)

| | | | | |
|---|---|---|---|---|
| ich (er/sie) | sei | | ich (er/sie) | wäre |
| du | seiest | | du | wärest |
| wir (sie, Sie) | seien | | wir (sie, Sie) | wären |
| ihr | seiet | | ihr | wäret |

| | |
|---|---|
| Sie behauptete, ihre Englischkenntnisse **seien** gut.<br>She maintained that her knowledge of English was good. | Wenn er Politiker **wäre**, würde er die Grenzen abschaffen.<br>If he were a politician, he would do away with frontiers. |

| | |
|---|---|
| Er sagte, er **sei** mit seiner neuen Stelle sehr zufrieden. | Sie **wäre** schon in Köln, wenn sie eine Wohnung gefunden hätte. |
| He said he was quite satisfied with his new job. | She would already be in Cologne if she had found a flat. |

## 98 b. haben (I, 4, 5, 10; II, 12)

**Present** (I, 4, 5)                    **Preterite** (I, 10)

| ich | habe | ich | hatte |
|---|---|---|---|
| du | hast | du | hattest |
| er/sie | hat | er/sie | hatte |
| wir (sie, Sie) | haben | wir (sie, Sie) | hatten |
| ihr | habt | ihr | hattet |

| | |
|---|---|
| **Haben** wir noch Rotwein? | Haben Sie eine Dampferfahrt auf dem Rhein gemacht? – Leider nicht, dafür **hatten** wir keine Zeit mehr. |
| Have we any red wine left? | |
| Er **hat** Hunger. | |
| He's hungry. | Did you go for a trip on the Rhine? No, unfortunately not, we hadn't any time left for that. |
| | Warum ist sie nicht in Urlaub gefahren? **Hatte** sie kein Geld? |
| | Why didn't she go away on holiday? Didn't she have any money? |

**Present perfect**                    **Past perfect**

| ich | habe . . . gehabt | ich | hatte . . . gehabt |
|---|---|---|---|
| du | hast | du | hattest |
| er/sie | hat | er/sie | hatte |
| wir (sie, Sie) | haben | wir (sie, Sie) | hatten |
| ihr | habt | ihr | hattet |

Sie **hat** Glück **gehabt**. Sie hat die Stelle sofort bekommen.

She was lucky. She got the job immediately.

Er ist aus der Partei ausgetreten. Welche Gründe **hat** er eigentlich dafür **gehabt**?

He has resigned from the party. What reasons did he have for doing that?

Er **hatte** immer Glück (**gehabt**), bevor ihm dieser Unfall passierte.

He had always been lucky before he had this accident.

**Future**

| | | |
|---|---|---|
| ich | werde . . . haben | Future perfect: wird . . . gehabt haben (see note p. 33) |
| du | wirst | |
| er/sie | wird | |
| wir (sie, Sie) | werden | |
| ihr | werdet | |

Sie will Pilotin werden. Sie **wird** es in diesem Beruf nicht leicht **haben**.

She wants to be a pilot. It won't be easy for her in that job.

Sie spricht perfekt Deutsch. – Dann **wird** sie auf der Universität keine Schwierigkeiten **haben**.

She speaks perfect German. – Then she won't have any difficulty at the university.

**Present subjunctive**

| | |
|---|---|
| er/sie | habe |

**Past subjunctive** (II, 12)

| | |
|---|---|
| ich (er/sie) | hätte |
| du | hättest |
| wir (sie, Sie) | hätten |
| ihr | hättet |

Er sagte, die Arbeit **habe** noch Zeit.

He said there was no need to hurry with the work.

Ich würde mir ein Wochenendhaus kaufen, wenn ich Geld **hätte**.

I'd buy myself a weekend cottage if I had the money.

59

In der Zeitung steht, die Stadt
**habe** zuwenig Geld für das neue
Krankenhaus.

The newspaper says the town hasn't got
enough money for the new hospital.

## 99  c. werden (II, 2, 7)

**Present** (II, 2, 7)

| ich | werde |
|---|---|
| du | wirst |
| er/sie | wird |
| wir (sie, Sie) | werden |
| ihr | werdet |

**Preterite** (II, 2, 7)

| ich | wurde |
|---|---|
| du | wurdest |
| er/sie | wurde |
| wir (sie, Sie) | wurden |
| ihr | wurdet |

Sie **wird** Lehrerin.

She's going to be a teacher.

Gemälde **werden** immer wert-voller.

Paintings are increasing in value.

Sie wollte Ärztin werden, dann
**wurde** sie doch Lehrerin.

She wanted to be a doctor, but then she
became a teacher after all.

Zuerst war das Wetter herrlich,
aber dann **wurde** es wieder kälter.

At first the weather was glorious, but
then it got colder again.

**Present perfect** (II, 7)

| ich | bin . . . geworden |
|---|---|
| du | bist |
| er/sie | ist |
| wir (sie, Sie) | sind |
| ihr | seid |

**Past perfect**

| ich | war . . . geworden |
|---|---|
| du | warst |
| er/sie | war |
| wir (sie, Sie) | waren |
| ihr | wart |

| | |
|---|---|
| Obwohl er nicht wollte, **ist** er schließlich doch Lehrer **geworden**.<br><br>Although he didn't want to, he eventually became a teacher after all. | Als er nach Deutschland zurückkam, mußte er feststellen, daß das Leben teurer **geworden war**.<br><br>When he returned to Germany, he found that life had got more expensive. |

**Present subjunctive**  **Past subjunctive**

| | | | |
|---|---|---|---|
| er/sie | werde | ich (er/sie) | würde |
| | | du | würdest |
| | | wir (sie, Sie) | würden |
| | | ihr | würdet |

| | |
|---|---|
| Er behauptet, das Leben **werde** immer interessanter.<br><br>He maintains that life is getting more and more interesting. | Er erzählte mir, er **würde** gern Architekt.<br><br>He told me he would like to be an architect. |

### d. The use of the auxiliary verbs

**100** (1) As an auxiliary, *sein* is used to form the present perfect and the past perfect tenses of certain verbs (see p. 17 ff., 29 ff.). It sometimes also forms the passive (see p. 45).

| | |
|---|---|
| Present perfect:<br>Sie **ist** ins Kino **gegangen**. | She has gone to the cinema. |
| Past perfect:<br>Er hatte einen Unfall. Er **war** zu schnell **gefahren**. | He had an accident. He had been driving too fast. |
| Passive:<br>In einem Computer **sind** Daten **gespeichert**. | Data are stored in a computer. |

**101**  (2) *Sein* as an independent verb:

| | |
|---|---|
| Sie **ist** Lehrerin. | She is a teacher. |
| Dieses Buch **ist** sehr interessant. | This book is very interesting. |

**102**  (3) As an auxiliary, *haben* is used to form the present perfect and past perfect tenses of most verbs.

| | |
|---|---|
| Present perfect: | |
| Er **hat** früher viel Klavier **gespielt**. | At one time he often played the piano. |
| Past perfect: | |
| Er kam zu spät. Das Stück **hatte** schon **angefangen**. | He came too late. The play had already started. |

**103**  (4) *Haben* as an independent verb:

| | |
|---|---|
| Er **hat** Hunger. | He's hungry. |
| Er **hat** eine neue Gitarre. | He has got a new guitar. |

**104**  (5) As an auxiliary, *werden* is used to form the future, the subjunctive (*würde* + infinitive) and the passive.

| | |
|---|---|
| Future: | |
| Ich **werde** ihm sofort **schreiben**. | I'll write to him at once. |
| Subjunctive: | |
| Ich **würde** gern zu Hause **bleiben**. | I'd like to stay at home. |
| Passive: | |
| Hier **wird** eine U-Bahn **gebaut**. | An underground (railway) is being built here. |

**105**  (6) *Werden* as an independent verb:

| | |
|---|---|
| Er **wurde** mit 24 Jahren Premier-minister. | He became prime minister at the age of twenty-four. |

| | |
|---|---|
| Es **wird** jetzt kühler. | It's getting cooler now. |
| Sie **wurde** ganz blaß. | She turned quite pale. |
| Gemälde **werden** immer wertvoller. | Paintings are increasing in value. |
| Er **wird** Lehrer. | He's going to be a teacher. |
| Obwohl er nicht wollte, **ist** er schließlich doch Lehrer **geworden**. | Although he didn't want to, he eventually became a teacher after all. |

Note: Before nouns denoting a profession, *werden* is used to express both *to be* (for future, intended profession) and *to become* (present, actual profession); the article is omitted. See also examples on p. 60 ff.


## 7. The Modal Verbs

**06** **a. dürfen** (I, 19; II, 14; III, 10, 19)

**Present** (I, 19)                    **Preterite**

| | | | |
|---|---|---|---|
| ich (er/sie) | darf | ich (er/sie) | durfte |
| du | darfst | du | durftest |
| wir (sie, Sie) | dürfen | wir (sie, Sie) | durften |
| ihr | dürft | ihr | durftet |

| | |
|---|---|
| Wie lange **dürfen** Ihre Kinder fernsehen? | Bernd freute sich, daß er allein verreisen **durfte**. |
| How long are your children allowed to watch television? | Bernd was happy that he was allowed to travel alone. |
| **Darf** ich Ihnen helfen? | Niemand weiß, ob er den Erfolg seiner Forschungen noch genießen **durfte**. |
| May I help you? | No one knows whether he could still enjoy the success of his research. |

| Present subjunctive (III, 19) | Past subjunctive (II, 14; III, 10) |
|---|---|
| ich (er/sie)    dürfe <br> (all other persons are used in past subjunctive form) | ich (er/sie)    dürfte <br> du    dürftest <br> wir (sie, Sie)    dürften <br> ihr    dürftet |

| | |
|---|---|
| Er sagte, er **dürfe** keinen Wein trinken. <br> He said he wasn't allowed to drink any wine. | Wenn es nach mir ginge, **dürften** unsere Kinder keine Party geben. <br> If I had my way, our children wouldn't be allowed to give a party. <br> **Dürfte** ich Sie um einen Gefallen bitten? <br> Might I ask a favour of you? <br> Ihre Reise **dürfte** sehr interessant gewesen sein. (= Ich nehme an, daß Ihre Reise sehr interessant war.) <br> Your trip must have been very interesting. |

**107  b. können** (I, 8, 12; II, 12; III, 19)

| Present (I, 8) | | Preterite (I, 12) | |
|---|---|---|---|
| ich (er/sie) | kann | ich (er/sie) | konnte |
| du | kannst | du | konntest |
| wir (sie, Sie) | können | wir (sie, Sie) | konnten |
| ihr | könnt | ihr | konntet |

| | |
|---|---|
| **Kann** ich bitte Herrn Meier sprechen?<br>Can I speak to Mr Meier, please?<br>Eine Weltreise **kann** ich mir nicht leisten.<br>I can't afford a world trip. | Er hatte Kopfschmerzen. Deshalb **konnte** er nicht ins Büro gehen.<br>He had a headache. So he couldn't go to the office.<br>Wir **konnten** die Wohnung nicht mieten. Sie war zu teuer.<br>We couldn't rent the flat. It was too expensive. |

**Present subjunctive (III, 19)**  **Past subjunctive (II, 12)**

| | | | | |
|---|---|---|---|---|
| ich (er/sie) | könne | | ich (er/sie) | könnte |
| (all other persons are used in past | | | du | könntest |
| subjunctive form) | | | | |
| | | | wir (sie, Sie) | könnten |
| | | | ihr | könntet |

| | |
|---|---|
| Er sagte, daß er das nicht gestatten **könne**.<br>He said he couldn't permit that. | Was **könnten** wir uns alles leisten, wenn wir kein Haus gebaut hätten!<br>What couldn't we afford if we hadn't built a house!<br>**Könnten** wir uns heute abend treffen?<br>Could we meet this evening? |

**108  c. müssen** (I, 8, 12; II, 14; III, 19)

**Present (I, 8)**  **Preterite (I, 12)**

| | | | |
|---|---|---|---|
| ich (er/sie) | muß | ich (er/sie) | mußte |
| du | mußt | du | mußtest |
| wir (sie, Sie) | müssen | wir (sie, Sie) | mußten |
| ihr | müßt | ihr | mußtet |

| | |
|---|---|
| Er **muß** morgen nach Köln (fahren). | Wir **mußten** zu Hause bleiben. Unser Auto war kaputt. |
| He has to go to Cologne tomorrow. | We had to stay at home. Our car had broken down. |
| Wir **müssen** den Wagen zur Reparatur bringen. | |
| We must take the car to be repaired. | |

**Present subjunctive** (III, 19)     **Past subjunctive** (II, 14)

| ich (er/sie) müsse (all other persons are used in past subjunctive form) | ich (er/sie) | müßte |
|---|---|---|
| | du | müßtest |
| | wir (sie, Sie) | müßten |
| | ihr | müßtet |

| | |
|---|---|
| Er sagte, daß er noch einen Brief schreiben **müsse**. | Claudia liegt im Krankenhaus. Ich **müßte** sie jetzt endlich mal besuchen. |
| He said he still had to write a letter. | Claudia's in hospital. I really ought to go and see her now. |
| | Mußt du den Brief heute noch schreiben? – Ich **müßte** eigentlich, aber ich habe keine Lust mehr. |
| | Do you have to write the letter today? – I ought to really, but I don't feel much like it any more. |

**109   d. sollen** (I, 14; II, 2, 14; III, 19)

**Present** (I, 14; II, 2)     **Preterite** (I, 14)

| ich (er/sie) | soll | ich (er/sie) | sollte |
|---|---|---|---|
| du | sollst | du | solltest |
| wir (sie, Sie) | sollen | wir (sie, Sie) | sollten |
| ihr | sollt | ihr | solltet |

Dein Vater hat angerufen. Du **sollst** nach Hause kommen.
Your father rang. He says you're to go home.

Ich habe gehört, die Schnellbahn **soll** für die Strecke von Hamburg nach München nur vier Stunden benötigen.
I have heard that the high-speed express trains should only need four hours for the stretch from Hamburg to Munich.

Er **sollte** doch ins Reisebüro gehen und die Theaterkarten holen.
He was supposed to go to the travel agent's and get the theatre tickets.

Sie **sollte** eigentlich auf mich warten, aber ich habe sie nicht mehr gesehen.
She was actually supposed to wait for me, but I didn't see her any more.

**Present subjunctive** (III, 19)

ich (er/sie)     solle
(all other persons are used in past subjunctive form)

**Past subjunctive** (II, 2)

(as preterite above)

Er meinte, sie **solle** doch allein ins Kino gehen, er müsse noch arbeiten.
He said she should go to the cinema alone, he still had some work to do.

Die Flugzeuge haben wieder Verspätung. Man **sollte** überhaupt nur mit der Bahn fahren.
The planes are delayed again. One should actually only travel by train.

Du **solltest** nicht so viel rauchen.
You shouldn't smoke so much.

**110   e. wollen** (I, 9, 12)

**Present** (I, 9)

| ich (er/sie) | will |
| du | willst |
| wir (sie, Sie) | wollen |
| ihr | wollt |

**Preterite** (I, 12)

| ich (er/sie) | wollte |
| du | wolltest |
| wir (sie, Sie) | wollten |
| ihr | wolltet |

| | |
|---|---|
| Wir fahren morgen nach Salzburg. Wir **wollen** in Österreich Urlaub machen. | Wir **wollten** gestern einen Ausflug machen. Aber meine Eltern sind plötzlich gekommen. |
| We're going to Salzburg tomorrow. We want to spend our holiday in Austria. | We wanted to go on an outing yesterday. But then my parents suddenly arrived. |
| Wenn du nicht **willst**, brauchst du heute nicht einzukaufen. | |
| You don't have to go shopping today if you don't want to. | |

**Present subjunctive**  **Past subjunctive**

| | |
|---|---|
| ich (er/sie)     wolle (all other persons are used in past subjunctive form) | (as preterite above) |

| | |
|---|---|
| Er sagte, er **wolle** in die Politik gehen. | Ich **wollte** fragen, ob die Besprechung morgen stattfindet. |
| He said he wanted to go in for politics. | I would like to ask if the meeting is taking place tomorrow. |

*Ich wollte* ... here means *Ich möchte* ... (see also p. 73)

**111  f. mögen** (I, 5)          **möchte** (I, 5)

| ich (er/sie) | mag | ich (er/sie) | möchte |
|---|---|---|---|
| du | magst | du | möchtest |
| wir (sie, Sie) | mögen | wir (sie, Sie) | möchten |
| ihr | mögt | ihr | möchtet |

| | |
|---|---|
| Er **mag** keinen Kaffee. | **Möchten** Sie einen Kaffee? |
| He doesn't like coffee. | Would you like some coffee? |
| | Ich **möchte** bitte Herrn Meier sprechen. |
| | I would like to speak to Mr Meier, please. |

68

## g. The use of the modal verbs

**12** (1) *dürfen* and *können*

*Dürfen* and *können* are frequently confused, because they often express similar ideas and are in some cases interchangeable.

*Dürfen* expresses permission and prohibition.

| | |
|---|---|
| **Darf** ich hier rauchen? | May I smoke here? |
| Nein, hier **dürfen** Sie nicht rauchen. (Hier ist Rauchen verboten.) | No, you may not smoke here. (Smoking is not permitted here.) |
| **Darf** Hans heute ins Kino? | May Hans go to the cinema today? |
| Er **darf** erst ins Kino, wenn er seine Hausaufgaben gemacht hat. | He can't go to the cinema until he has finished his homework. |
| Nach der Landung **durften** sich die Kinder das Cockpit ansehen. | After the landing the children were allowed to go and look at the cockpit. |

*Können* expresses possibility or capability.

| | |
|---|---|
| **Kann** man hier schwimmen? | Is there anywhere to swim here? |
| **Können** Sie Klavier spielen? | Can you play the piano? |
| **Können** Sie mir sagen, wo das Museum ist? | Can you tell me where the museum is? |
| **Können** Sie Englisch? | Do you speak English? |
| Ich **kann** nichts dafür. | I can't help it. |

In questions *dürfen* and *können* are often freely interchangeable.

| | |
|---|---|
| **Kann** ich mal telefonieren? <br> = **Darf** ich mal telefonieren? <br> (The speaker knows there is a telephone nearby.) | Can I make a phone call? |
| **Darf** ich mal Ihren Paß sehen? <br> = **Kann** ich mal Ihren Paß sehen? | May I see your passport, please? |

| But: | |
|---|---|
| **Kann** man hier (irgendwo) telefonieren? | Is there anywhere I can phone from here? |
| = Gibt es hier ein Telefon? | = Is there a telephone round here? |

*Dürfte* and *könnte* are politer forms of *darf* and *kann*.

| | |
|---|---|
| **Dürfte** ich mal kurz telefonieren? | Could I possibly make a short phone call, please? |
| **Könnte** ich Sie heute abend anrufen? | Might I phone you this evening? |

In the subjunctive, *dürfen* and *können* also express assumption.

| | |
|---|---|
| Das **dürfte** wohl stimmen. | That is probably correct. |
| = Das **könnte** wohl stimmen. | |
| ( = Ich glaube, daß das stimmt.) | ( = I believe that is correct.) |
| Sie **dürfte** jetzt vierzig sein. | She must be about forty now. |

**113** (2) *müssen* and *sollen*

*Müssen* and *sollen* are used to express duty or obligation.

| | |
|---|---|
| Ich **muß** morgen nach Köln fliegen. | I have to fly to Cologne tomorrow. |
| Die Kinder **sollen** sofort ihre Hausaufgaben machen. | The children are to do their homework immediately. |
| Sie **muß** jetzt einen Brief schreiben. | She must write a letter now. |
| Er **soll** den Damen den Tee bringen. | He is to take the ladies their tea. |

Whereas *müssen* can also express a duty or obligation one has set oneself, an intention in fact *(Ich muß noch schnell einkaufen)*, *sollen* indicates a demand made by someone else.

| | |
|---|---|
| Ich **muß** mal eben telefonieren. (Mir fällt gerade ein, daß ich noch telefonieren wollte.) | I've just got to make a phone call. (It has just occurred to me that I still have a phone call to make.) |
| Ich **soll** nächstes Jahr nach Amerika reisen. (Meine Firma schickt mich nächstes Jahr nach Amerika.) | Next year I am to go on a trip to America. (My firm is sending me to America next year.) |
| Sie **soll** heute nachmittag die Werkstatt anrufen. (Ich habe ihr gesagt, daß sie heute nachmittag die Werkstatt anrufen soll.) | She's to ring the workshop this afternoon. (I told her to ring the workshop this afternoon.) |
| Herr Meyer, Sie **sollen** sofort Ihre Frau anrufen. (Ihre Frau hat darum gebeten, daß Sie sofort anrufen.) | Mr Meyer, you're to ring your wife straight away. (Your wife has asked you to ring her straight away.) |

In the subjunctive, *müssen* and *sollen* both express a wish or idea which cannot be realized at all, or only with difficulty.

| | |
|---|---|
| Der Beckenbauer **müßte** man sein! | Beckenbauer's the man to be! |
| Man **sollte** überhaupt nur noch mit der Bahn fahren! | These days one should really only travel by train. |

In the past subjunctive, *sollen* very often expresses a reproach.

| | |
|---|---|
| Sie **sollten** den Herren den Whisky bringen! (Warum haben Sie es nicht getan?) | You were supposed to take the gentlemen some whisky! (Why haven't you done it?) |
| **Sollten** Sie nicht gestern die Werkstatt anrufen? (Und nicht heute!) | Weren't you supposed to ring the workshop yesterday? (And not today!) |

71

Note also these idiomatic uses of *sollen*:

| | |
|---|---|
| Was **sollte** ich bloß tun? | Whatever could I do? |
| Was **soll** das? | What's it all about? |
| Was **soll's**? | What's the point? |
| Das **sollte** ein Witz sein. | It was meant as a joke. |
| Er **soll** klug sein. | He's supposed to be clever. |
| Er **soll** sehr reich sein. | He is said to be very rich. |
| Compare: | |
| Er **soll** es getan haben. | He is said to have done it. |
| Er **muß** es getan haben. | He must have done it. |

The negative of *müssen* denotes lack of obligation and cannot translate the English *must not*.

| | |
|---|---|
| Du **mußt** nicht hingehen, wenn du nicht willst. | You don't have to go if you don't want to. |
| Man **muß** nicht immer die teuersten Plätze haben. | One needn't always take the most expensive seats. |
| But: | |
| Hier **darfst** du nicht rauchen. | You mustn't smoke here. |

Contrast the negative of *sollen*:

| | |
|---|---|
| Du **sollst** nicht mitkommen. | You are not to come along. |
| Das **sollte** er nicht sagen. | He shouldn't say that. |
| Das **hätte** er nicht sagen **sollen**. | He oughtn't to have said that. |
| Du **sollst** nicht töten. | Thou shalt not kill. |

**114** (3) **wollen** and **mögen**

*Wollen* and *mögen* both express an intention or wish – but with different chances of its being realized.

| | |
|---|---|
| Ich **will** nächste Woche Urlaub machen. (Ich habe die feste Absicht, nächste Woche nicht zu arbeiten.) | I want to go on holiday next week. (I have no intention of working next week.) (The speaker is sure nothing will interfere, because it rests with him when he goes on holiday.) |
| Ich **möchte** nächste Woche Urlaub machen (, wenn es geht). | I would like to go on holiday next week (if it is possible). (The speaker has the wish or intention, but he doesn't yet know for sure if the wish can be fulfilled – this doesn't only depend on himself, but also on circumstances or even other people.) |

Other uses of *wollen* and *mögen*:

| | |
|---|---|
| Ich **wollte** gerade gehen. | I was just about to leave. |
| Das **will** er gesehen haben. | He claims to have seen it. |
| Was **wollen** Sie damit sagen? | What do you mean by that? |
| Nichts **zu wollen**! | Nothing doing! |
| Das **mag** sein. | That may be. |
| Wo **mag** er wohl sein? | I wonder where he is. |
| Das **mag** wohl zwanzig Jahre her sein. | That must be about twenty years ago. |

**15** (4) *mögen*

This is most commonly used in the past subjunctive form with present meaning as a polite request or inquiry (*ich möchte . . .*).

| | |
|---|---|
| **Möchten** Sie Kaffee oder Tee? | Would you like coffee or tea? |
| Ich **möchte** fragen, . . . | I would like to ask . . . |
| = Ich **würde** gern . . . | |
| = Ich **wollte** fragen, . . . | |

73

The other forms of *mögen* have the meaning of *gern haben (ich (er/sie) mag, wir/sie mögen; er mochte; er hat gemocht).*

| | |
|---|---|
| Ich **mag** keinen Tee. (Ich trinke nicht gern Tee.) | I don't like tea. |
| Er **mag** sie. (Er hat sie gern.) | He likes her. |

**116** (5) Present perfect of the modal verbs (cf. p. 51)

The modal verbs form the present perfect with the infinitive instead of the past participle.

| | |
|---|---|
| Eine große Reise **habe** ich mir nicht **leisten können**. | I couldn't afford a big trip. |
| Ich **habe** gestern noch **arbeiten müssen**. | I still had to work yesterday. |
| Er **hat** nach Hause **kommen sollen**. | He had to come home. |

The past participle is only used in expressions where the modal verb functions as a complete finite verb.

| | |
|---|---|
| Das **habe** ich nicht **gewollt**. | That's not what I wanted. |

**117 h. Word order**

74

## 8. lassen

**18  a. Forms** (II, 10)

**Present** (II, 10)                                    **Preterite**

| ich | lasse ihn kommen | ich (er/sie) | ließ ihn kommen |
|---|---|---|---|
| du (er/sie) | läßt | du | ließt (ließest) |
| wir (sie, Sie) | lassen | wir (sie, Sie) | ließen |
| ihr | laßt | ihr | ließt |

**Present perfect**

| ich | habe das Buch im Büro gelassen |
|---|---|
| du | hast |
| er/sie | hat |
| wir (sie, Sie) | haben |
| ihr | habt |

**b. The use of „lassen"**

**19  (1)** *lassen* + infinitive (II, 10, 13)

| | |
|---|---|
| Seine Eltern **lassen** ihn nicht allein **verreisen**. (= erlauben nicht, daß er allein verreist.) | His parents don't let him travel alone. (= don't allow him to travel alone.) |
| Viele Gastarbeiter **lassen** ihre Familien **nachkommen**. (= veranlassen, daß ihre Familien nachkommen.) | Many foreign workers have their families come and join them. (= arrange for them to come.) |

**20  (2)** *sich lassen* + infinitive (III, 17, 18)

| | |
|---|---|
| Hans **läßt sich** die Haare **schneiden**. | Hans is having his hair cut. |

| Ich **lasse mich belehren**. (Man kann mich belehren.) | I am willing to take advice. |
| Ein echter Rembrandt **läßt sich** mit nichts **vergleichen**. (. . . kann mit nichts verglichen werden. cf. p. 48) | There is nothing to be compared with a genuine Rembrandt. |
| Die nationale Politik **läßt sich** heute nicht mehr von der Weltpolitik **trennen**. (. . . kann nicht mehr von der Weltpolitik getrennt werden. cf. p. 48) | Today national politics can no longer be separated from world politics. |

**121** (3) If *lassen* is combined with a finite verb, the past participle is replaced in both perfect tenses by the infinitive (cf. p. 51 ff.).

| Herr Meier **hat sich** einen neuen Anzug **machen lassen**. | Mr Meier has had a new suit made. |

(4) some idiomatic phrases with *(sich) lassen*:

| **Lassen** Sie **sich** nicht stören. | Don't let me disturb you. |
| Sie **läßt** herzlich grüßen. | She sends her best regards. |
| **Lassen** Sie **sich** Zeit. | Take your time. |

## 9. The Reflexive Verbs

Reflexive verbs are far more common in German than in English. The English reflexive verb is invariably transitive with a reflexive pronoun as direct object that passes the action back to the subject (e. g. *She is washing herself*). In German, the reflexive pronoun can be either in the accusative as direct object (*Ich wasche mich*) or in the dative as indirect object (*Ich sehe mir den Krimi an*). There are many German reflexive verbs whose English equivalent is non-reflexive: they can be rendered by an ordinary verb (*sich erinnern – to remember*), by a passive form (*sich interessieren – to be interested*) or by a verbal phrase (*sich irren – to make a mistake*).

**a. Forms** (I, 10, 11, 15)

**22  Present** (I, 10, 11, 15)

| Accusative | | Dative | |
|---|---|---|---|
| sich interessieren für: | | sich wünschen: | |
| ich | interessiere mich für Sport | ich | wünsche mir ein Buch |
| du | interessierst dich | du | wünschst dir |
| er/sie | interessiert **sich** | er/sie | wünscht **sich** |
| wir | interessieren uns | wir | wünschen uns |
| ihr | interessiert euch | ihr | wünscht euch |
| sie, Sie | interessieren **sich** | sie, Sie | wünschen **sich** |

(See also Reflexive Pronouns, p. 198 ff., and Personal Pronouns, p. 159 ff.)

**23  Present perfect and past perfect**

The present perfect and past perfect are formed with *haben.*

| | |
|---|---|
| Wofür **hat** er **sich** eigentlich **interessiert**? | What was he actually interested in? |
| Schade, daß er nicht kommen konnte. Ich **hatte mich** so auf seinen Besuch **gefreut**. | A pity he couldn't come! I had been so looking forward to his visit. |

**b. Verbs with a reflexive pronoun in the accusative and dative** (I, 10, 11, 15)

**24  (1) Accusative**

| | |
|---|---|
| sich ärgern über | sich setzen |
| sich beschäftigen mit | sich überschlagen |
| sich bewerben um | sich **um**sehen |

| | |
|---|---|
| sich eignen für | sich unterhalten über |
| sich entscheiden für | sich unterziehen |
| sich erinnern an | sich verabreden mit |
| sich freuen auf/über | sich verbeugen |
| sich fühlen | sich verhalten |
| sich interessieren für | sich versammeln |
| sich irren | sich **vor**stellen |
| sich melden | sich **weiter**bilden |
| sich richten gegen/nach | sich widmen |

**125** (2) Dative

| | |
|---|---|
| sich etwas **ab**gewöhnen | sich etwas leisten |
| sich etwas **an**sehen | sich **vor**kommen |
| sich etwas brechen | sich etwas wünschen |

The reflexive pronoun is in the accusative if it is the only object in the sentence or if the second object is dependent on a preposition.

| | |
|---|---|
| Ich habe **mich** (acc.) geirrt. | I made a mistake. |
| Du beschäftigst **dich** (acc.) viel **mit deinen Kindern**. | You spend a lot of time with your children. |

The reflexive pronoun is in the dative if the sentence already contains an accusative object.

| | |
|---|---|
| Ich möchte **mir** (dat.) heute **die Ausstellung** ansehen. | I'd like to go and see the exhibition today. |

Compare:

| | |
|---|---|
| Wasch **dich** bitte. | Please go and wash. |
| Wasch **dir** bitte **die Hände**. | Please go and wash your hands. |

Note this use of the definite article in German to render the English possessive when referring to parts of one's own body. *Er wäscht seine Hände.* = He is washing his (someone else's) hands.

78

## c. Reflexive verbs and verbs used reflexively (III, 3, 9, 12, 14, 15)

**26** In German there are reflexive verbs and verbs that are merely used reflexively.

**27** (1) Reflexive verbs are those whose reflexive pronoun cannot be substituted by any other word (e. g. *sich freuen*).

| | |
|---|---|
| **sich bewerben** Hast du *dich* um die Stelle *beworben?* | Have you applied for the job? |
| **sich irren** Er hat nicht recht gehabt. Er hat *sich geirrt.*[1] | He wasn't right there. He made a mistake. |
| **sich verhalten** Die Bevölkerung sollte *sich* umweltfreundlicher *verhalten.* | The population should be more pollution-conscious in their habits. |

**28** (2) Many verbs can be used either reflexively or non-reflexively. The variants often differ in meaning (III, 3, 9, 12, 14, 15).

| | |
|---|---|
| **(sich) kaufen** Das Buch sollte Manfred *sich* *kaufen.* | Manfred ought to buy himself the book. (Note this use of the reflexive pronoun as indirect object of a non-reflexive verb in English too.) |
| Die Pelzjacke sollte Manfred *dir* *kaufen.* | Manfred ought to buy you the fur jacket. |

| | |
|---|---|
| **sich vorstellen** Ich habe Ihre Anzeige gelesen und würde *mich* gern bei Ihnen *vorstellen.* | I read your advertisement and would like to come to your office and introduce myself. |
| Das Olympiastadion habe ich *mir* ganz anders *vorgestellt.* | I had imagined the Olympic Stadium to be quite different. |

---

[1] Note, however: *Er irrt, wenn er meint* . . . (He is wrong if he thinks . . .)

**jemand vorstellen**

Darf ich Ihnen *Herrn Baumann vorstellen*?

May I introduce Herr Baumann?

**sich informieren**

*Über* das neue Angebot muß ich *mich informieren*.

I must inform myself about the new offer.

**jemand informieren**

Bitte *informieren* Sie *ihn*, wenn Sie was Neues hören.

Please inform him if you hear anything new.

Note also: sich waschen, sich kämmen (accusative).

**Wasch dich** bitte.

Please go and wash.

**Wasch dir** bitte **die Hände**.

Please go and wash your hands.

Sie **wäscht** gerade **die Kinder**.

She's just washing the children.

---

**129**  (3) Some reflexive verbs only appear in idiomatic phrases.

Die Fünftagewoche **hat** eine sehr unerwünschte Folge **mit sich gebracht**, nämlich die Überstunden.

The five-day week has had an undesired result, and that is overtime.

Aus der Umfrage **ergab sich**, daß . . .

The inquiry revealed that . . .

Es **handelt sich um** die Stelle der Fremdsprachen-Korrespondentin.

I mean the vacancy for a foreign language correspondent.

---

## 10. Compound Verbs

**130**  **a. Forms (I, 7)**

**anrufen**

Sie *ruft* die Taxizentrale *an*.

She phones the taxi rank.

**einkaufen**

Er *kauft* für die Reise *ein*.

He is shopping for the trip.

Compound verbs, using prepositions as separable prefixes, are very common in English (e. g. *Put your coat on! The plane took off at 8.45*). So the concept of the German compound verb should not be difficult for the English-speaking student to grasp. The problems lie rather in distinguishing separable and inseparable prefixes and determining their position in the clause.

### b. Separable and inseparable prefixes (I, 7)

**131** (1) Inseparable prefixes

| be- | **be**antworten (beantwortet), **be**grüßen (begrüßt) |
|---|---|
| emp- | **emp**fangen (empfängt), **emp**finden (empfindet) |
| ent- | sich **ent**scheiden (entscheidet sich), **ent**stehen (es entsteht) |
| er- | sich **er**holen (erholt sich), **er**klären (erklärt) |
| ge- | **ge**fallen (gefällt), **ge**winnen (gewinnt) |
| miß- | **miß**raten (mißrät), sich **miß**verstehen (mißverstehen sich) |
| ver- | **ver**gessen (vergißt), **ver**reisen (verreist) |
| zer- | **zer**stören (zerstört) |

**132** (2) Separable prefixes (I, 7)

| ab- | **ab**holen (holt ab), **ab**schaffen (schafft ab) |
|---|---|
| an- | **an**kommen (kommt an), **an**rufen (ruft an) |
| auf- | **auf**passen (paßt auf), **auf**stehen (steht auf) |
| aus- | **aus**sehen (sieht aus), **aus**steigen (steigt aus) |
| bei- | **bei**tragen (trägt bei), **bei**treten (tritt bei) |
| da(r)- | **dar**stellen (stellt dar) |
| ein- | **ein**kaufen (kauft ein), **ein**laden (lädt ein) |
| fest- | **fest**stehen (es steht fest), **fest**stellen (stellt fest) |
| her- | **her**bringen (bringt her), **her**rühren (es rührt her) |
| herein- | **herein**kommen (kommt herein) |
| hin- | **hin**gehen (geht hin), **hin**schicken (schickt hin) |
| hinaus- | **hinaus**tragen (trägt hinaus) |

| | |
|---|---|
| los- | **los**gehen (geht los) |
| mit- | **mit**kommen (kommt mit), **mit**fahren (fährt mit) |
| nach- | **nach**denken (denkt nach), **nach**sehen (sieht nach) |
| um- | **um**rechnen (rechnet um), sich **um**sehen (sieht sich um) |
| vor- | **vor**bereiten (bereitet sich vor), **vor**schlagen (schlägt vor) |
| vorbei- | **vorbei**gehen (geht vorbei), **vorbei**kommen (kommt vorbei) |
| weg- | **weg**fahren (fährt weg), **weg**werfen (wirft weg) |
| weiter- | **weiter**fahren (fährt weiter), **weiter**gehen (geht weiter) |
| zu- | **zu**hören (hört zu), **zu**sehen (sieht zu) |
| zurück- | **zurück**fahren (fährt zurück), **zurück**geben (gibt zurück) |
| zusammen- | **zusammen**fassen (faßt zusammen), **zusammen**suchen (sucht zusammen) |

**133** Separable verbs can be recognized by the position of the stress.
If the prefix is unstressed, the verb is inseparable.
If the prefix is stressed (ánrufen), the verb is separable.
If the prefix is a polysyllabic word with the stress on the second syllable (zurückkommen), the verb is separable.

**134** (3) The separable prefix of a compound verb can also be another verb, a noun or an adjective.

**kennenlernen**
Er *lernte* im Urlaub viele Ausländer *kennen*.

He got to know a lot of foreigners during his holiday.

**spazierengehen**
Er *geht* jeden Abend *spazieren*.

He goes for a walk every evening.

**radfahren**
Er *fährt* jeden Abend *Rad*.

He rides his bicycle every evening.

| | |
|---|---|
| **fernsehen** | |
| *Sehen* Sie abends oft *fern*? | Do you often watch television in the evening? |
| **freigeben** | |
| Die Behörde *gibt* die Aufnahme zur Veröffentlichung *frei*. | The authorities have released the picture for publication. |

**135    c. Word order** (I, 7)

In a simple sentence, the separable prefix is placed at the end of the sentence and thus, together with the finite verb, forms a bracket for the sentence.

| | |
|---|---|
| Sie **ruft** die Taxizentrale **an**. | She phones the taxi rank. |
| Er **kommt** um 10 Uhr 20 in Frankfurt **an**. | He is arriving in Frankfurt at 10.20. |

In a dependent clause, however, the separable prefix joins the verb in its position at the end of the clause.

| | |
|---|---|
| Er hat gesagt, **daß** er morgen **anruft**. | He said he'll ring up tomorrow. |
| Kennen Sie den Herrn, **der** gerade zur Tür **reinkommt**? | Do you know the gentleman who is just coming through the door? |

Note:
separable:

| anrufen | | **Ruf** | bitte Manfred | **an**! |
|---|---|---|---|---|
| | Ich | **rufe** | jetzt Manfred | **an**. |
| **rad**fahren | Er | **fährt** | gern | **Rad**. |

inseparable:

| erklären | | **Erklär** | mir das bitte! | |
|---|---|---|---|---|
| | Sie | **erklärt** | ihm die Aufgabe. | |
| verreisen | Wir | **verreisen** | morgen. | |

## 11. Verbs and their Objects

**136**  (1) As in English, there are very many transitive verbs in German which take an accusative (direct) object. But a number of verbs, often with transitive English equivalents, take a dative object, one or two even govern the genitive. As in English, many verbs take a preposition before the object, the case of which is governed by the preposition. These verbal combinations, including the case of the object and, where necessary, the preposition, must be learnt by heart – or absorbed by constant practice.

| | |
|---|---|
| Accusative:<br>Sie schreibt **einen Brief**. | She is writing a letter. |
| Dative:<br>Er hilft **seiner Mutter**. | He is helping his mother. |
| Genitive:<br>Dieses Gesetz bedarf **der Zustimmung** des Bundesrats. | This law must be approved by the Upper House. |
| Preposition:<br>Sie unterhalten sich **über ihre Kinder**. | They are talking about their children. |

**137**  (2) Some verbs can be used with different prepositions, each producing a different meaning.

| | |
|---|---|
| **gelten als**<br>Das neue Gesetz *gilt als* (ein) Fortschritt.<br>(Man hält es für einen Fortschritt.) | The new law is considered an improvement. |
| **gelten für**<br>Das neue Gesetz *gilt für* Jugendliche unter 18.<br>(Es betrifft Jugendliche unter 18.) | The new law applies to young people under 18. |

**138** Note: Nouns and adjectives can also govern a certain preposition, e. g.:

---

**Interesse an** + dat.

Das *Interesse an* Sprachen wächst.  The interest in languages is growing.

**verantwortlich, zuständig für** + acc.

Sind Sie *für* die Organisation *ver-* *antwortlich*?  Are you responsible for the organization?

Nein, *dafür* war ich früher mal *zu-* *ständig*.  No, I used to be in charge of that.

**zufrieden mit** + dat.

Sind Sie *mit* Ihrer Wohnung *zu-* *frieden*?  Are you satisfied with your flat?

---

**139**  **a. Verbs governing the dative**

**angehören**

Er hat *der Partei* zehn Jahre *ange-* *hört*.  He was a member of the party for ten years.

**begegnen**

Ich bin *ihm* zufällig *begegnet*.  I happened to meet him.

**beitreten**

Er ist *dem Club beigetreten*.  He joined the club.

**danken**

Er *dankt seinen Kollegen* für die Hilfe.  He thanks his colleagues for their help.

**dienen**

Jede Politik muß *dem Frieden dienen*.  Any policy must help to further peace.

**entsprechen**

Das *entspricht meinen Vorstel-* *lungen*.  That complies with my conception (of it).

**gefallen**

*Gefällt dir* das Buch?  Do you like the book?

85

**gehören**

Gehört das Büro *deinem Vater?*　　Does the office belong to your father?

**gelingen**

Das Experiment ist *ihm gelungen.*　　His experiment was a success.

**gestatten**

*Gestatten* Sie *mir* eine Frage.　　Permit me to ask a question.

**glauben**

Ich *glaube ihm* nicht.　　I don't believe him.

**gratulieren**

Ich *gratuliere dir* zum Geburtstag.　　May I wish you many happy returns of the day.

**helfen**

Kann ich *Ihnen helfen?*　　Can I help you?

**sich nähern**

Sie *näherten sich der Stadt.*　　They approached the city.

**nutzen**

Das *nutzt* nur *der Opposition.*　　That's only any use to the Opposition.

**passen**

Das hat *mir* nicht *gepaßt.*　　I didn't like that at all.

**schaden**

Rauchen *schadet der Gesundheit.*　　Smoking is harmful to health.

**schmecken**

Das Essen *schmeckt mir* nicht.　　I don't like this food.

**zuhören**

Wir *hörten ihm* aufmerksam *zu.*　　We listened to him attentively.

**40  b. Verbs taking prepositions**

**abbringen von** + dat.

Kannst du ihn nicht *von* seinem   Can't you get him to change his mind?
Entschluß *abbringen*?

**abhängen von** + dat.

*Von* der Prüfung *hängt* viel *ab*.   A lot depends on the exam.

**achten auf** + acc.

*Achten* Sie mehr *auf* Ihre Gesund-   Pay more attention to your health.
heit.

**sich ärgern über** + acc.

*Ärgere dich* doch nicht *über* ihn!   Don't let him upset you!

**sich äußern über** + acc.

Er *äußert sich* positiv *über* deine   He commented favourably on your
Arbeit.   work.

**sich amüsieren über** + acc.

*Worüber amüsierst* du *dich*?   What are you smiling about?

**ankommen auf** + acc.

Es *kommt auf* das Wetter *an*, ob wir   It depends on the weather if we go for an
einen Ausflug machen.   excursion or not.

**arbeiten an** + dat.

Die Firma *arbeitet an* einem neuen   The firm is working on a new project.
Projekt.

**auffordern zu** + dat.

Die Regierung *fordert zum* Sparen   The government is making appeals (to
*auf*.   the public) to save money.

**aufmerksam machen auf** + acc.

Er *macht* uns *auf* die Gefahr *auf-*   He draws our attention to the danger.
*merksam*.

**aufrufen zu** + dat.

Die Gewerkschaft *rief zu* einem   The union called a strike.
Streik *auf*.

**aushelfen mit** + dat.

Können Sie mir *mit* ein paar Mark   Can you lend me a few marks?
*aushelfen*?

87

**sich auswirken auf** + acc.

Das Rauchen *wirkt sich* nachteilig *auf* die Gesundheit *aus*.

Smoking has a bad effect on health.

**begrenzen auf** + acc.

Das Problem der Gastarbeiter ist nicht *auf* die Bundesrepublik *begrenzt*.

The problem of foreign workers is not only limited to West Germany.

**begründen mit** + dat.

Er *begründete* die Maßnahme *mit* den gestiegenen Kosten.

He named higher costs as the reason for the measure.

**beitragen zu** + dat.

Jeder kann *zur* Reinhaltung der Umwelt *beitragen*.

Everyone can contribute towards keeping the environment clean.

**benutzen zu** + dat.

Die Nordsee wird oft *zur* Beseitigung von Abfällen *benutzt*.

The North Sea is often used for the disposal of waste.

**berichten über** + acc.

Der Sprecher *berichtet über* die Tagesereignisse.

The speaker is reporting on the events of the day.

**sich beschäftigen mit** + dat.

Er *beschäftigt sich* viel *mit* seinen Kindern.

He spends a lot of time with his children.

**sich beschränken auf** + acc.

Er *beschränkte sich auf* einen kurzen Bericht.

He limited himself to a brief report.

**bestehen aus** + dat.

*Woraus besteht* diese Soße?

What does this sauce consist of?

**sich beteiligen an** + dat.

Er hat *sich an* der Demonstration *beteiligt*.

He took part in the demonstration.

**betrachten als** + acc.

Er *betrachtet* das Theater *als* seinen Lebensinhalt.

He lives for the theatre.

**bewegen zu** + dat.

Was *bewegt* die Sportler (*dazu*), immer neue Rekorde aufzustellen?

What makes athletes always want to set up new records?

**sich bewerben um** + acc.

Sie *bewirbt sich um* die Stelle als Sekretärin.

She's applying for the secretary's post.

**bezeichnen als** + acc.

Soziologen *bezeichnen* unsere Gesellschaft *als* Freizeitgesellschaft.

Sociologists describe our society as a leisure society.

**sich beziehen auf** + acc.

*Worauf bezieht sich* Ihre Frage?

What does your question refer to?

**bitten um** + acc.

Er wird *um* Auskunft *gebeten*.

He is asked for information.

**denken an/über** + acc.

Haben Sie schon *an* Ihren Urlaub *gedacht*?

Have you already thought about your holiday?

Was *dachten* die Zeitgenossen *über* die Erfindung des Telefons?

What did (his) contemporaries think about the invention of the telephone?

**dienen als** + acc.

Dieser Raum *dient als* Arbeitszimmer.

This room serves as a study.

**diskutieren über** + acc.

Die Klasse *diskutiert über* die Politik.

The class is discussing politics.

**sich eignen für** + acc.

Er *eignet sich* bestimmt *für* diesen Beruf.

He is definitely well suited for this profession.

**einladen zu** + dat.

Die Partei hat *zu* einer Versammlung *eingeladen*.

The party issued an open invitation to the meeting.

**sich einstellen auf** + acc.

Er hat *sich* schnell *auf* die neue Situation *eingestellt*.

He quickly adapted to the new situation.

**empfinden als** + acc.

Die neuen Gesetze *empfinden* wir *als* Fortschritt. — We see the new laws as progress.

**sich entscheiden für** + acc.

Er *entscheidet sich für* den Beruf des Arztes. — He decides to become a doctor.

**sich entwickeln zu** + dat.

Die Firma *entwickelte sich zu* einem Großunternehmen. — The firm developed into a large business concern.

**sich ergeben für** + acc.

*Für* das Projekt *ergeben sich* Schwierigkeiten. — There are difficulties arising for this project.

**sich erinnern an** + acc.

*Erinnerst* du *dich* noch *an* Klaus? — Do you still remember Klaus?

**erwarten von** + dat.

Was *erwartet* ihr *von* der Firma? — What do you expect from the firm?

**fehlen an** + dat.

In vielen Ländern *fehlt* es *an* Nahrungsmitteln. — In many countries there is a lack of food.

**fragen nach** + dat.

Er *fragte* seine Schüler *nach* ihrem Traumberuf. — He asked his pupils about their dream profession.

**freigeben zu** + dat.

Das Foto ist *zur* Veröffentlichung *freigegeben* worden. — The photo has been released for publication.

**sich freuen auf/über** + acc.

*Freut* er *sich* schon *auf* das Wochenende? — Is he already looking forward to the weekend?

*Freust* du *dich über* mein Geschenk? — Are you happy about my present?

**gehören zu** + dat.

*Zur* Europäischen Gemeinschaft *gehören* neun Staaten. — There are nine countries belonging to the European Community.

**gelangen zu** + dat.

Die Erfindung *gelangte zu* großer Bedeutung.

The discovery attained great importance.

**gelten als/für** + acc.

Sie *gilt als* moderne Frau.

She is considered to be an up-to-date woman.

Die Bestimmung *gilt für* ganz Europa.

The regulation applies to the whole of Europe.

**sich gewöhnen an** + acc.

Wir haben *uns an* die neue Wohnung schon *gewöhnt*.

We have already got used to the new flat.

**halten für** + acc.

Er *hält sich für* einen modernen Lehrer.

He thinks himself an up-to-date teacher.

**sich handeln um** + acc.

*Handelt* es *sich* (= *geht* es) *um* uns?

Is it about us?

**helfen bei** + dat.

Wir *helfen* euch *beim* Umzug.

We'll help you with the move.

**herauskommen bei** + dat.

Was ist denn *bei* der Umfrage *herausgekommen*? – *Dabei* ist nichts *herausgekommen*.

What was revealed in the poll? Nothing was revealed.

**sich hinwegsetzen über** + acc.

*Darüber* sollte man *sich hinwegsetzen*.

That should be disregarded.

**hinweisen auf** + acc.

Er *wies auf* die Bestimmung *hin*.

He referred to the regulations.

**sich informieren über** + acc.

Apotheker müssen *sich über* neue Arzneimittel *informieren*.

Pharmacists must inform themselves on new medicines.

**sich interessieren für** + acc.

*Interessiert* sie *sich für* Musik?

Is she interested in music?

**kämpfen um (für)** + acc.

Sie *kämpfen um (für)* die Unabhängigkeit.

They are fighting for independence.

**kandidieren für** + acc.

Er *kandidiert für* den Bundestag.

He is standing for Parliament.

**sich kümmern um** + acc.

Kannst du *dich um* die Gäste *kümmern?*

Can you take care of the guests?

**leiden an/unter** + dat.

Sie *leidet an* einer schweren Krankheit.

She is suffering from a serious illness.

Sie *leidet unter* der Einsamkeit.

She suffers from loneliness.

**machen zu** + dat.

Er *machte* ihn *zum* Minister.

He made him a Minister.

**nachdenken über** + acc.

Er hat lange *über* das Problem *nachgedacht.*

He pondered the problem for a long time.

**neigen zu** + dat.

Er *neigt zu* Übertreibungen.

He tends to exaggerate.

**passen zu** + dat.

Die Mode *paßt zu* uns.

The fashion suits us.

**profitieren von** + dat.

Er hat *von* seinem Auslandsaufenthalt viel *profitiert.*

He gained a lot from his stay abroad.

**rechnen mit** + dat.

Es muß *mit* Entlassungen *gerechnet* werden.

Dismissals must be expected.

**reden von** + dat.

*Reden* wir *von* etwas anderem.

Let's talk about something else.

**sich richten gegen** + acc.
**nach** + dat.

Der Antrag *richtet sich gegen* die Gewerkschaft.

The proposal is levelled at the union.

Die Höhe des Stipendiums *richtet sich nach* dem Einkommen der Eltern.

The size of the scholarship depends on the parents' income.

**schätzen auf** + acc.

Das Gemälde wurde *auf* eine halbe Million *geschätzt*.

The painting was estimated at half a million.

**sich schützen vor** + dat.

*Schützen* Sie *sich vor* der Kälte!

Protect yourself from the cold.

**sorgen für** + acc.

Er muß *für* seinen alten Vater *sorgen*.

He must take care of his old father.

**stammen aus/von** + dat.

Sie *stammt aus* Dänemark.

She comes from Denmark.

Das Bild *stammt* noch *von* meinen Eltern.

This picture belonged to my parents.

**sterben an** + dat.

*An* welcher Krankheit ist er *gestorben*?

Which disease did he die of?

**stoßen auf** + acc.

Sein Antrag *stieß auf* Widerstand.

His proposal met with resistance.

**streben nach** + dat.

Sie *streben nach* sozialer Gerechtigkeit.

They are striving for social justice.

**sich stützen auf** + acc.

Der Abgeordnete *stützte sich auf* die Rede des Ministers.

The Member based his arguments on the Minister's speech.

**teilnehmen an** + dat.

Ich konnte *an* der Versammlung nicht *teilnehmen*.

I couldn't take part in the meeting.

**träumen von** + dat.

Er *träumt von* der Prüfung.

He is dreaming of the exam.

**übergehen zu** + dat.

Alle Automobilfabriken sind *zum* Fließband *übergegangen*.

All motor-car factories have changed over to the assembly line.

**sich unterhalten über** + acc.
Habt ihr *euch über* den neuen Film *unterhalten?*

Did you talk about the new film?

**sich verabreden mit** + dat.
Hat er *sich mit* ihr *verabredet?*

Has he made a date with her?

**verbinden mit** + dat.
Können Sie mich *mit* Herrn Meyer *verbinden?*

Can you put me through to Mr Meyer?

**verfügen über** + acc.
Er *verfügt über* ausreichende Geldmittel.

He has sufficient funds at his disposal.

**vergleichen mit** + dat.
Kann man die Verantwortung eines Lokführers *mit* der eines Piloten *vergleichen?*

Can you compare the responsibility of an engine driver with that of a pilot?

**sich verständigen mit** + dat.
Beethoven mußte *sich* schriftlich *mit* seiner Umwelt *verständigen.*

Beethoven had to communicate in writing.

**sich verstehen mit** + dat.
Ich *verstehe mich mit* meinen Nachbarn sehr gut.

I get along very well with my neighbours.

**wählen zu** + dat.
Er ist *zum* Fußballer des Jahres *gewählt* worden.

He has been elected Footballer of the Year.

**warten auf** + acc.
Er *wartet auf* sein Taxi.

He is waiting for his taxi.

**sich wenden an** + acc.
*Wenden* Sie *sich* bitte *an* Frau Schulz.

Please get in touch with Mrs Schulz.

**werden aus** + dat.
Wir wissen nicht, was *aus* ihm *geworden* ist.

We don't know what became of him.

**wissen über** + acc.

Er möchte mehr *über* sie *wissen.*  He would like to know more about her.

**zählen zu** + dat.

Er *zählt zu* den berühmtesten Piani-  He is one of the most famous pianists in
sten der Welt.  the world.

# The Noun

German nouns have several unfamiliar aspects for English-speaking students: grammatical gender independent of sex, for example, the declension of nouns, the intricate pattern of plural formation and then the coordination of all these by agreement in gender, number and case. But however complex it may seem at first, there is a clear system governing much of the German noun, and once learned, it is often easily mastered.

## 1. Gender

**141    a. Grammatical gender**

There are three grammatical genders: masculine, neuter and feminine. They are indicated by means of the article (*der, das, die*).

| | |
|---|---|
| masculine: | der Brief |
| neuter: | das Buch |
| feminine: | die Wohnung |

With persons, the grammatical gender usually corresponds to the sex, except in the case of diminutives, which are always neuter (see p. 98).

| | | |
|---|---|---|
| der Mann | die Frau | Exceptions: |
| der Vater | die Mutter | |
| der Sohn | die Tochter | das Weib |
| | | das Fräulein |
| der Fotograf | die Fotografin | das Mädchen |
| der Lehrer | die Lehrerin | das Kind |
| | | |
| der Schüler | die Schülerin | das Staatsoberhaupt |
| der Mitarbeiter | die Mitarbeiterin | das Mitglied |

**142    b. Rules for determining gender**

With many nouns there is no way of recognizing the gender at all. So every noun must be learnt together with its definite article (*der, das, die*). Rules can be made, however, for the following groups of nouns:

**Masculine**

**43** (1) the days of the week, the months and the seasons,

> der Montag, der Dienstag, der Mittwoch, der Donnerstag, der Freitag,
> der Samstag (Sonnabend), der Sonntag
>
> der Januar, der Februar, der März, der April, der Mai, der Juni, der Juli,
> der August, der September, der Oktober, der November, der Dezember
>
> der Frühling, der Sommer, der Herbst, der Winter
> but:
> die Woche, das Jahr

**44** (2) the points of the compass,

> der Osten, der Süden, der Westen, der Norden

**45** (3) brand names of motor vehicles,

> der BMW, der VW, der Mercedes, der Opel

**46** (4) most nouns ending in *-en*,

> der Hafen, der Kuchen, der Laden, der Schaden, der Wagen

**Neuter**

**47** (1) nouns formed from other parts of speech, which do not denote people,

> das Baden, das Einkaufen, das Essen, das Leben, das Rauchen
> das Gute, das Interessante, das Neue
> das Dänische, das Englische, das Französische
> das Blaue, das Grüne, das Rote

**148**  (2) diminutives ending in *-lein* and *-chen,*

> das Büchlein  (das Fräulein
> das Bildchen  das Mädchen)
> das Hütchen

**149**  (3) nouns ending in *-(i)um* and *-ment,*

> das Datum, das Einkaufszentrum, das Gymnasium, das Museum, das Studium
> das Appartement, das Argument, das Experiment

## Feminine

**150**  (1) the names of ships and aircraft,

> die Bremen, die Europa
> die Boeing, die Caravelle, die Iljuschin, die Trident

**151**  (2) nouns ending in *-heit, -keit, -schaft, -ung,*

> die Einzelheit, die Gelegenheit, die Gesundheit, die Menschheit
>
> die Geschwindigkeit, die Gewissenhaftigkeit, die Schwierigkeit, die Tätigkeit, die Ungerechtigkeit
>
> die Eigenschaft, die Gesellschaft, die Mannschaft
>
> die Beschäftigung, die Einladung, die Empfehlung, die Entschuldigung, die Verantwortung, die Verwaltung, die Zeitung

**152**  (3) most nouns ending in *-enz, -ie, -ik, -ion, -tät.*

> die Konferenz, die Konkurrenz, die Korrespondenz
> die Akademie, die Chemie, die Garantie, die Industrie, die Fotografie

> die Fabrik, die Grafik, die Kritik, die Mathematik, die Musik, die Politik, die Technik
>
> die Diskussion, die Inflation, die Konstruktion, die Organisation, die Position, die Produktion
>
> die Aktivität, die Intensität, die Qualität, die Realität

## Special cases

**153** (1) Some masculine nouns denote both male and female persons.

> der Boß, der Gast, der Mensch

**154** (2) Compound nouns follow the gender of the last component.

> der Lärm – das Flugzeug: der Flugzeuglärm
> das Geschäft – die Lebensmittel: das Lebensmittelgeschäft
> die Abteilung – der Export: die Exportabteilung
> der Satellit – die Nachrichten: der Nachrichtensatellit

## 2. Number

### a. Singular and plural

**155** Almost all nouns have singular and plural forms.

The following nouns appear **only in the singular**:

**156** (1) the names of materials or substances,

> das Eis, der Kaffee, die Salami, der Tee, der Whisky

**157** (2) collective nouns,

> die Bevölkerung, das Gepäck, die Polizei, das Publikum

**158** (3) abstract nouns.

> der Durst, der Hunger
>
> das Tempo (but note also in music: die Tempi), der Verkehr, das Wetter
> die Abschaffung, der Bedarf, die Erholung
>
> Also nouns formed from infinitives:
> das Tennisspielen, das Skifahren

The following nouns appear **only in the plural:**

**159** (1) certain geographical names,

> die Alpen, die Niederlande, die USA

**160** (2) groups of people,

> die Eltern, die Leute

**161** (3) miscellaneous.

> die Ferien, die Festspiele
>
> die Kenntnisse, die Kosten, die Papiere (meaning documents etc.), die Unterlagen
>
> die Lebensmittel
>
> die Antiquitäten, die Möbel

**162 b. Formation of the plural** (I, 22)

In English most nouns form their plural by adding -*(e)s*; German has eight different ways of forming the plural (quoted for grammar purposes in the nominative). The definite article in the nominative plural is always *die*.

| (1) | - | no change | der Lehrer – die Lehrer |
| (2) | ˙˙ | umlaut only | der Mantel – die Mäntel |

| (3) | -e | -e ending | der Tag – die Tag**e** |
|---|---|---|---|
| (4) | ⸚e | -e ending + umlaut | der Platz – die Pl**ä**tz**e** |
| (5) | -er | -er ending | das Kind – die Kind**er** |
| (6) | ⸚er | -er ending + umlaut | das Haus – die H**äuser** |
| (7) | -(e)n | -n or -en ending | die Stunde – die Stunde**n** |
| | | | der Student – die Student**en** |
| (8) | -s | -s ending | der Krimi – die Krimi**s** |

The surest way to master the plural form of a German noun is to learn it along with the gender and absorb it by constant practice. However, a plural form can frequently be deduced from the type + gender + (sometimes) ending of the noun, as should be clear from the following examples:

**63** (1) no change (der Lehrer – die Lehrer)
Masculine nouns ending in *-er* derived from verbs and denoting the performer of the action,

> der Arbeiter, der Autofahrer, der Einwohner, der Leiter, der Maler, der Richter, der Sprecher

many other masculine and neuter nouns ending in *-el*, *-en* or *-er*,

> das Fenster, der Keller, der Schlüssel, der Wagen, das Zimmer

neuter nouns with prefix *Ge-* and suffix *-e* derived from verbs and denoting object of action,

> das Gebäude, das Gemälde

all diminutives ending in *-chen* and *-lein*.

> das Büchlein, das Häuschen, das Fräulein, das Mädchen

**164** (2) umlaut only (der Mantel – die Mäntel)
Masculine nouns ending in *-el*, *-en* or *-er* with stem vowel *a* or *o*,

> der Apfel, der Flughafen, der Garten, der Vogel

the following four nouns denoting close family relationships:

> der Bruder, die Mutter, die Tochter, der Vater

**165**  (3) *-e* ending (der Tag – die Tag**e**)
Many masculine and neuter monosyllables,

> der Brief, der Hund, der Preis, der Punkt, der Schuh
> das Bein, das Brot, das Haar, das Paar, das Pferd, das Schiff

neuter nouns with prefix *Ge-* derived from verbs and denoting the object of the action.

> das Geschenk, das Getränk

> Note: das Erlebnis – die Erleb**nisse**
> das Ergebnis – die Ergeb**nisse**
> das Zeugnis – die Zeug**nisse**

**166**  (4) *-e* ending + umlaut (der Platz – die Plä**tze**)
Many masculine monosyllables, especially derivatives from verbs (+ compounds),

> der Arzt, der Gast, der Hof, der Sohn, der Flug, der Satz, der Sprung, der Zug, der Anzug, der Ausflug, der Bahnhof
> Note: die Nuß – die N**üsse**

a number of feminine monosyllables.

> die Bank, die Hand, die Kraft, die Nacht, die Stadt, die Wand

**167**  (5) *-er* ending (das Kind – die Kind**er**)

> das Bild, das Kleid, das Licht, das Schild

This group consists mainly of neuter monosyllables.

**68** (6) *-er* ending + umlaut (das Haus – die Häuser)
Many neuter monosyllables,

> das Buch, das Dach, das Dorf, das Glas, das Land, das (Post)amt, das
> (Motor)rad

a few masculine monosyllables,

> der Mann, der Mund

nouns with the suffix *-tum*.

> der Irrtum

**69** (7) *-n* or *-en* ending (die Stunde – die Stunden, der Student – die Studenten)
All feminine nouns ending in *-e* take an *-n* ending,

> die Anzeige, die Briefmarke, die Dame, die Familie, die Minute, die
> Reise, die Schule

most other feminine nouns take *-en* (except those ending in *l* and *r*),

> die Fabrik, die Gefahr, die Nachricht, die Zahl, die Zeit (-en)
> die Kartoffel, die Mauer (-n)

all feminine nouns ending in *-ung* and any feminine abstract nouns with
suffixes *-schaft*, *-heit*, *-keit* and *-ei*, if they can be pluralized, take the ending
*-en*,

> die Empfehlung, die Erklärung, die Sendung, die Wohnung
> die Möglichkeit, die Partei

some common masculine nouns of the weak declension (see p. 108 ff.)
already ending in *-e*, take an *-n* ending,

> der Gedanke, der Junge, der Name

other masculine nouns of the weak declension, especially those denoting human beings, take an *-en* ending (cf. p. 109),

der Fürst, der Mensch

only a handful of neuter nouns take an *-(e)n* ending.

das Auge, das Interesse (-n)
das Bett, das Hemd (-en)

Note: die Ansagerin – die Ansager**innen**
die Lehrerin – die Lehrer**innen**
die Freundin – die Freund**innen**

**170**  (8) *-s* ending (der Krimi – die Krimis)

das Auto, das Hotel, das Kino, das Radio, das Restaurant, das Studio, das Ticket

Only foreign words take an *-s* ending in the plural (see p. 106 ff.). Note: An *s* is added to family names to indicate all members of a household.

| Am Sonntagmorgen klingelt bei Kaufmann**s** (Meier**s**) das Telefon. | On Sunday morning the Kaufmanns' (Meiers') telephone rings. |

Plural of abbreviations:

| der Pkw | – die Pkw**s** |
| der Lkw | – die Lkw**s** |
| der BMW | – die BMW**s** |

**Special cases**

**171** Terms ending in *-mann*:

| der Fach**mann** | – die Fach**leute** |
|---|---|
| der Kauf**mann** | – die Kauf**leute** |

This classification of noun plurals is not exhaustive and there do exist exceptions to the various groups. It should therefore be considered as a guide rather than a set of rules; the following summary should help facilitate learning further:

(1) Most feminine nouns take an *-(e)n* plural, except some common monosyllables which take *-e*.

(2) No change or umlaut only for masculine and neuter nouns ending in *-el*, *-en*, *-er*. Diminutives (*-chen*, *-lein*) do not change.

(3) Most masculine monosyllables (plus a number of neuter and feminine monosyllables) add *-e*, with or without umlaut.

(4) The nouns with *-er* plural ending (with or without umlaut) are mainly neuter.

(5) Common masculine nouns of the weak declension take an *-(e)n* plural.

**c. Plural forms of foreign words**

**172** (1) *-e* ending

Masculine nouns ending in *-är*, *-eur*,

| der Million**är** | – die Million**äre** |
|---|---|
| der Ingen**ieur** | – die Ingen**ieure** |

neuter nouns ending in *-ment*.

| das Argu**ment** | – die Argu**mente** |
|---|---|
| das Experi**ment** | – die Experi**mente** |

**173**  (2) -*(e)n* ending

Masculine nouns ending in -*oge, -ant, -ent, -ist,*

| | |
|---|---|
| der Geologe | – die Geologen |
| der Psychologe | – die Psychologen |
| der Demonstrant | – die Demonstranten |
| der Passant | – die Passanten |
| der Dirigent | – die Dirigenten |
| der Polizist | – die Polizisten |
| der Journalist | – die Journalisten |

neuter nouns ending in -*(i)um,*

| | |
|---|---|
| das Gymnasium | – die Gymnasien |
| das Einkaufszentrum | – die Einkaufszentren |

feminine nouns ending in -*enz, -ie, -ik, -ion, -tät.*

| | |
|---|---|
| die Konferenz | – die Konferenzen |
| die Akademie | – die Akademien |
| die Graphik | – die Graphiken |
| die Diskussion | – die Diskussionen |
| die Aktivität | – die Aktivitäten |

**174**  (3) -*s* ending

Foreign words from English,

| | |
|---|---|
| der Club | – die Clubs |
| das Hobby | – die Hobbies (or Hobbys) |
| die Party | – die Parties (or Partys) |
| das Team | – die Teams |

foreign words from French and Italian, especially those ending in a vowel.

| | |
|---|---|
| das Büro | – die Büros |
| der Chef | – die Chefs |
| das Foto | – die Fotos |
| das Kino | – die Kinos |
| der Park | – die Parks |
| das Radio | – die Radios |
| das Studio | – die Studios |

## 3. Declension

There are four cases in German, indicated by the article and sometimes also by an ending. These cases are:

(1) The nominative (Nom.), the case of the subject, also used predicatively after *sein, werden, bleiben, heißen* and *scheinen*.

(2) The accusative (Acc.), the case of the direct object, answering the question *wen* or *was?*. It is also used after certain prepositions (see p.215 ff.) and in many adverbial phrases (see p. 111).

(3) The dative (Dat.), the case of the indirect object, answering the question *wem?*. It also functions as object after certain verbs (see. p. 85 ff.) and follows many prepositions (see p. 217 ff.).

(4) The genitive (Gen.), the case of possession, answering the question *wessen?*. It is a close equivalent to the English possessive with *of, 's or s'*. The genitive also follows a few verbs (see p. 84) and a few prepositions (see p. 221) and is used in one or two adverbial phrases (see p. 111).

175  **a. Declension in the singular** (I, 6, 11, 14; II, 3)

| | | Masculine | Neuter | Feminine |
|---|---|---|---|---|
| Sing. | Nominative | der Lehrer | das Kind | die Lehrerin |
| | Accusative | den Lehrer | das Kind | die Lehrerin |
| | Dative | dem Lehrer | dem Kind | der Lehrerin |
| | Genitive | des Lehrers | des Kindes | der Lehrerin |

**176**  (1) There is only one singular ending, the *-(e)s* added to the genitive of masculine and neuter nouns.

*-es* is added to nouns ending in *-s*, *-ß* and *-z*.

| der Bus | – des Busses | der Paß | – des Passes |
|---------|--------------|---------|--------------|
| der Kurs | – des Kurses | der Platz | – des Platzes |

*-es* is often added to monosyllabic nouns.

| das Buch | – des Buches | das Kind | – des Kindes |
|----------|--------------|----------|--------------|
| der Freund | – des Freundes | das Haus | – des Hauses |
| but: der Film | – des Films | | |

**177**  (2) Words ending in *-nis* double the *-s* in the genitive (cf. p. 102).

| das Ergebnis | – des Ergebnisses |
|--------------|-------------------|
| das Erlebnis | – des Erlebnisses |
| das Zeugnis | – des Zeugnisses |

**178**  (3) Names of the months do not usually take an *-s* in the genitive.

| der Februar | – des Februar |
|-------------|---------------|
| der März | – des März |
| der September | – des September |

The names of the months also remain unchanged when used with *Anfang, Mitte, Ende.*

| Anfang September | Ende April | Mitte Mai |
|------------------|------------|-----------|

**179**  **The weak declension of masculine nouns with -(e)n ending** (cf. p. 114 ff)

| Nominative | der Junge | der Student |
|------------|-----------|-------------|
| Accusative | den Jungen | den Studenten |
| Dative | dem Jungen | dem Studenten |
| Genitive | des Jungen | des Studenten |

Masculine nouns of the weak declension take the ending -(e)n in the accusative, dative and genitive; -en is added to nouns ending in a consonant, -n to those ending in a vowel.

-en is added to

**180** (1)

> der Mensch (den, dem, des Menschen)
>
> but:
> der Herr, den Herrn, dem Herrn, des Herrn

**181** (2) foreign words ending in -ant, -ent, -ist etc.

> der Demonstrant (den, dem, des Demonstranten)    der Architekt
> der Dirigent                                     der Astronaut
> der Polizist, der Journalist                     der Fotograf

-n is added to

**182** (1) nouns ending in -e,

> der Experte, der Fluglotse, der Kollege, der Vorsitzende

**183** (2) nouns indicating certain nationalities,

> der Deutsche, der Franzose, der Jugoslawe, der Portugiese, der Türke

**184** (3) professions ending in -oge.

> der Geologe, der Psychologe, der Soziologe

Some nouns in this group also take an -s in the genitive.

| Nominative | der Name | der Gedanke |
|---|---|---|
| Accusative | den Namen | den Gedanken |
| Dative | dem Namen | dem Gedanken |
| Genitive | des Namens | des Gedankens |

**185  b. Declension in the plural** (I, 14; II, 3)

| Pl. Nom. | die Tage | die Plätze | die Studenten |
|---|---|---|---|
| Acc. | die Tage | die Plätze | die Studenten |
| Dat. | den Tagen | den Plätzen | den Studenten |
| Gen. | der Tage | der Plätze | der Studenten |
| Nom. | die Lehrer | die Mäntel | |
| Acc. | die Lehrer | die Mäntel | |
| Dat. | den Lehrern | den Mänteln | |
| Gen. | der Lehrer | der Mäntel | |
| Nom. | die Kinder | die Häuser | die Krimis |
| Acc. | die Kinder | die Häuser | die Krimis |
| Dat. | den Kindern | den Häusern | den Krimis |
| Gen. | der Kinder | der Häuser | der Krimis |

The plural form of the noun remains the same throughout, except in the dative, where -*n* is added.

No -*n* is added when
**186**  (1) the plural already ends in -*n*,

> die Student**en** – den Student**en**

**187**  (2) the nominative plural ends in -*s*.

> die Krimi**s** – den Krimi**s**

Note:

(1) Nouns in apposition
A noun must be in the same case as the noun or pronoun with which it stands in apposition.

> Herr Schulz, **unser neuer Kollege**,    Mr Schulz, our new colleague, is sick.
> ist krank.

| | |
|---|---|
| Kennen Sie Herrn Schulz, **unseren neuen Kollegen**? | Do you know Mr Schulz, our new colleague? |
| Nächsten Sonntag gehe ich mit Herrn Schulz, **unserem neuen Kollegen**, zum Fußball. | Next Sunday I'm going to a football match with Mr Schulz, our new colleague. |

After *als* or *wie*, the case of a noun in apposition depends on the sense.

| | |
|---|---|
| **Ich** kannte ihn schon **als Junge**. | I knew him as a boy (= when I was a boy). |
| Ich kannte **ihn** schon **als Jungen**. | I knew him as a boy (= when he was a boy). |

(2) Adverbial phrases

in the accusative:
Many phrases expressing time, price, measure etc. stand in the accusative.

| | |
|---|---|
| Er wohnte **einen Monat** bei uns. | He stayed with us for one month. |
| Es regnete **den ganzen Tag**. | It rained all day. |
| Die Strecke ist **einen Kilometer** lang und kostet **eine Million**. | The track is a kilometre long and costs a million (marks). |
| **Nächstes Jahr** fahre ich nach Marokko. | Next year I'm going to Morocco. |

in the genitive:
The genitive is used in a few phrases to show indefinite time.

| | |
|---|---|
| **Eines Tages** traf er seinen alten Freund wieder. | One day he met his old friend again. |

### c. Declension of proper nouns (II, 9)

**188** (1) Personal names
Personal names do not generally take an article. In colloquial German, however, one can say:

| | |
|---|---|
| Wo ist denn **der Hans**? | Wherever's Hans? |
| **Der Beckenbauer** müßte man sein! | Beckenbauer's the man to be! |
| Hast du **die Claudia** gesehen? | Have you seen Claudia? |

The genitive singular ending is *-s*. There is no ending in the accusative or dative.

| | |
|---|---|
| **Evas** neue Wohnung ist ziemlich groß. | Eva's new flat is quite big. |
| **Michaels** Schwester hat jetzt eine neue Stelle. | Michael's sister has got a new job now. |
| Ich habe **Jochen** heute getroffen. | I met Jochen today. |
| Hast du **Brigitte** das Buch schon zurückgegeben? | Have you already given the book back to Brigitte? |

The genitive always appears before the noun to which it refers.

| | |
|---|---|
| **Wolfs Rekord** gilt schon lange nicht mehr. | Wolf's record was beaten long ago. |

Titles and Christian names appearing before surnames remain unchanged.

| | |
|---|---|
| **Frau Fischers Mann** ist oft im Ausland. | Mrs Fischer's husband is often abroad. |
| **Dr. Müllers Bruder** spielt sehr gut Klavier. | Dr Müller's brother plays the piano very well. |
| Ich habe gestern **Manfred Wolfs Schwester** gesehen. | I saw Manfred Wolf's sister yesterday. |

112

Only the word *Herr* is declined.

| | |
|---|---|
| **Herrn Baumanns Firma** produziert noch. | Mr Baumann's firm is still manufacturing. |

The genitive is often expressed by *von + dative*.

| | |
|---|---|
| Gilt der **Rekord von Manfred Wolf** noch? | Does Manfred Wolf still hold the record? |
| Der **Wagen von Herrn Bauer** ist schon alt. | Mr Bauer's car is already old. |

This use of *von + dative* is particularly frequent with nouns ending in *-s* or *-z*, where the genitive ending cannot be recognized.

| | |
|---|---|
| Läuft der **Wagen von Fritz** noch? | Is Fritz's car still running? |
| Sind die **Eltern von Hans** verreist? | Have Hans' parents gone away? |

**189** (2) Geographical names
Masculine and neuter geographical names also take an *-(e)s* ending in the genitive. The alternative form *von + dative* is frequent.

| | |
|---|---|
| die **Länder Südamerikas** | the countries of South America |
| die **Größe Europas** | the size of Europe |
| die **Entfernung des Mondes** | the distance of the moon |
| die **Hauptstadt von Italien** | the capital of Italy |
| der **Bürgermeister von Berlin** | the Mayor of Berlin |

## d. Declension of nouns formed from adjectives and participles

**190  Definite article**

|        |       | Masculine | Neuter | Feminine |
|--------|-------|-----------|--------|----------|
| Sing.  | Nom.  | der Neue  | das Neue | die Neue |
|        | Acc.  | den Neuen | das Neue | die Neue |
|        | Dat.  | dem Neuen | dem Neuen | der Neuen |
|        | Gen.  | des Neuen | des Neuen[1] | der Neuen |
| Pl.    | Nom.  | die Neuen | – | die Neuen |
|        | Acc.  | die Neuen | – | die Neuen |
|        | Dat.  | den Neuen | – | den Neuen |
|        | Gen.  | der Neuen | – | der Neuen |

**191  Indefinite article**

|        |       | Masculine | | Neuter | Feminine | |
|--------|-------|-----------|---|--------|----------|---|
| Sing.  | Nom.  | ein    | Neuer | (etwas) Neues | eine  | Neue  |
|        | Acc.  | einen  | Neuen | (etwas) Neues | eine  | Neue  |
|        | Dat.  | einem  | Neuen | (etwas) Neuem | einer | Neuen |
|        | Gen.  | eines  | Neuen | –             | einer | Neuen |
| Pl.    | Nom.  |        | Neue  | –             |       | Neue  |
|        | Acc.  |        | Neue  | –             |       | Neue  |
|        | Dat.  |        | Neuen | –             |       | Neuen |
|        | Gen.  |        | Neuer | –             |       | Neuer |

Nouns formed from adjectives and participles (e. g. *der Angestellte*) take an article like any other noun. They are declined, however, like adjectives. Compare these two nominative forms as used with the definite and indefinite article:

---

[1]  As in phrases like *Der Reiz des Neuen* (the charm of novelty).

114

```
der Neue          – ein Neuer
der Angestellte   – ein Angestellter
```

This group of nouns also includes

**192** (1) masculine and feminine (persons),

```
der Abgeordnete/die Abgeordnete (ein Abgeordneter/eine Abgeordnete)
der Bekannte/die Bekannte        (ein Bekannter/eine Bekannte)
der Berufstätige/die Berufstätige (ein Berufstätiger/eine Berufstätige)
```

**193** (2) neuter (abstract nouns).

```
das Besondere, das Gute, das Interessante, das Schöne
```

# The Article

**194   1. The definite and the indefinite article**

*Der, das die* are known as the definite article,
*ein, ein, eine* the indefinite article.
The article always precedes a noun.

Whereas the English *the* is invariable, the German definite article changes
its form to agree with its noun in gender, number and case. Similarly, while
*a(n)* remains invariable, the German indefinite article agrees with the noun
in gender and case; *ein(e)*, which can also mean "one", has no plural (see p.
119 ff.).

**a. Declension of the definite article** (I, 2, 3, 6, 14; II, 3)

**195   Singular**

Masculine: **der**

| N | der | **Der** Student wohnt in Berlin. The student lives in Berlin. |
|---|---|---|
| A | den | Dort sehen Sie **den** Fernsehturm. There you see the TV tower. |
| D | dem | Er bringt **dem** Gast einen Kaffee. He brings the guest some coffee. |
| G | des | Der Rekord **des** Sportlers war eine große Leistung. The sportsman's record was a great achievement. |

Neuter: **das**

| N | das | **Das** Büro ist zu klein. The office is too small. |
|---|---|---|
| A | das | Dort sehen Sie **das** Rathaus. There you see the Town Hall. |
| D | dem | Er spielt mit **dem** Kind. He is playing with the child. |
| G | des | Den Namen **des** Kindes weiß ich nicht mehr. I have forgotten the name of the child. |

**96** Feminine: **die**

| N | die | **Die** Sekretärin arbeitet in Köln. |
|---|---|---|
| | | The secretary works in Cologne. |
| A | die | Ich kenne **die** Straße nicht. |
| | | I don't know the street. |
| D | der | Er hilft **der** Dame. |
| | | He is helping the lady. |
| G | der | Das ist die Meinung **der** Bundesregierung. |
| | | That is the opinion of the Federal Government. |

**Plural**

Masculine, Neuter, Feminine: **die**

| N | die | **Die** Zigaretten sind hier. |
|---|---|---|
| | | The cigarettes are here. |
| A | die | Ich hole **die** Gläser. |
| | | I'll fetch the glasses. |
| D | den | Sie bringt **den** Gästen Kaffee. |
| | | She brings the guests some coffee. |
| G | der | Kennen Sie die Ansichten **der** Fachleute? |
| | | Do you know the expert's views? |

**97 b. The use of the definite article**

In German the definite article appears before nouns denoting persons or things that are generally known or have already been mentioned in the context concerned. It can often have the force of the English demonstratives *this* and *that*.

| | |
|---|---|
| **Das Stadion in Berlin** ist groß. | The stadium in Berlin is large. |
| **Den Film** möchte ich mir ansehen. | I want to see that film. |
| **Die Frau** möchte ich gerne kennenlernen. | I'd like to meet that woman. |

It always appears with superlatives and ordinal numbers.

| | |
|---|---|
| Das ist **das höchste Gebäude** der Stadt. | That's the tallest building in the town. |
| Das ist **der schnellste Rennwagen** der Welt. | That is the fastest racing car in the world. |
| Sie wollen Herrn Zinn sprechen? Fahren Sie bitte in **den dritten Stock**. | You want to speak to Mr Zinn? Please take the lift to the third floor. |
| In **der zweiten Urlaubswoche** erholt man sich am besten. | You get the best rest in the second week of the holiday. |

### Special uses of the definite article in German

(1) Frequently before abstract nouns and nouns used in a general sense,

| | |
|---|---|
| **Das Leben** wird immer interessanter. | Life gets more and more interesting. |
| Er hält nichts von **der Ehe.** | He takes a dim view of marriage. |
| **Der Mensch** und **die Technik.** | Man and technology. |

(2) with parts of the body where English uses a possessive (cf. p. 88),

| | |
|---|---|
| Er wäscht sich gerade **die Hände**. | He is just washing his hands. |

(3) before seasons, months, days of the week, meals, streets, and places of public resort,

| | |
|---|---|
| Er kam **im Januar**, also **im Winter**. | He came in January, hence in winter. |
| Das sagte sie mir **am Montag**, beim Mittagessen. | She told me that on Monday – during lunch. |
| Das mußt du in **der Carnaby Street** kaufen. | You must buy that in Carnaby Street. |
| Ich gehe ganz gern in **die Schule**. | I quite like going to school. |

118

(4) before the names of countries when feminine or plural,

| | |
|---|---|
| Ich fahre in **die Schweiz**. | I am going to Switzerland. |
| Waren Sie schon in **den USA**? | Have you been to the USA? |

(5) in certain stock phrases.

| | |
|---|---|
| Er fährt **ins Ausland**. | He is going abroad. |
| Ich fahre lieber mit **der Bahn**. | I prefer to go by train. |
| Er liegt schon **im Bett**. | He has already gone to bed. |

(6) The German definite article replaces the English indefinite article when used distributively.

| | |
|---|---|
| Das kostet vier Mark **das Meter**. | That costs four Marks a metre. |

**c. Declension of the indefinite article** (I, 4, 5, 16)

**98 ein-** (Singular only)

Masculine

| N | ein | **Ein** Urlaub zu Hause kann auch schön sein. A holiday at home can be nice too. |
|---|---|---|
| A | einen | Ich trinke **einen** Kaffee. I'll have a coffee. |
| D | einem | Sie kommt mit **einem** neuen Freund. She is coming with a new boy-friend. |
| G | eines | Er arbeitet im Büro **eines** Architekten. He is working in an architect's office. |

Neuter

| N | ein | **Ein** Originalgemälde kostet viel Geld. An original painting costs a lot of money. |
|---|---|---|
| A | ein | Ich möchte **ein** Bier. I'd like a beer. |

| D | einem | Er arbeitet in **einem** Hotel. |
| | | He is working in a hotel. |
| G | eines | Er arbeitet in der Küche **eines** großen Hotels. |
| | | He is working in the kitchen of a large hotel. |

### Feminine

| N | eine | **Eine** berufstätige Frau arbeitet mehr als ein Mann. |
| | | A woman with a job works more than a man. |
| A | eine | Sie hat **eine** neue Wohnung. |
| | | She's got a new flat. |
| D | einer | Ich komme in **einer** Stunde. |
| | | I'll come in an hour ('s time). |
| G | einer | Sie arbeitet in der Verwaltung **einer** kleinen Fabrik. |
| | | She is working in the administration department of a small factory. |

### kein-

The German indefinite article also has a negative form *kein-*, meaning *no*, *not a*, *not any*. *Kein-* can also be used in the plural.

## 199 Singular

Masculine

| N | kein | **Kein** Mensch war da. |
| | | Not a soul was there. |
| A | keinen | Ich möchte aber **keinen** Kaffee. |
| | | But I don't want any coffee. |
| D | keinem | Er ist mit **keinem** Vorschlag zufrieden. |
| | | He isn't satisfied with any suggestion. |
| G¹ | (keines) | |

---

¹ The genitive forms *keines, keiner* are uncommon; they are only used with certain verbs, e. g. *bedürfen*: *Das bedarf keines Vertrages, keines Wortes, keiner Erwähnung.* – That needs no contract, word, mentioning.

## Neuter

| N | kein | **Kein** Taxi war zu finden. |
|---|---|---|
|  |  | There wasn't a taxi anywhere. |
| A | kein | Möchtest du **kein** Bier? |
|  |  | Don't you want any beer? |
| D | keiner | Das findest du in **keinem** Wörterbuch. |
|  |  | You won't find that in a dictionary. |
| G¹ | (keines) |  |

## Feminine

| N | keine | **Keine** Reise war schöner. |
|---|---|---|
|  |  | No trip was better. |
| A | keine | Sie hat **keine** Antwort bekommen. |
|  |  | She hasn't received an answer. |
| D | keiner | Er hat an **keiner** Versammlung teilgenommen. |
|  |  | He took part in no meeting. |
| G¹ | (keiner) |  |

**00  Plural**

Masculine, Neuter, Feminine

| N | keine | **Keine** Deutschkenntnisse erforderlich. |
|---|---|---|
|  |  | No knowledge of German required. |
| A | keine | Er kann **keine** Fremdsprachen. |
|  |  | He can't speak any foreign languages. |
| D | – |  |
| G | – |  |

---

¹ See footnote, p. 120.

## 201 d. The use of the indefinite article

The indefinite article appears before nouns pointing out a person or an object as representative of a class.

| | |
|---|---|
| München hat **eine schöne Innenstadt**, die wollen wir uns morgen ansehen. | Munich has a beautiful old city centre; we're going to see it tomorrow. |
| Sie hat **einen Mantel** gekauft, der mir nicht gefällt. | She has bought a coat I don't like. |
| Sie wünscht sich **eine Handtasche**. | She wants a handbag. |
| Sie haben noch **eine Stunde Zeit**. | You have still an hour. |

The indefinite article does not appear with plural nouns.

| | | |
|---|---|---|
| Sing.: | Ich habe noch **eine Frage**. | I still have a question. |
| Pl.: | Haben Sie noch **Fragen**? | Do you have any other questions? |
| Sing.: | Ich kaufe mir **einen Gebrauchtwagen**. | I'm going to buy a second-hand car. |
| Pl.: | Er verkauft **Gebrauchtwagen**. | He sells second-hand cars. |

## 2. The omission of the article

The article is omitted

## 202 (1) when used in a partitive sense (i. e. implying English *some* or *any*) or to denote an indefinite quantity,

| | |
|---|---|
| Er trinkt gern **Wein**. | He likes drinking wine. |
| Haben wir noch **Bier**? | Have we any beer left? |
| Brauchen wir noch **Brot**? | Do we need any more bread? |
| But: | |
| Er hat **eine Flasche Bier** getrunken. | He drank a bottle of beer. |

122

**203** (2) After *sein, werden* and *bleiben* and after *als* before nouns denoting a profession or nationality, unless there is a defining adjective,

| | |
|---|---|
| Mein Vater ist **Lehrer.** | My father is a teacher. |
| Sie wird **Sekretärin.** | She's going to be a secretary. |
| Ihre Ausbildung als **Pilotin** war teuer. | Her training as a pilot was expensive. |
| But: | |
| Er ist **ein guter Lehrer.** | He is a good teacher. |
| Sie ist **die neue Sekretärin des Chefs.** | She's the boss's new secretary. |

**204** (3) with nouns in the accusative that form a unit with the verb,

| | |
|---|---|
| Er **hat Hunger.** | He is hungry. |
| Er **hat Geld.** | He has got money. |
| Er **hat Zeit.** | He has got time. |
| Der Zug **hat Verspätung.** | The train is late. |
| Ich **habe** 14 Tage **Urlaub.** | I have a fortnight's holiday. |
| Er **liest** jeden Abend **Zeitung.** | He reads the paper every evening. |
| Sie **fährt** gerne **Ski.** | She likes skiing. |
| But: | |
| Er hat immer **den größten Hunger** (von allen). | He is always the hungriest (of all). |
| Er liest **die Süddeutsche Zeitung.** | He reads the Süddeutsche Zeitung. |

**205** (4) with many prepositional phrases,

| | |
|---|---|
| **Auf Landstraßen** darf nicht schneller als 100 km/h gefahren werden. | On country roads one may not drive faster than 100 k.p.h. |
| **Nach Auffassung der Regierung** sollte mehr gespart werden. | In the government's opinion, people should save more. |

| | |
|---|---|
| Er verbringt seinen Urlaub **mit Wandern und Fotografieren**. | He spends his holiday going on rambles and taking photographs. |
| Die Geschäfte sind **ohne Unterbrechung** geöffnet. | The shops are open all day. |
| Er ist **bis nächste Woche** verreist. | He will be away until next week. |

**206** (5) with names of continents, countries and towns,

| | |
|---|---|
| Waren Sie schon in **Südamerika**? | Have you ever been to South America? |
| Der Student kommt aus **Afrika**. | The student comes from Africa. |

| | |
|---|---|
| Er kommt aus **Frankreich**. | He comes from France. |
| Sie verbringen ihren Urlaub in **England**. | They are spending their holiday in England. |
| Wir fliegen morgen nach **Berlin**. | We are flying to Berlin tomorrow. |
| **Köln** liegt am Rhein. | Cologne is on the Rhine. |
| But: | |
| In den Ferien fahren wir in **die Schweiz** (die Türkei, die Tschechoslowakei; die Niederlande (pl.), die USA (pl.). | In the holidays we are going to Switzerland (Turkey, Czechoslovakia, the Netherlands, the U.S.A.). |

(6) in certain expressions of time,

| | |
|---|---|
| **Ende Mai** war ich in England. | I was in England at the end of May. |
| **Anfang des Monats** werde ich bezahlt. | I get paid at the beginning of the month. |

**207** (7) in slogans and headlines.

| | |
|---|---|
| Einkaufen ohne **Auto**. | Shopping without a car. |
| Urlaub nach **Wunsch**. | Holiday as you please. |

124

### 3. The contraction of the definite article with a preposition (I, 14)

**08** (1) *Dem, der, das* and *den* can be fused with a preceding preposition. The following contractions are possible:

| | |
|---|---|
| *dem + preposition:* | am, beim, hinterm[1], im, überm[1], unterm[1], vom, vorm[1], zum |
| *der + preposition:* | zur |
| *das + preposition:* | ans, aufs[1], durchs[1], fürs[1], hinters[1], ins, übers[1], ums[1], unters[1], vors[1] |
| *den + preposition:* | hintern[1], übern[1], untern[1] |

**09** (2) Contraction always appears in certain set phrases,

| | |
|---|---|
| Jeder kann **zur** Reinhaltung der Luft **beitragen**. (beitragen zu) | Everyone can contribute towards keeping the air clean. |
| Er ist **zum** Fußballer des Jahres **gewählt** worden. (wählen zu) | He was elected Footballer of the Year. |
| **Im Hinblick auf** die hohen Kosten wurde das Projekt abgelehnt. | In view of the high costs, the project was turned down. |

and with nouns formed from infinitives.

| | |
|---|---|
| Du sollst **beim Essen** nicht immer reden. | You mustn't always talk when you're eating. |
| Er hat sich **beim Skifahren** das Bein gebrochen. | He broke his leg when he was skiing. |
| Er hat keinen Spaß **am Lernen**. | He doesn't enjoy learning. |

---

[1] Normally limited to colloquial speech.

**210**    (3) The use of contraction depends on whether or not the definite article is stressed. (= Identification)

| | |
|---|---|
| unstressed:<br>Er war gestern **im** Kino. | He was at the cinema yesterday. |
| stressed:<br>Warst du schon **in dem neuen** Kino? | Have you been to the new cinema yet? |
| unstressed:<br>Kommt doch **am** nächsten Wochenende! | Do come next weekend! |
| stressed:<br>**An dem** Wochenende bin ich zu Hause. | I'll be at home that weekend. |

With proper names the contracted form appears because identification by means of the definite article is unnecessary.

| | |
|---|---|
| Wir waren ein paar Tage **am** Rhein. | We went to the Rhine for a few days. |
| Er hat eine Reise **zum** Fudschijama gemacht. | He went on a trip to Mount Fuji. |

**211**    (4) Contraction is not possible when the noun acts as antecedent to a relative clause.

| | |
|---|---|
| Ich war **in dem** Restaurant, **das** du mir gezeigt hast. | I was in the restaurant you showed me. |
| Bis **zu dem** Turm, **den** man da hinten sieht, sind es zwanzig Minuten. | It's twenty minutes to the tower you see over there. |
| Wir haben **bei dem** Ober bestellt, **der** uns immer bedient. | We gave our order to the waiter who always serves us. |

126

# The Adjective

Adjectives can be used either attributively (as in *the new airport*) or predicatively (as in *the airport is new*). In their positive form (see p. 134), all English adjectives are invariable; German adjectives are only invariable if used predicatively (*der Flughafen ist neu*) – where used attributively, they must be declined.

## 1. Declension

### a. Declension after a definite article (I, 17, 23; II, 4, 7)

12 Singular (I, 17, 23; II, 4, 7)

Masculine

| N | -e | Der neue Flughafen wurde in zwei Jahren gebaut.<br>The new airport was built in two years. |
|---|---|---|
| A | -en | Kennen Sie den neuen Flughafen?<br>Have you seen the new airport yet? |
| D | -en | Wir haben von dem neuen Flughafen gelesen.<br>We have read about the new airport. |
| G | -en | Der Bau des neuen Flughafens ist für 1980 geplant.<br>The construction of the new airport is planned for 1980. |

Neuter

| N | -e | Das neue Rathaus ist sehr modern.<br>The new Town Hall is very modern. |
|---|---|---|
| A | -e | Hast du das neue Rathaus schon gesehen?<br>Have you seen the new Town Hall yet? |
| D | -en | Er arbeitet in dem neuen Rathaus.<br>He is working in the new Town Hall. |
| G | -en | Die moderne Fassade des neuen Rathauses gefällt mir gut.<br>I like the modern façade of the new Town Hall. |

Feminine

| N | -e | Die neue Mitarbeiterin ist Fremdsprachenkorrespondentin. |
|---|---|---|
| | | The new colleague is a foreign language correspondent. |
| A | -e | Er hat die neue Mitarbeiterin zum 1. Januar eingestellt. |
| | | He employed the new colleague as from January 1st. |
| D | -en | Wir haben mit der neuen Mitarbeiterin gerade telefoniert. |
| | | We have just talked to the new colleague on the telephone. |
| G | -en | Den Namen der neuen Mitarbeiterin habe ich vergessen. |
| | | I've forgotten the new colleague's name. |

## 213 Plural

Masculine, Neuter, Feminine

| N | -en | Die neuen Verkehrsbestimmungen gelten seit einer Woche. |
|---|---|---|
| | | The new traffic regulations have been in force for a week. |
| A | -en | Wir kennen die neuen Bestimmungen genau. |
| | | We know the new regulations in detail. |
| D | -en | Wir sind mit den neuen Bestimmungen einverstanden. |
| | | We agree to the new regulations. |
| G | -en | Das Ergebnis der letzten Untersuchungen wird bald veröffentlicht. |
| | | The result of the latest investigations will be published soon. |

**214** (1) After a definite article, adjectives take the ending *-e* or (in the Dat. and Gen. Sing. and in all cases in the plural) *-en*.

**215** (2) After *alle* (pl.), *derjenige, derselbe, dieser, jeder, jener, mancher* and *welcher*, adjectives take the same endings as they would after the definite article.

| | |
|---|---|
| **Alle** interessant**en** Reisen sind ausgebucht. | All the interesting trips are booked out. |
| Das ist **derselbe** freundliche Herr wie gestern. | That's the same friendly gentleman as yesterday. |
| Dieses Land hat **dasselbe** moderne Schulsystem wie wir. | This country has the same modern educational system as we do. |
| Kennen Sie **diesen** jung**en** Mann? | Do you know this young man? |
| **Diese** neu**en** Bestimmungen sind uns bekannt. | We are familiar with these new regulations. |
| **Welcher** berühmte Komponist wurde im Jahre 1770 geboren? | Which famous composer was born in 1770? |
| **Welche** konkret**en** Ergebnisse erreicht wurden, ist nicht bekannt. | What definite results were achieved, is not known. |

## b. Declension after an indefinite article (I, 15; II, 5)

**216** **Singular** (I, 15; II, 5)

Masculine

| N | -er | Das war ein teur**er** Ausflug. *That was an expensive outing.* |
|---|---|---|
| A | -en | Wir haben einen klein**en** Ausflug nach Salzburg gemacht. *We have been on a little outing to Salzburg.* |
| D | -en | Wir sind gerade von einem klein**en** Spaziergang zurückgekommen. *We have just come back from a short walk.* |
| G | -en | Das sind die Erinnerungen eines berühmt**en** Musikers. *Those are the memories of a famous musician.* |

## Neuter

| N | -es | Ein rotes Kleid gefällt ihr bestimmt.<br>A red dress would be sure to please her. |
|---|---|---|
| A | -es | Sie hat sich ein langes Kleid gekauft.<br>She has bought herself a long dress. |
| D | -en | Sie ist in einem langen Kleid gekommen.<br>She came in a long dress. |
| G | -en | Er hat im Empfang eines großen Hotels gearbeitet.<br>He worked at the reception desk of a large hotel. |

## Feminine

| N | -e | Eine weite Flugreise ist teuer.<br>A long journey by plane is expensive. |
|---|---|---|
| A | -e | Plant ihr dieses Jahr eine weite Reise?<br>Are you planning a long trip this year? |
| D | -en | Sie macht eine Berlin-Reise mit einer interessanten Stadtrundfahrt.<br>She is doing a trip to Berlin with an interesting tour of the city. |
| G | -en | Das sind die Vorteile einer längeren Freizeit.<br>Those are the advantages of more leisure time. |

After *kein-* and after possessives (see p. 186ff.), adjectives take the same endings as they would after an indefinite article. The plural forms of the adjective end in *-en* in all cases – as after a definite article.

| | |
|---|---|
| **Ihr** neuer Freund ist Architekt. | Her new boy-friend is an architect. |
| **Unser** neues Geschäft liegt in der Innenstadt. | Our new shop is in the town centre. |
| Kennen Sie schon **unsere** neue Mitarbeiterin? | Have you met our new colleague yet? |
| **Meine** neuen Kollegen sind sehr hilfsbereit. | My new colleagues are very helpful. |
| Das ist **kein** großer Verlust. | That's no great loss. |
| Wir brauchen **kein** großes Haus. | We don't need a large house. |
| Wir machen **keine** großen Parties mehr. | We don't give any more big parties. |

## c. Declension without an article (I, 15; II, 17, 20)

**217** **Singular** (II, 17, 20)

Masculine

| N | -er | Guter Wein ist teuer.<br>Good wine is expensive. |
|---|-----|--------------------------------------------------|
| A | -en | Er hatte großen Erfolg.<br>He had great success. |
| D | -em | Das ist ein Gemälde von großem Wert.<br>That is a painting of great value. |
| G | -en | Das ist ein Beweis guten Geschmacks.<br>That is a proof of good taste. |

Neuter

| N | -es | Das ist wirklich großartiges Theater.<br>That's really first-rate theatre. |
|---|-----|----------------------------------------------------------------------------|
| A | -es | Wir hatten gutes Wetter.<br>We had good weather. |
| D | -em | Es handelt sich um eine Stelle mit überdurchschnittlichem Gehalt.<br>This is a post with above average salary. |
| G | -en | Das ist das Ergebnis ständigen Übens.<br>That is the result of constant practice. |

Feminine

| N | -e  | Junge Französin sucht Stelle in kleiner Firma.<br>Young French girl seeks post in small firm. |
|---|-----|-----------------------------------------------------------------------------------------------|
| A | -e  | Die Arbeit erfordert große Gewissenhaftigkeit.<br>The work demands great conscientiousness. |
| D | -er | Stelle in deutscher Firma gesucht.<br>Post wanted in German firm. |
| G | -er | Das ist das Ergebnis guter Zusammenarbeit.<br>That is the result of good cooperation. |

131

**218** **Plural** (I, 15; II, 17, 20)

Masculine, Neuter, Feminine

| N | -e | Große Aufträge sind selten.<br>Large commissions are rare. |
|---|---|---|
| A | -e | Die Firma hat große Aufträge bekommen.<br>The firm was given large commissions. |
| D | -en | Von großen Firmen kamen wichtige Aufträge.<br>Important commissions came from large firms. |
| G | -er | Das ist eine Reihe interessanter Projekte.<br>That is a series of interesting projects. |

**219** (1) Where there is no article, the adjective ending indicates case and gender.

Note also the following expressions (cf. III, 6):

| bei steigenden Kosten | while costs rise |
|---|---|
| bei passender Gelegenheit | at a suitable opportunity |
| mit steigendem Alter | with increasing age |

**220** (2) Adjectives after *einige, einzelne, mehrere, viele* and *wenige* have the same endings as adjectives without an article (III, 3).

| Das ist die Auffassung **einiger (mehrerer)** prominenter Politiker. | That is the opinion of some (several) prominent politicians. |
|---|---|
| Ich habe **einige (mehrere)** interessante Anzeigen in der Zeitung gelesen. | I have read some (several) interesting advertisements in the newspaper. |
| Sie hat **mehrere** gute Angebote bekommen. | She got several good offers. |
| Es wurden **mehrere** neue Weltrekorde aufgestellt. | Several new world records were set up. |
| Die Mode bringt in diesem Jahr nur **wenige** schöne Modelle. | This year's fashion only offers a few nice models. |

| | |
|---|---|
| Auf der Messe wurden **viele** ver-wertbare Erfindungen gezeigt. | Many realizable inventions were ex-hibited at the Fair. |
| Eine Messe mit **vielen** verwertba-**ren** Erfindungen. | A fair with many realizable inventions. |

## d. Special forms

**221**  (1) Adjectives ending in *-er* and *-el* lose the *-e-* when an ending is added.

| | |
|---|---|
| teu**er**: | ein teu**res** Kleid |
| dunk**el**: | ein dunk**les** Zimmer |

**222**  (2) *Hoch* changes *-ch* to *-h-* when declined.

| | |
|---|---|
| hoch: | ein ho**hes** Gebäude |

**223**  (3) Adjectives formed by adding *-er* to names of towns do not change.

| | |
|---|---|
| Das ist der Köln**er** Dom. | That's Cologne Cathedral. |
| Ich wohne in der Berlin**er** Straße. | I live in Berlin Street. |

## e. The use of the adjective (II, 4)

**224**  (1) Predicative adjectives remain unchanged.

| | |
|---|---|
| Die Reise war **schön**. | The trip was lovely. |
| Das Wetter wird **schlecht**. | The weather's getting bad. |
| Zigaretten sind **schädlich**. | Cigarettes are harmful. |

**225**  (2) Adjectives with the function of an adverb remain unchanged.

| | |
|---|---|
| Er fährt sehr **schnell**. | He drives very fast. |
| Sie spielt **gut** Klavier. | She plays the piano well. |
| Sie spricht **ausgezeichnet** Eng-lisch. | She speaks English excellently. |

**226** (3) Attributive adjectives are declined.

| | |
|---|---|
| Sie wünscht sich eine **braune** Tasche. | She wants a brown handbag. |
| Er interessiert sich für **alte** Autos. | He is interested in old cars. |
| Sehen Sie die **hohen** Gebäude dahinten? | Do you see the tall buildings over there? |

**227** (4) After the indefinite pronouns *etwas, mehr, nichts, viel, wenig* the adjective is declined and capitalized.

| | |
|---|---|
| Die Ausstellung ist **nichts Besonderes**. | The exhibition is nothing special. |
| Er hat **viel Interessantes** gesehen. | He has seen a lot of interesting things. |

## 2. The Comparison of Adjectives

### a. Comparative and superlative (I, 19, 20; II, 4)

**228** (1) Adjectives have positive, comparative and superlative forms. German forms the comparative by adding *-er*, the superlative by adding *-st* to the positive form. These endings are used regardless of the number of syllables the adjective may have, and there is no equivalent to the English comparison with *more* and *most*. (*Mehr* is only used before an adjective to mean *rather*, *meist(ens)* to mean *mostly*. For the use of *mehr* with nouns, see p. 176.)

| | | |
|---|---|---|
| schön | schön**er** | (der, das, die) schön**ste** |
| klein | klein**er** | (der, das, die) klein**ste** |
| interessant | interessant**er** | (der, das, die) interessant**este** |

**229** (2) The comparative is declined when the adjective is used attributively; when used predicatively it is invariable.

| | |
|---|---|
| Wir brauchen eine **größere** Wohnung. | We need a larger flat. |
| Unsere Wohnung ist **kleiner** (als eure). | Our flat is smaller (than yours). |
| Das Empire State Building ist **höher** (als der Eiffelturm). | The Empire State Building is taller (than the Eiffel Tower). |

**30** (3) The superlative is declined whether it is used attributively or in the predicate. It always appears with the definite article.

| | |
|---|---|
| **Das schnellste Flugzeug** fliegt 3000 Stundenkilometer. | The fastest aeroplane flies 3000 km per hour. |
| Der Fernsehturm ist **das höchste Gebäude** der Stadt. | The television tower is the tallest building in the town. |
| Dieser Krimi ist **der interessanteste,** den ich je gesehen habe. | This thriller is the most interesting one I have ever seen. |
| Dieses Gebäude ist **das höchste** der Stadt. | This building is the tallest in the town. |

The combination *am* + *-en* can also appear in the predicate.

| | |
|---|---|
| Dieses Gebäude ist **am höchsten.** | This building is the tallest. |
| Auf Autobahnen wird **am schnellsten** gefahren. (Adverb) | People drive fastest on the motorways. |

**b. Special forms** (I, 20, 21, 22, 23, 24; II, 21)

**31** (1) Adjectives ending in *-er* and *-el* drop the *-e-* in the comparative (cf. p. 133).

| | | |
|---|---|---|
| teu**er** | teu**rer** | (teuerste) |
| dunk**el** | dunk**ler** | (dunkelste) |

**232** (2) Some monosyllabic adjectives take an umlaut.

| | | |
|---|---|---|
| alt | **älter** | **ält**este |
| groß | **größer** | **größ**te |
| jung | **jünger** | **jüng**ste |
| lang | **länger** | **läng**ste |

**233** (3) Irregular comparison:

| | | |
|---|---|---|
| hoch | höher | höchste (am höchsten) |
| gern | lieber | liebste (am liebsten) |
| gut | besser | beste (am besten) |
| viel | mehr | meiste (am meisten) |

**234** (4) The comparative forms *mehr* and *weniger* have no endings.

| | |
|---|---|
| Er hat **mehr** Zeit als ich. | He has more time than I. |
| Die Studenten brauchen **mehr** Geld für ihr Studium. | The students need more money for their studies. |
| Er hat jetzt **weniger** Freizeit als früher. | He has less free time now than before. |

**c. Forming comparisons** (I, 19; II, 21)

**235** (1) Dissimilarity is expressed by the comparative with *als*[1].

| | |
|---|---|
| Er hat einen **interessanteren** Beruf **als** ich. | He has a more interesting job than I. |
| Die Kirche ist **höher als** das Rathaus. | The church is taller than the town hall. |
| Er kam **früher als** verabredet. | He came earlier than arranged. |

---

[1] In some regions often interchanged with *wie*: Er ist größer *wie* ich.

| Die Hochschule hat **mehr** Studenten, **als** wir gedacht haben. | The university has more students than we thought. |
| Das Buch ist **interessanter, als** ich geglaubt habe. | The book is more interesting than I thought. |

**236** (2) Similarity is expressed by the positive form of the adjective with *so . . . wie.*

| Schreibe bitte **so** schnell **wie** möglich.[1] | Please write as soon as possible. |
| Er spricht **so** gut deutsch, **wie** er schreibt. | He speaks German as well as he writes it. |

### 3. The Numerals

**237** **a. The cardinal numbers** (I, 4, 5, 20)

| 0 | null | 10 | zehn | 20 | zwanzig |
|---|------|----|------|----|---------|
| 1 | eins | 11 | elf | 21 | **ein**undzwanzig |
| 2 | zwei | 12 | zwölf | 22 | zweiundzwanzig |
| 3 | drei | 13 | dreizehn | 23 | dreiundzwanzig |
| 4 | vier | 14 | vierzehn | 24 | vierundzwanzig |
| 5 | fünf | 15 | fünfzehn | 25 | fünfundzwanzig |
| 6 | sechs | 16 | **sechzehn** | 26 | sechsundzwanzig |
| 7 | sieben | 17 | **siebzehn** | 27 | siebenundzwanzig |
| 8 | acht | 18 | achtzehn | 28 | achtundzwanzig |
| 9 | neun | 19 | neunzehn | 29 | neunundzwanzig |

| 30 | dreißig |
|----|---------|
| 40 | vierzig |
| 50 | fünfzig |
| 60 | **sech**zig |

---

[1] Common in older German: Schreibe so schnell *als* möglich.

| 70 | **sieb**zig | | |
|----|-----------|---|---|
| 80 | achtzig | | |
| 90 | neunzig | | |
| | | | |
| 100 | hundert | 1 000 | tausend |
| 101 | hunderteins | 1 001 | tausendeins |
| 102 | hundertzwei | | |
| | | 1 100 | tausendeinhundert |
| | | 1 101 | tausendeinhunderteins |
| | | | |
| | | 2 000 | zweitausend |
| | | 3 000 | dreitausend |
| | | | |
| | | 10 000 | zehntausend |
| 200 | zweihundert | 20 000 | zwanzigtausend |
| 300 | dreihundert | | |
| 400 | vierhundert | 100 000 | hunderttausend |
| 500 | fünfhundert | 1 000 000 | eine Million |

Note:

In German numerals, the decimal is represented by a comma.

| | |
|---|---|
| 10,5 Gramm | 10.5 grams |

The comma used in English to separate groups of three figures is represented in German by a period or a space.

| | |
|---|---|
| 10.000 (10 000) | 10,000 |

**238** (1) Questions asking how much? are introduced by *wieviel?*

| | |
|---|---|
| **Wieviel Geld** hast du dabei (= bei dir)? – 50 Mark. | How much money have you got on you? 50 marks. |

Questions asking how many? are introduced by *wie viele?*

| | |
|---|---|
| **Wie viele Sprachen** sprechen Sie? | How many languages do you speak? |
| – Zwei. | Two. |

**239** (2) Some nouns denoting measures or amounts appear in the singular.

| | |
|---|---|
| Er trank **drei Glas Bier**. | He drank three glasses of beer. |
| Sie nahm **vier Stück Zucker**. | She took four lumps of sugar. |

Compare, however:

| | |
|---|---|
| Ich möchte mir **zwölf Weingläser** kaufen. | I would like to buy twelve wineglasses. |

**240** (3) Written as figures, numerals appear in the same order as in English, but when spoken or written in full, the units precede the tens. They are connected by *und*.

| | |
|---|---|
| 23 | drei**und**zwanzig |
| 31 | ein**und**dreißig |

**241** (4) The number 1 used in conjunction with tens is *ein*; if it is the last unit stated in a number, it is *eins*.

| | |
|---|---|
| 41 | **ein**undvierzig |
| 101 | hundert**eins** |

**242** (5) The following numbers are feminine nouns and take an *-(e)n* ending in the plural:

| | |
|---|---|
| 1 000 000 | eine Million |
| 2 000 000 | zwei Million**en** |
| 1 000 000 000 | eine Milliarde |
| 2 000 000 000 | zwei Milliarde**n** |

139

**243** (6) The cardinal number 1 is declined. When used attributively, it has the same declension as the indefinite article.

| | |
|---|---|
| Ich möchte **einen Espresso**. | I would like an espresso. |
| Sie haben **eine Tochter**. | They have one daughter. |

Declension when used as a noun:

| | |
|---|---|
| **Einer der Bewerber** war perfekt in Englisch. | One of the applicants was perfect in English. |
| Die Firma konnte nur **einen der Bewerber** einstellen. | The firm could only employ one of the applicants. |

Numbers placed after the noun are invariable.

| | |
|---|---|
| Wir sind bei **Lektion eins**. | We are on Lesson One. |
| Fragen Sie bitte in **Zimmer drei**. | Please ask in Room Three. |

**244** (7) **Years** are read as follows:

| | |
|---|---|
| 1976 | neunzehnhundertsechsundsiebzig |
| 1832 | achtzehnhundertzweiunddreißig |

Years are used either alone or with the phrase *im Jahr(e)*.

| | |
|---|---|
| Goethe wurde (im Jahre) 1749 geboren. | Goethe was born in 1749. |

**245** (8) **Times of day** (I, 5 and I, p. 156)

For stating the times of day, German distinguishes between official and colloquial expressions.

For official purposes the 24-hour day is used.

| | |
|---|---|
| Es ist elf Uhr. | It is 11 a. m. |
| Es ist zwanzig Uhr. | It is 8 p. m. |

140

In colloquial language, however:

| | |
|---|---|
| Es ist ein Uhr (mittags, nachts). Or: Es ist eins. | It's one o'clock (in the morning, after-noon). |
| Es ist acht Uhr (morgens, abends). Or: Es ist acht. | It's eight o'clock (in the morning, eve-ning). |

In official expressions of time, as in timetables etc., the minutes stand *after* the hour.

| | |
|---|---|
| Der Zug fährt um 9.15 Uhr (neun Uhr fünfzehn). | The train leaves at 9.15. |
| Das Flugzeug geht um 17.10 (siebzehn Uhr zehn). | The plane takes off at 5.10 p. m. |

In colloquial language, the minutes stand before the hour.

| | |
|---|---|
| Es ist jetzt 5 vor 4. | It's now five to four. |
| Es ist jetzt 20 vor 7. | It's now twenty to seven. |

When using the prepositions *vor* and *nach*, note that the shortest time interval is expressed – this sometimes results in different phrases from the English ones.

| | |
|---|---|
| Es ist jetzt Viertel vor 2.[1] | It's now a quarter to two. |
| Es ist jetzt Viertel nach 2.[2] | It's now a quarter past two. |
| Es ist jetzt fünf vor halb 3. | It's now twenty-five minutes past two. |
| Es ist jetzt halb 3. | It's now half past two. |
| Es ist jetzt 5 Minuten nach halb drei. | It's now twenty-five to three. |

---

[1] Alternatively: *Es ist jetzt dreiviertel zwei.*
[2] Alternatively, however: *Es ist jetzt Viertel drei.*

**246  b. The ordinal numbers** (I, 14, 18)

| der, das, die | **erste** | elfte | einundzwanzigste |
|---|---|---|---|
| | zweite | zwölfte | zweiundzwanzigste |
| | **dritte** | dreizehnte | |
| | vierte | vierzehnte | dreißigste |
| | fünfte | fünfzehnte | vierzigste |
| | sechste | sechzehnte | |
| | **siebte** | siebzehnte | hundertste |
| | **achte** | achtzehnte | tausendste |
| | neunte | neunzehnte | zehntausendste |
| | zehnte | zwanzigste | millionste |

Note: To write an ordinal number, a period is placed after the numeral.

**247**  (1) The ordinal numbers from 2 to 19 take the endings *-t-*, from 20 upwards the ending *-st-*.

Ordinal numbers are declined like adjectives.

| | |
|---|---|
| Gehen Sie bitte in den zweit**en** Stock. | Please go to the second floor (AE third floor). |
| Fahren Sie bitte die zweit**e** Straße nach rechts und dann geradeaus. | Turn right at the second street and then drive straight on. |

**248**  (2) **Dates** (I, 18)

| | |
|---|---|
| Heute ist der 4. 9. (oder: der 4. September; der vierte September). | Today is September 4th. |
| Sie hat am 14. 4. Geburtstag (oder: am 14. April; am vierzehnten April). | Her birthday is on April 14th. |

142

Year numbers are written and read either without any preposition at all, or are preceded by the phrase *im Jahre*.

| | |
|---|---|
| Beethoven starb (im Jahre) 1827 (= achtzehnhundertsiebenundzwanzig). | Beethoven died in 1827. |

The words for day and month are not used when complete dates are read aloud as here:

Berlin, den 13. 10. 1976 (as in letter-head – read: Berlin, den dreizehnten zehnten neunzehnhundertsechsundsiebzig)

Note:

| | |
|---|---|
| Der **wievielte** ist heute? – Heute ist der 5. (Mai.) (Or: Den wievielten haben wir heute? – Heute haben wir den 5. Mai.) | What's the date today? Today is the 5th (May). |

**249** **c. Fractions**

| | | | |
|---|---|---|---|
| $1/2$ | ein halb- (die Hälfte) | $1^1/2$ | eineinhalb |
| $1/3$ | ein Drittel | $2^1/2$ | zweieinhalb |
| $1/4$ | ein Viertel | $2^2/3$ | zweizweidrittel |
| $3/4$ | drei Viertel | $1/100$ | ein Hundertstel |

**250** (1) Only *halb-* is declined. The other fractions are invariable.

| | |
|---|---|
| Er war ein halb**es** Jahr im Ausland. | He was abroad for six months. |
| Wir haben nur noch ein halb**es** Pfund Kaffee. | We've only got half a pound of coffee left. |
| Der Zug kommt in einer halb**en** Stunde. | The train arrives in half an hour. |

143

| | |
|---|---|
| Er war ein zehntel Sekunde[1] schneller. | He was a tenth of a second faster. |
| Unsere Gäste kommen in ungefähr einer dreiviertel[2] Stunde. | Our guests will arrive in about three quarters of an hour. |

**251** (2) As nouns, fractions are all neuter – with the one exception of *die Hälfte*.

| | |
|---|---|
| Ozeane produzieren etwa **zwei Drittel** unseres Sauerstoffbedarfs. | Oceans produce about two thirds of our oxygen needs. |
| Viele verbringen ca. **die Hälfte** ihrer Freizeit vor dem Fernseher. | Many people spend about half their free time in front of the television. |
| **Ein Viertel** ihres Geldes geben die meisten für Lebensmittel aus. | Most people spend a quarter of their money on food. |

**252 d. Ordinal adverbs**

| | | |
|---|---|---|
| 1. | erstens | first(ly) |
| 2. | zweitens | second(ly) |
| 3. | drittens | third(ly) |

Ordinal adverbs are used in enumerations.

| | |
|---|---|
| Ich brauche keinen Fernseher, denn **erstens** ist das Programm oft schlecht und **zweitens** habe ich zuwenig Zeit. | I don't need a television set, because firstly the programme is often bad, and secondly I haven't got enough time. |

---

[1] Also written *Zehntelsekunde*.
[2] *drei* and *viertel* are usually written together as one word.

144

| Nur wenige würden sich ein Ge- mälde kaufen, wenn sie viel Geld hätten: 1. **(Erstens)** tut nach Mei- nung vieler ein guter Farbdruck dieselben Dienste, und 2. **(zwei- tens)** würden die meisten das Geld lieber für Reisen ausgeben. | Only a few people would buy themselves a painting if they had a lot of money: firstly, many people think that a good colour print serves the same purpose, and secondly, most people would rather spend the money on travelling. |
| --- | --- |

## 253   e. Frequentative adverbs

| einmal | once |
| --- | --- |
| zweimal | twice |
| dreimal | three times |

| Wir waren schon **dreimal** in den USA. | We have already been to the U.S.A. three times. |
| --- | --- |
| Jetzt habe ich schon **zweimal** ge- schrieben und noch keine Antwort erhalten. | Now I've written twice and still haven't got an answer. |
| Wir mußten **dreimal** klingeln, bis sie uns hörten. | We had to ring three times before they heard us. |

# The Adverb

**254** (1) In English, adverbs are often formed by adding *-ly* to the corresponding adjective; German adverbs, which are always indeclinable, frequently have the same form as the adjective (II, 4). Adverbs can also be formed from other parts of speech through the addition of a suffix (e. g. *abends, manchmal, kürzlich, einigermaßen*). Other commonly used German adverbs are simple monosyllables (*bald, nie, dann, noch* etc.).

| | |
|---|---|
| Er hat **schlecht** geschlafen. | He has slept badly. |
| Der Zug ist **pünktlich** angekommen. | The train arrived on time. |
| Er war **kürzlich** in Rom. | He was recently in Rome. |
| Er kommt **bald**. | He is coming soon. |
| **Sonntags** ist er nie zu Hause. | He is never at home on Sundays. |

**255** (2) Adverbs with the same form as adjectives can be put into the comparative and superlative.

| | |
|---|---|
| Er fährt **schnell**. | He drives fast. |
| Er ist heute **schneller** als sonst gefahren. | Today he drove faster than usual. |
| Auf der Autobahn wird **am schnellsten** gefahren. | People drive fastest on the motorways. |

**256** (3) There are three main types of adverb: adverbs of place (*hier, da, dort* etc.), adverbs of time (*damals, früher* etc.) and adverbs of manner (*gern, umsonst, vergeblich* etc.).

146

|        | Das Taxi | kommt.    |
|--------|----------|-----------|
| Jetzt  | kommt    | das Taxi. |

|        | Sie  | ruft |              |
|--------|------|------|--------------|
| Gleich | ruft | sie  |              |

das Hotel **an**.

das Hotel **an**.

|         | Die Post | ist       |
|---------|----------|-----------|
| Da vorn | ist      | die Post. |

da vorn.

With statements, the main verb must always be the second idea in the sentence.

If two or more adverbs (or adverbial phrases) occur in a sentence, the normal word order is: time – manner – place. (Contrast English word order here!)

| Wir gehen heute abend dahin. | We are going there this evening. |
| Jeden Morgen fährt er mit dem Bus in die Stadt. | Every morning he goes to town by bus. |

If two or more adverbs of the same type occur in a sentence, the more general precedes the more specific.

| Er kommt jeden Tag um 6 Uhr zurück. | He returns every day at six. |

Note that the subject and finite verb of a main clause cannot be separated by an adverb in German, as they can in English.

| Wir gehen oft ins Theater. | We often go to the theatre. |

147

**258  1. Adverbs of place**

With adverbs of place, distinguish between adverbs of *location* (question: *wo?*) and those of *motion* (question: *wohin?* or *woher?*).

**259  Question: wo?**

| | |
|---|---|
| **hier** | |
| Der Brief liegt *hier*. | The letter is lying here. |
| **da, dort** | |
| *Da* ist das Postamt. | There is the post office. |
| Wir sind oft *dort*. | We're often there. |
| **draußen** | |
| Ich bleibe noch ein bißchen *draußen*. | I'll stay outside a little longer. |
| **drinnen** | |
| Hier *drinnen* ist es schön warm. | It's nice and warm in here. |
| **außen** | |
| Der Mantel hat *außen* Leder – | The coat has leather on the outside |
| **innen** | |
| – und *innen* Pelz. | and fur on the inside. |
| **drüben** | |
| Da *drüben* steht mein Wagen. | My car is over there. |
| **oben** | |
| Er ist *oben* im 5. Stock. | He is up on the 5th floor. |
| **unten** | |
| Wir sind *unten* im Parterre. | We're down on the ground floor. |
| **mitten** | |
| Wir wohnen *mitten* in der Stadt. | We live right in the centre of town. |
| **rechts** | |
| *Rechts* vom Eingang ist ein Schild. | At the right of the entrance there is a sign. |
| **links** | |
| In England fährt man *links*. | In England they drive on the left. |

148

**vorn**

Da *vorn* ist ein Restaurant.　　　　There's a restaurant up there.

**hinten**

Da *hinten* ist der Bahnhof.　　　　Back there is the railway station.

**überall**

Wir waren *überall*.　　　　We went everywhere.

**irgendwo**

*Irgendwo* wird er schon sein.　　　　He'll be somewhere.

**nirgendwo**

Wir haben ihn *nirgendwo (= nir-*　　We haven't seen him anywhere.
*gends)* gesehen.

## 260　Question: wohin?/woher?

**hierhin (hierher)**

Lege die Briefe *hierhin (hierher)*.　　Put the letters here.

**dahin (dorthin)**

Lege die Briefe *dahin (dorthin)*.　　Put the letters there.

**hinaus/herein**
**(= raus) (= rein)**

Geh mit *hinaus (= raus)*. Komm　　Go outside (with them). Come in.
*herein (= rein)*.

**nach/von draußen**

Er geht *nach draußen*. Er kommt　　He is going outside. He is coming from
*von draußen*.　　　　　　　　outside.

**nach außen/nach innen**

Das Fenster geht *nach außen* und　　The window opens in and out.
*nach innen* auf.

**hinüber/herüber**
**(= rüber)**

Wir fahren auf die Insel *hinüber* (= *rüber*).

We're going over to the island.

Er kommt von Dänemark *herüber* (= *rüber*).

He's coming over from Denmark.

**hinauf/herauf**
**(= rauf)**

Er geht die Treppe *hinauf* (= *rauf*).

He is going up the stairs.

Er kommt die Treppe *herauf* (= *rauf*).

He is coming up the stairs.

**hinunter/herunter**
**(= runter)**

Er geht die Treppe *hinunter* (= *runter*).

He is going down the stairs.

Er kommt die Treppe *herunter* (= *runter*).

He is coming down the stairs.

**nach oben/nach unten**

Er fährt mit dem Fahrstuhl *nach oben/nach unten*.

He's taking the lift up/down.

**mitten**

Die Autobahn führt *mitten* durch die Stadt.

The motorway leads right through the city.

**nach/von rechts**

Das Auto fuhr *nach rechts/nach links*.

The car turned off to the right/left.

**nach/von links**

Das Auto kam *von rechts/von links*.

The car came from the right/left.

**nach/von vorn**

Sieh *nach vorn*. Das Auto kam *von vorn*.

Look straight ahead. The car came from the front.

| | |
|---|---|
| **nach/von hinten** | |
| Schau mal *nach hinten*. | Look behind you. |
| **überall hin** | |
| Ich möchte *überall hin*. | I'd like to go everywhere. |
| **irgendwohin** | |
| Wir fahren jetzt *irgendwohin*. | We're driving round just anywhere. |
| **nirgendwohin** | |
| Er möchte *nirgendwohin*. | He doesn't want to go anywhere. |
| **weg** | |
| Gehst du heute abend *weg*? | Are you going out tonight? |

Note:

**261** (1) *hin*- denotes a motion away from the speaker, *her*- a motion towards the speaker.

| | |
|---|---|
| Wo gehst du **hin**? | Where are you going? |
| (Or: **Wohin** gehst du?) | |
| Wo kommst du **her**? | Where do you come from? |
| (Or: **Woher** kommst du?) | |

**262** (2) In colloquial German, *hin*- und *her*- are abbreviated to *r*-.

| | |
|---|---|
| Er kommt die Treppe **runter**. | He's coming down the stairs. |
| (= **herunter**) | |
| Wir gehen noch eine halbe Stunde **raus**. (= **hinaus**) | We're going out for half an hour. |

**263** (3) *hin*- and *her*- and the combination of *hin*- and *her*- with a preposition frequently form a unit with the verb (III, 4, 13).

| | |
|---|---|
| Kommst du zu der Party? Wenn du kommst, **komme** ich auch **hin**. | Are you coming to the party? If you come, I'll go too. |

| | |
|---|---|
| Heute abend ist die Versammlung. Können Sie für mich **hingehen**? | The meeting is tonight. Can you go for me? |
| Wir können den Wagen nicht holen. **Bringen** Sie ihn doch bitte **her**. | We can't fetch the car. Please bring it here. |
| Haben Sie den schweren Koffer allein **hergeschleppt**? | Did you carry the heavy suitcase here alone? |
| Er ist gerade **hinausgegangen**. | He has just gone out. |
| Ihm ist der Löffel **heruntergefallen**. | He has dropped his spoon. |

The same applies for *weg*.

| | |
|---|---|
| Hat schon jemand die Post **weggebracht**? | Has anyone taken the post? |

## 2. Adverbs of time

264 **a. Denoting an event in the past**

| | |
|---|---|
| **damals** | |
| Ein Gulden war *damals* (im 18. Jahrhundert) soviel wert wie heute 20 bis 30 Mark. | At that time (in the 18th century) a gulden was worth as much as 20 to 30 marks today. |
| **früher** | |
| *Früher* war alles anders. | It was all different in the old days. |
| **ehemals** | |
| Er war *ehemals* ein bekannter Dichter. | He was once a well-known poet. |
| **kürzlich/neulich/vor kurzem** | |
| Er war *kürzlich* (= *neulich, vor kurzem*) in Rom. | He was recently in Rome. |

| | |
|---|---|
| **(so)eben/gerade** | |
| Sie ist *(so)eben* (= *gerade*) ange- kommen. | She has just arrived. |

## 265  b. in the present

| | |
|---|---|
| **(so)eben/gerade** | |
| Er kommt *(so)eben (gerade)* ins Zimmer. | He is just coming into the room. |
| Die Sekretärin schreibt *gerade* einen Brief. | The secretary is just writing a letter. |
| **jetzt** | |
| Es ist *jetzt* 5 Uhr. | It is now 5 o'clock. |
| **nun** | |
| Was machen wir *nun*? | What shall we do now? |
| **heute** | |
| *Heute* ist Sonntag. | Today is Sunday. |
| **heute morgen/mittag/nachmittag/abend** | |
| *Heute abend* gehen wir ins Theater. | This evening we're going to the theatre. |
| **heutzutage** | |
| *Heutzutage* ist vieles anders. | Nowadays many things are different. |

## 266  c. in the future

| | |
|---|---|
| **bald** | |
| Ich bin *bald* wieder da. | I'll be back soon. |
| **gleich/sofort** | |
| Ich bin *gleich* (= *sofort*) fertig. | I'll be finished in a second. |
| **heute/morgen (abend, früh, mittag), übermorgen** | |
| Wir fahren *übermorgen* nach London. | The day after tomorrow we're going to London. |

**einmal**

Kommt doch *einmal* (= *mal*) zu uns! — Come and see us sometime.

**später**

*Später* wirst du dir Vorwürfe machen. — Later you'll be sorry.

**künftig**

Werden Roboter *künftig* die Arbeiter am Fließband ersetzen? — Will robots replace workers on the assembly line in the future?

**267   d. in relationship to another point in time**

**zuerst – dann**

*Zuerst* war ich dafür, *dann* dagegen. — At first I was for it, then against.

**zunächst**

Hören Sie *zunächst* die Nachrichten. — First here is the news.

**vorher, zuvor**

Ich sage meine Meinung sofort, aber *vorher* (= *zuvor*) habe ich noch eine Frage. — I'll give my opinion right away, but first I have another question.

Er ist schneller gelaufen als je *zuvor*. — He ran faster than ever before.

**dann**

Ich habe meine Prüfung gemacht und bin *dann* ein Jahr nach England gegangen. — I took my exams and then went to England for a year.

**danach**

Sie haben drei Monate Probezeit. *Danach* sind Sie fest angestellt. — You'll have three months probation. After that you'll be on the regular staff.

**da**

Niemand ahnte etwas. *Da* geschah plötzlich das Unglück.

Nobody suspected anything. Then suddenly the accident happened.

**nachher**

Und *nachher* bitte einen Kaffee!

And after that some coffee, please!

**hinterher**

Er war *hinterher* froh, daß er nichts gesagt hatte.

Afterwards he was glad he hadn't said anything.

**zuletzt**

*Zuerst* kamen die Damen, dann die Kinder und *zuletzt* die Herren.

First came the ladies, then the children and finally the gentlemen.

**schließlich**

Die Besprechung dauerte zwei Stunden. Der Diskussionsleiter faßte *schließlich* die Ergebnisse zusammen.

The conference lasted two hours. Then finally the discussion leader summarized the results.

**inzwischen**

Ich mache das Abendessen, *inzwischen* kannst du ja telefonieren.

I'll make supper and in the meantime you can phone.

**bisher**

Ich hatte *bisher* keine Zeit, dich anzurufen.

Up to now I haven't had any time to ring you up.

**seitdem**

Ich war *seitdem* (seit unserem letzten Treffen) so beschäftigt, daß ich dich nicht anrufen konnte.

Since then (since our last meeting) I have been so busy that I haven't been able to ring you up.

**268  e. Frequency and repetition**

**nie**

Ich war noch *nie* in Griechenland.

I have never been to Greece.

**niemals**

Er würde *niemals* viel Geld für eine Reise ausgeben.

He'd never spend a lot of money on travelling.

**selten, fast nie, kaum**
Er ist nur *selten* (= *fast nie, kaum*)
zu Hause.

He is only seldom (hardly ever) at home.

Schneller geht's *kaum (noch)*.

It could hardly be quicker.

**manchmal**
Sie spielt *manchmal* Klavier.

She sometimes plays the piano.

**ab und zu, öfters**
Kinder sollten *ab und zu* (= *öfters*)
im Haushalt helfen.

Children should help with the house-
work now and then (often).

**oft, häufig**
Er kommt *oft* (= *häufig*) zu spät.

He often (frequently) comes too late.

**meistens, fast immer**
Sonntags geht er *meistens* (= *fast
immer*) zum Fußball.

On Sundays he generally (nearly always)
goes to the football match.

**immer, ständig**
Fahren Sie *immer* geradeaus,
dann kommen Sie zum Rathaus.

Drive straight on, then you'll get to the
town hall.

Er ist *immer* (= *ständig*) unter-
wegs.

He's always (constantly) on the move.

**jederzeit**
Sie können mich *jederzeit* anrufen.

You can phone me any time.

**stets**
Sie ist *stets* gut gekleidet.

She is always well dressed.

**einmal, zweimal . . .**
Er hat mich schon *zweimal* ge-
fragt, ob ich mitkomme.

He has already asked me twice if I'm
going too.

**jedesmal**
Er ist *jedesmal* Zweiter.

He's second every time.

**mehrmals**
Er hat *mehrmals* den Preis ge-
wonnen.

He has won the prize several times.

**wieder**

In 2 Tagen bin ich *wieder* da.     I'll be back again in two days.

**erneut**

Sein Vorschlag wurde *erneut* ab-     His suggestion was rejected again.
gelehnt.

**täglich, wöchentlich, monatlich, jährlich**

Er verdient *monatlich* DM     He earns 2000 marks a month.
2000,–.

**montags, dienstags . . .**

Sprechstunde *dienstags* von 9–12     Consultation Tuesdays 9–12 a. m.
Uhr.

**morgens, mittags, nachmittags, abends**

*Abends* sehen wir immer fern.     In the evening we always watch television.

## 269    f. Point in time and duration

**früh – spät**

Er steht *früh* auf und geht     He gets up early and still goes to bed
trotzdem *spät* ins Bett.     late.

**erst – schon (bereits)**

Es ist *erst* 9 Uhr.     It is only 9 o'clock.

Es ist *schon* (= *bereits*) 3 Uhr     It's already 3 o'clock in the afternoon.
nachmittags.

**lange**

Wir haben schon *lange* nichts     It's been a long time since we heard from
mehr von Ihnen gehört.     you.

**längst**

Der Brief hätte *längst* da sein     The letter should have arrived ages ago.
müssen.

**weiterhin**

Ich wünsche Ihnen *weiterhin* viel     I wish you continued success.
Erfolg.

| | |
|---|---|
| **monatelang, jahrelang** | |
| Er hat *monatelang* auf sein Geld gewartet. | He waited for his money for months. |

## 270 3. Interrogative adverbs

Interrogative adverbs are always placed at the beginning of the sentence.

| | |
|---|---|
| **wo** | |
| *Wo* wohnt er? In Köln? | Where does he live? In Cologne? |
| **woher** | |
| *Woher* sind Sie? Aus München? | Where do you come from? Munich? |
| **wohin** | |
| *Wohin* fliegt er? Nach Hamburg? | Where is he flying? To Hamburg? |
| **wann** | |
| *Wann* geht das Flugzeug? Um elf? | When does the plane leave? At eleven? |
| **wie lange** | |
| *Wie lange* bleiben Sie in Salzburg? – Nur eine Woche. | How long are you staying in Salzburg? – Only a week. |
| **wie** | |
| *Wie* heißen Sie, bitte? | What's your name, please? |
| *Wie* spät ist es eigentlich? | What's the time anyway? |
| *Wie* hat Ihnen die Reise gefallen? | How did you like the trip? |
| **warum** | |
| *Warum* machen Sie keinen Urlaub? – Weil ich sparen muß. | Why don't you take a holiday? – Because I must save money. |
| **wieviel** | |
| *Wieviel* hat er gewonnen? Eine Million? | How much did he win? A million? |
| **wie viele** | |
| *Wie viele* Sprachen werden in Ihrem Land gesprochen? | How many languages are spoken in your country? |

# Pronouns and Determiners

A pronoun is a word used instead of a noun; a determiner is a limiting adjective. The categories of pronouns and determiners run parallel in German and English: pronouns can be personal (*I, you* etc.), interrogative (*What* do you think?), demonstrative (*These* are much nicer), relative (The man *who* told me . . .), *possessive* (That's *mine*), reflexive (Enjoy *yourself*!) and indefinite (e. g. *everyone, nothing*). Determiners include the interrogative adjectives (*Which* man do you mean?), the demonstrative adjectives (*That* man over there), the possessive adjectives (It's *my* room) and the indefinite adjectives (e. g. *every* day, *any* book), as well as the definite and indefinite articles (see p. 116 ff.).

Pronouns can be very similar to their corresponding determiners, and in some forms they are even identical. In German all determiners and most pronouns are declinable.

## 1. The Personal Pronouns

**a. Forms** (I, 1, 2, 4, 8, 9, 11, 12, 13, 14)

**1st Person**

**271  Singular**

| N | ich | **Ich** wohne in Köln.<br>I live in Cologne. |
|---|---|---|
| A | mich | Können Sie **mich** zum Bahnhof bringen?<br>Can you take me to the station? |
| D | mir | Der Koffer gehört **mir**.<br>The suitcase belongs to me. |
| G[1] | | |

---

[1] The personal pronoun rarely appears in the genitive (*meiner, deiner, seiner/ihrer* etc.). It follows one or two verbs, e. g. *gedenken: Überall wurde seiner gedacht.* – His memory was commemorated everywhere.

**272 Plural**

| N | wir | **Wir** haben lange auf euch gewartet.<br>We've been waiting for you a long time. |
|---|-----|---|
| A | uns | Warum habt ihr **uns** nicht angerufen?<br>Why didn't you phone us? |
| D | uns | Bleibt ihr heute bei **uns**?<br>Are you staying with us today? |
| G[1] | | |

## 2nd Person

**273 Singular**

| N | du | Was machst **du** morgen?<br>What are you doing tomorrow? |
|---|-----|---|
| A | dich | Ich hole **dich** um 6 Uhr ab.<br>I'll fetch you at six. |
| D | dir | Ich bringe **dir** das Buch morgen mit.<br>I'll bring you the book tomorrow. |
| G[1] | | |

**274 Plural**

| N | ihr | Seid **ihr** morgen zu Hause?<br>Are you at home tomorrow? |
|---|-----|---|
| A | euch | Wir möchten **euch** besuchen.<br>We would like to come and see you. |
| D. | euch | Wie ist das Wetter bei **euch**?<br>What's the weather like with you? |
| G[1] | | |

---

[1] The personal pronoun rarely appears in the genitive (*meiner, deiner, seiner/ihrer* etc.). It follows one or two verbs, e. g. *gedenken: Überall wurde seiner gedacht.* – His memory was commemorated everywhere.

**Singular**

| N | Sie | Wohin möchten **Sie**?<br>Where would you like to go? |
|---|---|---|
| A | Sie | Ich bringe **Sie** zum Bahnhof!<br>I'll take you to the station. |
| D | Ihnen | Kann ich **Ihnen** helfen?<br>Can I help you? |
| G[1] | | |

276 **Plural**

| N | Sie | Wann sind **Sie** (= Herr und Frau Meier) ange-<br>kommen?<br>When did you arrive? |
|---|---|---|
| A | Sie | Ich hole **Sie** sofort ab.<br>I'll come and fetch you right away. |
| D | Ihnen | Wie gefällt es **Ihnen** hier?<br>How do you like it here? |
| G[1] | | |

### 3rd Person

277 **Singular**

| N | er | es | sie | **Er** ist Journalist.<br>He is a journalist.<br>**Es** (das Studio) ist in Köln.<br>It's in Cologne.<br>**Sie** ist Lehrerin.<br>She is a teacher. |
|---|---|---|---|---|

---

[1] See footnote, p. 160.

| A | ihn | es | sie | Wir sehen **ihn** nächste Woche.<br>We'll be seeing him next week. |
| | | | | Ich habe **es** (das Buch) schon gelesen.<br>I've already read it. |
| | | | | Ich habe **sie** gestern getroffen.<br>I saw her yesterday. |
| D | ihm | (ihm) | ihr | Wie geht es **ihm**?<br>How is he? |
| | | | | Hast du **ihr** geschrieben?<br>Have you written to her? |
| G[1] | | | | |

### 278 Plural

| N | sie | Sie (die Eltern) sind nach Berlin gefahren.<br>They've gone to Berlin. |
| A | sie | Wir haben **sie** gestern zum Bahnhof gebracht.<br>We saw them off at the station yesterday. |
| D | ihnen | Die Reise wird **ihnen** bestimmt gefallen.<br>They are sure to enjoy the trip. |
| G[1] | | |

#### b. The 2nd Person

**279** (1) The familiar forms *du* (sing.) and *ihr* (pl.) are used in the family, to children, among friends and with close acquaintances.

**280** (2) In letter-writing, *du* and *ihr* and the corresponding possessives are written with initial capital letters in all cases.

| Zum Geburtstag wünsche ich **Dir** alles Gute. | I'd like to wish you many happy returns of the day. |

---

[1] The genitive forms of the personal pronoun *(meiner, deiner, seiner/ihrer* etc.) are rare. They can appear in a sentence like: *Es gibt hier viele Theater: Es gibt ihrer viele.* – There are a lot of theatres here; there are a lot of them.

| Wie geht es **Dir** und **Deiner** Familie. | How are you and your family? |
|---|---|
| Wie geht es **Euch**? | How are you (all)? |

**81** (3) *Sie* is used in formal address (cf. French *vous*) for both singular and plural. *Sie* and its corresponding possessives are always written with an initial capital letter; it requires the verb in the 3rd Pers. Pl.

| Können **Sie** mich morgen anrufen, Frau Fuchs? | Can you phone me tomorrow, Mrs Fuchs? |
|---|---|
| Haben Sie **Ihren** Paß? | Have you got your passport? |
| Woher kommen **Sie**, meine Herren? | Where do you come from, gentlemen? |

### c. The impersonal pronoun „es"

**82** (1) *Es* replaces a neuter noun. Unlike the English *it*, it cannot be used for all inanimate objects; objects of masculine gender are replaced by *er* in German, those of feminine gender by *sie*.

| Hier sehen Sie das Studio A. **Es** ist in München. | Here is Studio A. It is in Munich. |
|---|---|
| Warst du schon in dem neuen Restaurant? **Es** ist ziemlich teuer. | Have you been to the new restaurant yet? It's rather expensive. |
| Das neue Theaterprogramm ist da. Ich habe **es** Ihnen mitgebracht. | The new theatre programme is out. I've brought it for you. |
| But: Wo ist mein Paß? – **Er** liegt auf dem Tisch. | Where's my passport? – It's on the table. |
| Und meine Brieftasche? Ich finde **sie** nirgends. | And my wallet? I can't find it anywhere. |

163

**283** (2) When *es* is used to introduce a sentence, the form of the verb is determined by the noun and not by *es*.

| | |
|---|---|
| **Es** passieren zu viele Unfälle auf Landstraßen. <br> (Auf Landstraßen passieren zu viele Unfälle.) | Too many accidents occur on country roads. |
| **Es** ist niemand gekommen. <br> (Niemand ist gekommen.) | No one came. |
| **Es** haben zwanzig Personen an dem Kurs teilgenommen. <br> (An dem Kurs haben zwanzig Personen teilgenommen.) | Twenty people took part in the course. |

The same applies for passive sentences.

| | |
|---|---|
| **Es** wurde viel über das Gesetz diskutiert. <br> (Über das Gesetz wurde viel diskutiert. = Man hat viel über das Gesetz diskutiert.) | There was a lot of discussion about the law. |
| **Es** wurde mehr Urlaub gefordert. <br> (Mehr Urlaub wurde gefordert. = Man hat mehr Urlaub gefordert.) | More holiday time was demanded. |

Note:

Similarly, when *es* (or *das*) is used with *sein*, and the real subject is a personal pronoun, the verb agrees with the pronoun (contrast English usage!).

| | |
|---|---|
| **Bist du's,** Inge? <br> Der ganz hinten – **das bin ich**. | Is that you, Inge? <br> The one right at the back – that's me. |

**84** (3) *Es* anticipates a dependent clause.

| | |
|---|---|
| Ich finde **es** nicht richtig, daß eine Stewardeß mehr verdient als ein Lokführer. (Daß eine Stewardeß mehr verdient als ein Lokführer, finde ich nicht richtig.) | I don't think it's right that an air hostess earns more than an engine driver. |
| **Es** ist schwierig, jemand vom Rauchen abzubringen. (Jemand vom Rauchen abzubringen, ist schwierig.) | It's hard to get somebody to give up smoking. |
| **Es** scheint nicht möglich zu sein, alle Arbeit zu rationalisieren. (Alle Arbeit zu rationalisieren, scheint nicht möglich zu sein.) | It doesn't seem possible to rationalize all types of work. |

**85** (4) *Es* appears in the following expressions and phrases.

| | |
|---|---|
| Es regnet. | It's raining. |
| Es klingelt. | The bell's ringing. |
| Es ist schon spät. | It's late. |
| Es wird kälter. | It's getting colder. |
| Es bleibt schön. | It's going to stay fine. |
| Es geht mir gut. | I'm fine. |
| Es gefällt mir hier gut. | I like it here. |
| Was gibt es im Deutschen Museum zu sehen? | What is there to see in the Deutsche Museum? |
| Worum handelt es sich (geht es)? Um die Arbeit? | What is it about? Work? |
| Er hat es eilig. | He's in a hurry. |
| Er hat es im Leben schwer gehabt. | He has had a hard life. |

## d. Word order of pronoun objects

(1) Pronoun objects without prepositions precede all other objects, adverbs etc.; personal pronouns precede other pronouns.

| | |
|---|---|
| Sie hat mir heute Gulasch gekocht. | She made me some goulash today. |
| Ich gebe dir etwas mit. | I'll give you something to take with you. |

(2) Of several personal pronouns, the accusative precedes; of noun objects without prepositions, the person precedes the thing.

| | |
|---|---|
| Ich gebe es dir gern. | I'm happy to give it to you. |
| Ich habe meiner Schwester eine Handtasche geschenkt. | I have given my sister a handbag. |

## e. Pronominal adverbs (II, 1)

**286** (1) Certain prepositions combine with *da-* and *wo-* to form pronominal adverbs (*dar-* and *wor-* whenever the preposition begins with a vowel).

*Preposition + accusative:* wodurch – dadurch; wofür – dafür; wogegen – dagegen; worum – darum.

*Preposition + dative:* woraus – daraus; wobei – dabei; womit – damit; wonach – danach; wovon – davon; wozu – dazu.

*Preposition + accusative* or *dative:* woran – daran; worauf – darauf; worin – darin; worüber – darüber; worunter – darunter; wovor – davor.

**287** (2) They are used for prepositional expressions (preposition + noun) which refer to things. (For persons, the preposition is used with the 3rd Pers. of the personal pronoun.)

| | |
|---|---|
| Er beschäftigt sich **mit seinem Hobby**. | He occupies himself with his hobby. |
| **Womit** beschäftigt er sich? – Mit seinem Hobby. | What does he occupy himself with? – With his hobby. |

166

| | |
|---|---|
| Beschäftigt er sich oft mit seinem Hobby? – **Ja**, er beschäftigt sich oft **damit**. | Does he often occupy himself with his hobby? – Yes, he often occupies himself with it. |
| Compare: Er beschäftigt sich **mit seinem Sohn**. | He is occupied with his son. |
| **Mit wem** beschäftigt er sich? – Mit seinem Sohn. | Who is he occupied with? – His son. |
| Beschäftigt er sich oft mit seinem Sohn? – Ja, er beschäftigt sich oft **mit ihm**. | Is he often occupied with his son? – Yes, he is often occupied with him. |
| Können Sie sich noch an das Konzert erinnern? – Natürlich, **daran** (= an das Konzert) kann ich mich sehr gut erinnern. | Can you still remember that concert? – Of course, I remember it very well. |
| Achten Sie auf Ihre Gesundheit? – Natürlich achte ich **darauf** (= auf die Gesundheit). | Do you take care of your health? – Of course I take care of it. |
| Sind Sie für die Organisation verantwortlich? – Nein, **dafür** (= für die Organisation) war ich früher mal zuständig. | Are you responsible for the organization? – No, I used to be in charge of it. |

**288** (3) Pronominal adverbs anticipate a dependent clause (cf. *es*, p. 165).

| | |
|---|---|
| Man **ging dazu über**, in Gruppen zu arbeiten. | They changed over to group work. |
| Er **rechnet damit**, daß viele Arbeiter durch Roboter ersetzt werden. | He expects many workers to be replaced by robots. |
| Wie **kommst** du nur **darauf**, daß mich deine Arbeit nicht interessiert? | How did you get the idea that your work doesn't interest me? |
| Wie ist es nur **dazu gekommen**, daß er kaum noch Freunde hat? | How did it come about that he hardly has any friends left? |

167

## 2. The Interrogative Pronouns and Adjectives

**289**  **a. wer, was** (I, 1, 8, 14)

| N | wer | **Wer** ist am Apparat?<br>Who's speaking? |
|---|---|---|
| A | wen | **Wen** ruft sie an? Herrn Meier?<br>Who is she phoning? Mr Meier? |
| D | wem | Mit **wem** hast du eben gesprochen?<br>Who have you just been speaking to? |
| G | wessen | **Wessen**Tasche ist das?<br>Whose bag is that? |
| N | was | **Was** ist passiert?<br>What has happened? |
| A | was | **Was** möchten Sie lesen?<br>What would you like to read? |
| D | – | |
| G | – | |

**b. welch-; was für ein-** (II, 7, 17, 19)

**290**  **Singular**

Masculine

| N | welcher | **Welcher** Beruf interessiert Sie denn?<br>Which profession interests you, then? |
|---|---|---|
| A | welchen | Für **welchen** Beruf interessieren Sie sich?<br>Which profession are you interested in? |
| D | welchem | Mit **welchem** Zug kommt er eigentlich?<br>Which train is he taking? |
| G | welches[1] | |

---

[1] Not commonly used.

Neuter

| N | welches | **Welches** Arbeitsgebiet gefällt Ihnen besonders?<br>Which field of work do you prefer? |
|---|---|---|
| A | welches | **Welches** Hobby haben Sie?<br>Which hobby do you have? |
| D | welchem | Mit **welchem** Projekt haben Sie sich beschäftigt?<br>Which project have you been working on? |
| G | welches[1] | |

Feminine

| N | welche | **Welche** Firma hat Ihnen geschrieben?<br>Which firm has written to you? |
|---|---|---|
| A | welche | **Welche** Schule haben Sie besucht?<br>Which school did you attend? |
| D | welcher | Von **welcher** Firma kommen Sie?<br>Which firm do you come from? |
| G | welcher[1] | |

## 291 Plural

Masculine, Neuter, Feminine

| N | welche | **Welche** Sprachen werden verlangt?<br>Which languages are required? |
|---|---|---|
| A | welche | **Welche** Sprachen sprechen Sie?<br>Which languages do you speak? |
| D | welchen | An **welchen** Universitäten haben Sie studiert?<br>At which universities did you study? |
| G | welcher[1] | |

---

[1] Not commonly used.

## Masculine

| N | was für ein | **Was für ein** Motor ist das eigentlich?[1] |
|---|---|---|
| | | What sort of engine is that exactly? |
| A | was für einen | **Was für einen** Wagen hat er eigentlich?[1] |
| | | What sort of car has he got? |
| D | was für einem | In **was für einem** Betrieb arbeitet er? |
| | | What sort of firm does he work in? |
| G | was für eines[2] | |

## Neuter

| N | was für ein | **Was für ein** Unternehmen ist das? |
|---|---|---|
| | | What sort of enterprise is that? |
| A | was für ein | **Was für ein** Geschäft hat sie denn? |
| | | What sort of business does she have, then? |
| D | was für einem | In **was für einem** Restaurant wart ihr denn? |
| | | What sort of restaurant did you go to, then? |
| G | was für eines[2] | |

## Feminine

| N | was für eine | **Was für eine** Arbeit ist das eigentlich? |
|---|---|---|
| | | What sort of work is that exactly? |
| A | was für eine | Auf **was für eine** Schule geht sie denn? |
| | | What sort of school does she go to, then? |
| D | was für einer | In **was für einer** Firma arbeitet sie? |
| | | What sort of firm does she work in? |
| G | was für einer[2] | |

---

[1] In colloquial language also: *Was ist das eigentlich für ein Mann? – Was hat er eigentlich für einen Beruf?*
[2] Not commonly used.

**93** (1) *Welch-* asks about the person or object itself. *Was für ein-* and *was für* (pl.) ask about a definite characteristic of a person or object.

| | |
|---|---|
| **Mit welchem Zug** wird er kommen? Mit dem Vormittags- oder dem Nachmittagszug? | Which train is he coming on? The morning or afternoon train? |
| **Mit was für einem Zug** wird er kommen? Mit einem TEE (Trans European Express) oder mit einem Schnellzug? | What sort of train is he coming on? A TEE or an ordinary express train? |
| **Mit welcher Gesellschaft** bist du geflogen? Mit der Lufthansa? | Which airline did you fly with? Lufthansa? |
| **Mit was für einem Flugzeug** bist du geflogen? Mit einer Boeing 707? | What kind of plane did you fly on? A Boeing 707? |
| **Welchen Pullover** möchten Sie? Den roten oder den grünen? | Which jersey would you like? The red one or the green one? |
| **Was für einen Pullover** möchten Sie? Einen mit oder ohne Rollkragen? | What kind of jersey would you like? One with or without a polo-neck? |

**94** (2) Pronominal use

*Welch-* has the same forms whether used as determiner or pronoun.

| | |
|---|---|
| **Welcher** Beruf ist erstrebenswert?– Ich weiß nicht, **welcher** erstrebenswert ist. | Which profession is worth aspiring to? I don't know which one is worth aspiring to. |
| Für **welche** Firma arbeitet er eigentlich?– Ich weiß nicht, für **welche** er arbeitet. | Which firm is he working for exactly? I don't know which one he's working for. |

When used as a pronoun, *was für ein-* has different forms in the Nom. Masc. Sing. and in the Nom. and Acc. Neut. Sing. (cf. *einer*, p. 201 ff.). In the plural, *welche(n)* is used to replace *ein-*.

171

## 295 Singular

Masculine

| N | was für einer | Was für ein Motor ist das? – Ich weiß auch nicht, **was für einer** das ist.<br>What sort of engine is that? – I don't know what sort it is either. |
|---|---|---|

Neuter

| N | was für eins | Was für ein Unternehmen ist das? – Ich weiß auch nicht, **was für eins** das ist.<br>What sort of enterprise is that? – I don't know what sort it is either. |
|---|---|---|
| A | was für eins | Was für ein Geschäft hat sie eigentlich? – Ich weiß auch nicht, **was für eins** sie hat.<br>What sort of business does she have exactly? – I don't know what sort she has either. |

## 296 Plural

Masculine, Neuter, Feminine

| N | was für welche | Was für Leute sind das eigentlich? – Ich weiß auch nicht, **was für welche** das sind.<br>What sort of people are they exactly? – I don't know what sort they are either. |
|---|---|---|
| A | was für welche | Was für Interessen hat sie eigentlich? – Ich weiß auch nicht, **was für welche** sie hat.<br>What sort of interests does she have exactly? – I don't know what sort she has either. |
| D | was für welchen | Mit was für Plänen beschäftigt er sich eigentlich? – Wir wissen auch nicht, mit **was für welchen** er sich beschäftigt.<br>What sort of plans is he working on exactly? – We don't know what sort he's working on either. |
| G | – | |

## 3. The Demonstrative Pronouns and Adjectives

### a. der, das, die (I, 6, II, 23)

**97 Singular**

Masculine

| N | der | Ich habe den neuen Wein probiert. **Der** ist ausgezeichnet.<br>I have tasted the new wine. It's excellent. |
|---|---|---|
| A | den | **Den** werde ich mir besorgen.<br>I'm going to buy some of that. |
| D | dem | Mein Sohn spielt kein Instrument. **Dem** macht Musik keinen Spaß.<br>My son doesn't play an instrument. Music's no fun for him. |
| G | **dessen** | Ich habe Herrn Braun in der Versammlung gehört. **Dessen** Einstellung teile ich nicht.<br>I heard Mr Braun at the meeting. His is a view I don't share. |

Neuter

| N | das | **Das** ist ein gutes Restaurant.<br>That's a good restaurant. |
|---|---|---|
| A | das | Das Buch gefällt mir. **Das** nehme ich.<br>I like this book. I'll take it. |
| D | dem | Das ist teuer. Mit **dem** verglichen ist das Restaurant auf dem Fernsehturm billig.<br>That's expensive. The restaurant on the TV tower is cheap in comparison (with that). |
| G | **dessen** | Ich bin mir **dessen** sicher.<br>I'm quite sure of that. |

Feminine

| N | die | Deine neue Wohnung ist schick. **Die** würde mir auch gefallen.<br>Your new flat is very smart. I wouldn't mind it either. |
|---|---|---|
| A | die | **Die** würde ich auch mieten.<br>I would rent it too. |

| | | |
|---|---|---|
| D | der | In **der** würde ich mich auch wohlfühlen.<br>I would feel at home there too. |
| G | **deren** | Ich habe Frau Braun gesprochen. **Deren** Sorgen möchte ich nicht haben!<br>I've been speaking to Mrs Braun. I wouldn't like to have her problems! |

## 298 Plural

Masculine, Neuter, Feminine

| | | |
|---|---|---|
| N | die | Wo ist denn Familie Neumann? – **Die** kommen noch.<br>Where are the Neumanns? They're coming. |
| A | die | Und Klaus und Inge? – Ja, **die** haben wir auch eingeladen.<br>And Klaus and Inge? Yes, we invited them too. |
| D | **denen** | Mit **denen** haben wir auch Fasching gefeiert.<br>We celebrated Fasching with them too. |
| G | **deren,** | **Deren** Kinder sind heute bei den Eltern.<br>Their children are with their parents today. |
| | **derer**[1] | Das ist die Meinung **derer**, die gegen Reformen sind.<br>That is the opinion of those who are against reforms. |

**299** (1) The demonstrative pronouns *der, das, die* have no real equivalent in English. They have the same forms as the definite article *der, das, die* with only a few exceptions (see forms in bold type; cf. p. 116ff.).

*Der, das, die* takes the place of a personal pronoun and stands at the beginning of the sentence. The noun it refers to must have been previously mentioned.

| | |
|---|---|
| Kann man von hier aus den Dom sehen? – Ja, **der** ist sehr gut zu sehen. | Can you see the cathedral from here? – Yes, it can be seen very well. |
| Kennen Sie Herrn Berg? – Ja, **den** habe ich gestern kennengelernt. | Do you know Mr Berg? – Yes, I met him yesterday. |

---

[1] *Derer* is always used with a relative clause.

| Hast du die Karten? – Ach, **die** habe ich vergessen. | Have you got the tickets? – Oh, I forgot them. |

(2) *Das* can refer to all nouns in the singular or plural or to a whole clause or sentence.

| Der Herr dort links, **das** ist Herr Weiß. | The gentleman over there on the left, that's Mr Weiß. |
| Die Dame da hinten, **das** ist Frau Berg. | The lady back there, that's Mrs Berg. |
| Dieses Gemälde hier, **das** gehört einem Sammler. | This painting here, it belongs to a collector. |
| Was wollten die beiden Herren eigentlich? – **Das** waren zwei Studenten, die Zeitschriften verkaufen wollten. | What did the two gentlemen want anyway? – That was two students wanting to sell magazines. |
| Es tut uns leid, daß wir so spät gekommen sind. – **Das** macht nichts. | We're sorry we're so late. – That doesn't matter. |

**b. dieser, dieses, diese** (I, 19) / **jener, jenes, jene** (III, 18)

Declension is the same for pronoun and determiner.

**Singular**

Masculine

| N | dieser | **Dieser** Pullover gefällt mir gut. |
| | | I like this pullover very much. |
| A | diesen | **Diesen** Pullover nehme ich. |
| | | I'll take this pullover. |
| D | diesem | In **diesem** Zimmer fühle ich mich am wohlsten. |
| | | I feel most at home in this room. |
| G | dieses | Die Miete **dieses** Hauses beträgt DM 600,–. |
| | | The rent on this house is DM 600. |

Neuter

| N | dieses | Wie groß ist **dieses** Stadion?<br>How big is this stadium? |
| A | dieses | Ich kenne **dieses** Museum sehr gut.<br>I know this museum very well. |
| D | diesem | In **diesem** Kino war ich schon oft.<br>I have often been to this cinema. |
| G | dieses | Der Preis **dieses** Autos beträgt DM 15 000,–.<br>The price of this car ist DM 15,000. |

Feminine

| N | diese | **Diese** Karte ist kostenlos.<br>This ticket is free. |
| A | diese | **Diese** Gelegenheit mußt du nützen.<br>You must take this opportunity. |
| D | dieser | In **dieser** Straße war ich schon lange nicht mehr.<br>I haven't been in this street for ages. |
| G | dieser | Er ist ein Gegner **dieser** Politik.<br>He is an opponent of this policy. |

## 302 Plural

Masculine, Neuter, Feminine

| N | diese | **Diese** Probleme interessieren mich.<br>These problems interest me. |
| A | diese | Haben Sie **diese** Zeitungen schon gelesen?<br>Have you read these papers yet? |
| D | diesen | Haben Sie sich mit **diesen** Fragen schon beschäftigt?<br>Have you considered these questions yet? |
| G | dieser | Der Zweck **dieser** Maßnahmen ist klar.<br>The purpose of these measures is obvious. |

**03** (1) *Jener* is declined like *dieser*, but is only used in elevated style. It can be replaced by *der* or *derjenige* (= *diejenigen, die* . . .).

| | |
|---|---|
| Wir wollen der Vernunft voran-helfen, **jener** Vernunft, die uns den Frieden befiehlt. (= **der** Ver-nunft nämlich, die uns den Frieden befiehlt.) | We want to promote good sense, that sound judgement that bids us strive for peace. |
| Atlantis, **jener** sagenhafte Erdteil, von dem die alten Griechen be-richteten . . . (= **der; derjenige**) | Atlantis, that mythical continent of which the ancient Greeks related . . . |

**304** (2) *Dieser* and *jener* have the same endings as the definite article (cf. p. 116ff.). As demonstrative pronouns they translate *this/that one; these/those.*

| | |
|---|---|
| Wie findest du die Pullover? **Dieser** hier gefällt mir gut. **Diese** sind aber billiger. | What do you think of the pullovers? I like this one very much. But these are cheaper. |

(3) *Dieser* and *jener* are not exact equivalents of the English *this* and *that; this* can sometimes be rendered by the German definite article (see p. 116ff.), and as demonstrative pronoun *this/that* can translate *der/das/die* exactly (see p. 173ff.).

In general, *dieser* is used to refer to a particular person or thing; *jener* (not nearly as common as the English *that*) is used to differentiate or to indicate an alternative.

| | |
|---|---|
| **Diese** Verhältnisse, die wir jetzt haben, sind gut im Vergleich zu **jenen**, die wir viele Jahre lang hatten. | These conditions we have now are good compared with those we had for so many years. |

177

**305** (4) *Dies* – can summarize a preceding report.

| | |
|---|---|
| ... **Dies(es)** ist das Ergebnis der Untersuchung. | ...This is the result of the investigation. |
| ... Auf **diese** Weise kam er nach Deutschland. | ...In this way he came to Germany. |

**306** (5) When *dies-* refers to someone or something already familiar to the speaker, it can have a derogatory undertone.

| | |
|---|---|
| Er ist schlecht in der Schule. Was ist nur mit **diesem** Jungen los? | He is poor at school. Whatever's the matter with the boy? |
| Was soll ich denn mit **diesen** alten Möbeln? | Whatever shall I do with all this old furniture? |

### c. derselbe, dasselbe, dieselbe (II, 7)

Declension is the same for pronoun and determiner.

**307 Singular**

Masculine

| N | derselbe | War das der Herr von gestern? – Ja, das war **derselbe**. Was that the gentleman from yesterday? Yes, that was he. |
|---|---|---|
| A | denselben | Er hat noch **denselben** Wagen wie vor fünf Jahren. He's got the same car as he had 5 years ago. |
| D | demselben | Er ist in **demselben** Kurs wie ich. He is in the same course as I am. |
| G | desselben[1] | |

---

[1] Not commonly used.

Neuter

| N | dasselbe | Es ist jeden Tag **dasselbe**.<br>Every day it's the same. |
| A | dasselbe | Sie hatte **dasselbe** Kleid an wie gestern.<br>She was wearing the same dress as yesterday. |
| D | demselben | Er ißt immer in **demselben** Restaurant.<br>He always eats in the same restaurant. |
| G | desselben[1] | |

Feminine

| N | dieselbe | War das die Verkäuferin von gestern? – Ja, das war **dieselbe**.<br>Was that the assistant we had yesterday? – Yes, it's the same one. |
| A | dieselbe | Du hast **dieselbe** Geschichte schon einmal erzählt.<br>You've already told that story once. |
| D | derselben | Ich bin letztes Jahr in **derselben** Gegend gewesen.<br>I was in the same district last year. |
| G | derselben[1] | |

## 308 Plural

Masculine, Neuter, Feminine

| N | dieselben | Das sind **dieselben** Bestimmungen wie in anderen Ländern.<br>Those are the same regulations as in other countries. |
| A | dieselben | Er hat immer noch **dieselben** Probleme.<br>He still has the same problems. |
| D | denselben | Er trifft sich immer mit **denselben** Leuten.<br>He always gets together with the same people. |
| G | derselben[1] | |

*Derselbe* is a combination of the definite article *der, das, die* and *selb-*, which is declined like an adjective.

---

[1] Not commonly used.

Note:

In colloquial language *der- (das-, die-) selbe* and *der (das, die) gleiche* are frequently confused.

| | |
|---|---|
| Sie trug **dasselbe Kleid** wie gestern. | She wore the same dress as she did yesterday. |
| But: | |
| Sie trug **das gleiche Kleid** wie ihre Freundin. | She wore the same dress as her friend. |

### d. derjenige, dasjenige, diejenige (II, 15)

**309** (1) *Derjenige* is a combination of the definite article *der, das, die* and *jenig-*, which is declined like an adjective (cf. *derselbe*, p. 178 ff.).

**310** (2) *Derjenige* is usually followed by a relative clause.

| | |
|---|---|
| **Diejenigen** Studenten, **die** ihr Studium nicht selbst bezahlen können, werden unterstützt. | Those students who cannot pay for their studies themselves are given financial support. |
| Er ist **derjenige, der** von der Polizei gesucht wird. | He is the one the police are after. |
| Wir haben mit **denjenigen** gesprochen, **die** für diese Sendung verantwortlich sind. | We have spoken to the people who were responsible for this programme. |

### e. solcher, solches, solche (III, 1)

**311** (1) *Solcher* has the same endings as the definite article, *der, das, die* (cf. p. ff.), both as pronoun and determiner. *Solcher* points out the particular nature of a person or thing.

| | |
|---|---|
| Mit **solchen** Leuten will ich nichts zu tun haben. | I don't want to have anything to do with such people. |

| | |
|---|---|
| **Solche** alten Schlösser habe ich noch nie gesehen. | I have never seen such old castles. |
| Hast du die Blumen hier schon gesehen? – Ja, **solche** haben wir auch. | Have you ever seen these flowers? Yes, we have ones like that too. |

**312**  (2) After an indefinite article, *solch-* is declined like an adjective.

| | |
|---|---|
| Ein **solcher** Computer wäre ziemlich teuer. | A computer like that would be rather expensive. |
| An einem **solchen** Abend kann man doch nicht nach Hause gehen. | One can't go home on an evening like this. |

Before an indefinite article, *solch-* has no ending.

| | |
|---|---|
| **Solch ein** Computer wäre ziemlich teuer. (coll.: **So ein** Computer (**so einer**) wäre ziemlich teuer.) | A computer like that would be rather expensive. |
| **Solch ein** Gesetz ist nicht geplant. (coll.: **So ein** Gesetz (**so eins**) ist nicht geplant.) | No such law is planned. |

## 4. The Relative Pronouns

**313**  The demonstrative pronouns *der, das, die* and the interrogative pronouns *wer, was* are used as relative pronouns.

**a. der, das, die** (I, 19, 21; II, 9, 23; III, 13)

## 314 Singular

Masculine

| N | . . ., der | Der Bekannte, **der** mich gestern besucht hat, war ein Jahr in Südamerika.<br>The friend who came to see me yesterday was in South America for a year. |
|---|---|---|
| A | . . ., den | Der Film, **den** wir gestern gesehen haben, war ausgezeichnet.<br>The film we saw yesterday was excellent. |
| D | . . ., dem | Der Sportler, mit **dem** wir gesprochen haben, kommt aus Kanada.<br>The sportsman we were speaking to comes from Canada. |
| G | . . ., dessen | Herr Meier, **dessen** Betrieb ich neulich kennengelernt habe, besucht uns morgen.<br>Mr Meier, whose factory I visited the other day, is coming to see us tomorrow. |

Neuter

| N | . . ., das | Das ist ein Flugzeug, **das** 3000 Stundenkilometer fliegt.<br>That's a plane that flies 3000 km/hr. |
|---|---|---|
| A | . . ., das | Das Gebäude, **das** Sie dort sehen, war früher das Rathaus.<br>The building you see over there used to be the Town Hall. |
| D | . . ., dem | Das Gebäude, in **dem** wir gerade waren, ist noch älter als die Kirche.<br>The building we have just been in is even older than the church. |
| G | . . ., dessen | Wir besichtigen jetzt ein Haus, **dessen** Alter auf 350 Jahre geschätzt wird.<br>We're now going to visit a house whose age is estimated at 350 years. |

Feminine

| N | . . ., die | Wir besichtigen heute eine Kirche, **die** im 12. Jahrhundert erbaut wurde.<br>Today we're going to visit a church that was built in the twelfth century. |
|---|---|---|
| A | . . ., die | Die Kirche, **die** Sie dort sehen, ist über 700 Jahre alt.<br>The church you see over there is over 700 years old. |
| D | . . ., der | Die Dame, mit **der** ich gerade gesprochen habe, kommt aus Köln.<br>The lady I have just been speaking to comes from Cologne. |
| G | . . ., deren | Ist das die Firma, **deren** Besitzer verunglückt ist?<br>Is that the firm whose owner had an accident? |

**315 Plural**

Masculine, Neuter, Feminine

| N | . . ., die | Besucher, **die** zu spät kommen, müssen draußen warten.<br>Visitors who arrive too late must wait outside |
|---|---|---|
| A | . . ., die | Filme, **die** wir schon gesehen haben, interessieren uns nicht.<br>We are not interested in films we have already seen. |
| D | . . ., denen | Die Bekannten, mit **denen** wir uns treffen wollten, haben heute keine Zeit.<br>The friends we wanted to meet have no time today. |
| G | . . ., deren | Sind das die Kinder, **deren** Eltern verunglückt sind?<br>Are those the children whose parents had an accident? |

**316** (1) In German the relative pronoun must agree in gender and number with its antecedent in the main clause. The case depends on its function within the relative clause. Note that a relative pronoun can never be omitted in German, as it sometimes is in English.

| | |
|---|---|
| Der Film, **den** wir gestern gesehen haben, war ausgezeichnet. | The film we saw yesterday was excellent. |
| Die Kirche, **die** Sie dort sehen, ist über 700 Jahre alt. | The church you see over there is over 700 years old. |

**317**  (2) In phrases of time and place, *wo* often replaces the preposition *in* + relative pronoun.

| | |
|---|---|
| Er besuchte auch die Stadt, **in der** er zehn Jahre gelebt hatte. | He also visited the town in which he had lived for 10 years. |
| Er besuchte auch die Stadt, **wo** er zehn Jahre gelebt hatte. | He also visited the city where he had lived for ten years. |
| Er kam an dem Wochenende, **an dem** ich verreist war. (. . ., **wo** ich verreist war; or: . . ., **als** ich verreist war.) | He came the weekend I was away. |
| Das war in der Zeit, **in der** ich noch studiert habe. (. . ., **wo** ich noch studiert habe; or: . . ., **als** ich noch studiert habe.) | That was during the time when I was still studying. |

*Wo* is used to refer to the name of a country or town.

| | |
|---|---|
| Sie waren drei Wochen in der Türkei, **wo** sie viel herumgereist sind. | They were in Turkey for three weeks, where they travelled around a great deal. |
| Sie fährt nach Salzburg, **wo** jetzt die Festspiele stattfinden. | She is going to Salzburg, where the Festival is now on. |

**b. wer, was** (II, 11)

**318**  (1) *Wer* refers to a person who is not clearly defined. A demonstrative pronoun usually appears in the main clause.

184

| | |
|---|---|
| **Wer** viel raucht, (**der**) gefährdet seine Gesundheit. | Whoever smokes a lot, endangers his health. |
| **Wer** sich das Rauchen abgewöhnen will, (**der**) findet viele Hilfsmittel. | Anyone wanting to give up smoking will find many remedies. |
| **Wer** sich das Rauchen abgewöhnen will, **dem** empfehlen wir einen Anti-Rauch-Kurs. | Anyone who wants to give up smoking is recommended to join an anti-smoking course. |

If the relative pronoun and the demonstrative pronoun are in the same case, the demonstrative pronoun can be omitted.

| | |
|---|---|
| **Wer** viel raucht, gefährdet seine Gesundheit. | Whoever smokes a lot, endangers his health. |

**319** (2) *Was* refers to an antecedent of a general nature, usually an indefinite pronoun or an adjective.

| | |
|---|---|
| Das ist **alles, was** ich weiß. | That's all I know. |
| Es gibt **nichts, was** ihn interessiert. | There's nothing that interests him. |
| **Das Schönste, was** wir erlebt haben, war eine Fahrt zum Tegernsee. | The most enjoyable thing we experienced was a trip to the Tegernsee. |

## 5. The Possessive Adjectives and Pronouns (I, 7, 12, 13, 16; II, 6, 16)

### 1st Person

**320 Singular**

|   | Masc. | Neut. | Fem. |   |
|---|-------|-------|------|---|
| N | mein | mein | meine | Wo ist **mein** Paß?<br>Where's my passport?<br>Wann geht **mein** Flugzeug?<br>When does my plane leave?<br>**Meine** Besprechung ist um 11 Uhr.<br>My meeting is at 11 o'clock. |
| A | meinen | mein | meine | Ich brauche **meinen** Paß, **mein** Ticket und **meine** Brieftasche.<br>I need my passport, my ticket and my wallet. |
| D | meinem | meinem | meiner | Ich komme mit **meinem** Kollegen (**meiner** Kollegin).<br>I'm coming with my colleague.<br>Die Papiere habe ich in **meinem** Auto.<br>I've got the papers in my car. |
| G | meines | meines | meiner | Das sind die Papiere **meines** Kollegen (**meiner** Kollegin).<br>Those are my colleague's papers.<br>Ein Drittel **meines** Gehalts gebe ich für die Miete aus.<br>I spend a third of my salary on the rent. |

**321 Plural**

| N | meine | Sind das **meine** Papiere?<br>Are those my papers? |
|---|---|---|
| A | meine | Haben Sie **meine** Papiere gesehen?<br>Have you seen my papers? |
| D | meinen | Ich komme mit **meinen** Kollegen.<br>I'm coming with my colleagues. |
| G | meiner | Ich bringe zwei **meiner** Kollegen mit.<br>I'm bringing two of my colleagues along. |

**2nd Person**

**322 Singular**

| | Masc. | Neut. | Fem. | |
|---|---|---|---|---|
| N | dein | dein | deine | **Dein** Wagen ist kaputt?<br>Your car has broken down?<br>**Dein** Telefon klingelt.<br>Your telephone's ringing.<br>**Deine** Mutter kommt.<br>Your mother's coming. |
| A | deinen | dein | deine | Kannst du mir morgen **deinen** Wagen (**dein** Auto) geben?<br>Can I have your car tomorrow?<br>Triffst du **deine** Mutter?<br>Are you meeting your mother? |
| D | deinem | deinem | deiner | Du kommst also mit **deinem** Bruder (**deiner** Schwester).<br>So you're coming with your brother (your sister).<br>Kann ich mit **deinem** Auto fahren?<br>Can I take your car? |

|   | Masc. | Neut. | Fem. | |
|---|---|---|---|---|
| G | deines | deines | deiner | Ist das die Freundin **deines** Bruders (**deiner** Schwester)? <br> Is that your brother's (your sister's) girl-friend? <br> Was, du brauchst 10 Prozent **deines** Gehalts für Wein und Tabak? <br> What, you need 10% of your salary for wine and tobacco? |

**323 Plural**

|   |   | | | |
|---|---|---|---|---|
| N | deine | | | Sind das **deine** Schallplatten? <br> Are those your records? |
| A | deine | | | Zeig mir doch mal **deine** Platten! <br> Do show me your records! |
| D | deinen | | | Was willst du **deinen** Gästen zeigen? <br> What do you want to show your guests? |
| G. | deiner | | | Willst du einen Teil **deiner** Ferien bei uns verbringen? <br> Would you like to spend part of your holiday with us? |

**3rd Person**

**324 Singular**

|   | Masc. | Neut. | Fem. | |
|---|---|---|---|---|
| N | sein | sein | seine | **Sein** Kollege ist krank. <br> His colleague is sick. <br> **Sein** Taxi ist da. <br> His taxi's here. <br> **Seine** Frau hat angerufen. <br> His wife phoned. |

|     | Masc. | Neut. | Fem. |  |
|-----|-------|-------|------|--|
| A | seinen | sein | seine | Er braucht **seinen** Paß, **sein** Ticket und **seine** Brieftasche.<br>He needs his passport, his ticket and his wallet. |
| D | seinem | seinem | seiner | Er kommt mit **seinem** Kollegen (**seiner** Kollegin).<br>He's coming with his colleague.<br>Er ist in **seinem** Zimmer.<br>He's in his room. |
| G | seines | seines | seiner | Er hat das Auto **seines** Freundes (**seiner** Frau).<br>He's got his friend's (his wife's) car.<br>Einen Teil **seines** Gehalts gibt er für Reisen aus.<br>He spends part of his salary on travelling. |

## 25  Plural

|     |  |  |
|-----|--|--|
| N | seine | **Seine** Gäste sind da.<br>His guests are here. |
| A | seine | Haben Sie **seine** Gäste schon begrüßt?<br>Have you greeted his guests yet? |
| D | seinen | Er ist mit **seinen** Gästen unterwegs.<br>He is travelling around with his guests. |
| G | seiner | Einige **seiner** Freunde können nicht kommen.<br>Some of his friends can't come. |

|   | Masc. | Neut. | Fem. | |
|---|-------|-------|------|---|
| N | ihr | ihr | ihre | **Ihr** Beruf (**ihre** Tätigkeit) macht ihr Spaß.<br>She enjoys her profession (her job).<br>**Ihr** Geschäft liegt in der Innenstadt.<br>Her shop is in the centre of town. |
| A | ihren | ihr | ihre | Sie möchte **ihren** Beruf (**ihre** Tätigkeit) nicht aufgeben.<br>She doesn't want to give up her profession (her job).<br>Sie ist auf **ihr** Gehalt angewiesen.<br>She depends on her salary. |
| D | ihrem | ihrem | ihrer | Sie ist mit **ihrem** Beruf (**ihrem** Gehalt, **ihrer** Tätigkeit) zufrieden.<br>She is satisfied with her profession (her salary, her job). |
| G | ihres | ihres | ihrer | Eine Hausfrau verbringt den größten Teil **ihres** Tages mit Hausarbeit.<br>A housewife spends most of her day doing housework.<br>Sie gibt ein Viertel **ihres** Gehalts für Lebensmittel aus.<br>She spends a quarter of her salary on groceries.<br>Sie verbringt einen großen Teil **ihrer** Freizeit mit Lesen.<br>She spends much of her free time reading. |

| N | ihre | **Ihre** Hobbies sind Kino und Theater.<br>Her hobbies are films and the theatre. |
|---|------|---|
| A | ihre | Sie hat nur wenig Zeit für **ihre** Hobbies.<br>She only has a little time for her hobbies. |
| D | ihren | Sie beschäftigt sich viel mit **ihren** Kindern.<br>She spends a lot of time with her children. |
| G | ihrer | Sie kümmert sich um die Hausaufgaben **ihrer** Kinder.<br>She is concerned about her children's homework. |

## 1st Person

328 Singular

| | Masc. | Neut. | Fem. | |
|---|-------|-------|------|---|
| N | unser | unser | unsere | **Unser** Urlaub beginnt in einer Woche.<br>Our holiday begins in a week.<br>Das ist **unser** Gepäck.<br>That's our luggage.<br>**Unsere** Reise geht nach Österreich.<br>We're going on a trip to Austria. |
| A | unseren | unser | unsere | **Unseren** Urlaub (**unsere** Freizeit) verbringen wir mit Lesen.<br>We're spending our holiday (our free time) reading. |

|   | Masc. | Neut. | Fem. | |
|---|-------|-------|------|---|
|   |       |       |      | Ich habe **unser** Gepäck schon in den Kofferraum gelegt. <br> I've already put our luggage in the boot. |
| D | unserem | unserem | unserer | Wir verbringen den Urlaub bei **unserem** Sohn (**unserer** Tochter, in **unserem** Ferienhaus). <br> We're spending our holiday at our son's (at our daughter's, in our holiday home). |
| G | unseres | unseres | unserer | Einen Teil **unseres** Urlaubs verbringen wir zu Hause. <br> We're spending part of our holiday at home. <br><br> Die Hälfte **unseres** Geldes haben wir schon ausgegeben. <br> We've already spent half our money. <br><br> Die Hälfte **unserer** Reise ist schon vorbei. <br> Half our trip's already over. |

**329 Plural**

|   | | |
|---|---|---|
| N | unsere | **Unsere** Koffer sind gepackt. <br> Our cases are packed. |
| A | unsere | Wir haben **unsere** Koffer schon gepackt. <br> We've already packed our cases. |
| D. | unseren | Wir haben **unseren** Nachbarn den Hausschlüssel gegeben. <br> We've given the house key to our neighbours. |
| G | unserer | Die meisten **unserer** Nachbarn sind auch verreist. <br> Most of our neighbours have gone away too. |

**330 Singular**

|   | Masc. | Neut. | Fem. |   |
|---|-------|-------|------|---|
| N | euer | euer | eure | **Euer** Garten ist wirklich schön.<br>Your garden really is lovely.<br>Wo liegt **euer** Haus?<br>Where is your house?<br>Wie hoch ist **eure** Miete?<br>How high is your rent? |
| A | euren | euer | eure | Habt ihr noch **euren** Wagen (**euer** Haus, **eure** Wohnung)?<br>Have you still got your car (your house, your flat)? |
| D | eurem | eurem | eurer | Seid ihr mit **eurem** Wagen da?<br>Do you have your car here?<br>Wie lange wohnt ihr schon in **eurem** Haus (in **eurer** Wohnung)?<br>How long have you been living in your house (your flat)? |
| G | eures | eures | eurer | Ich habe die Freundin **eures** Bruders (**eurer** Schwester) neulich kennengelernt.<br>The other day I met your brother's (your sister's) girl-friend.<br>Die Lage **eures** Hauses ist sehr schön.<br>Your house is very nicely situated. |

**331 Plural**

|   |   |   |
|---|---|---|
| N | eure | Was machen **eure** Kinder?<br>How are your children getting on? |
| A | eure | **Eure** Bekannten kennen wir nicht.<br>We don't know your friends. |

| | | | | |
|---|---|---|---|---|
| D | | euren | | Wie geht es **euren** Eltern?<br>How are your parents? |
| G | | eurer | | Habt ihr das Geschäft **eurer** Eltern übernommen?<br>Have you taken over your parents' business? |

### 3rd Person

**332 Singular**

| | Masc. | Neut. | Fem. | |
|---|---|---|---|---|
| N | ihr<br>(Ihr) | ihr<br>(Ihr) | ihre<br>(Ihre) | **Ihr** Sohn (der Sohn von Meiers) (**ihre** Tochter) ist schlecht in der Schule.<br>Their (Meiers') son (their daughter) is weak at school. |
| A | ihren<br>(Ihren) | ihr<br>(Ihr) | ihre<br>(Ihre) | Die Eltern unterhalten sich über **ihren** Sohn (**ihr** Kind, **ihre** Tochter).<br>The parents are talking about their son (their child, their daughter). |
| D | ihrem<br>(Ihrem) | ihrem<br>(Ihrem) | ihrer<br>(Ihrer) | Die Kinder sind in **ihrem** Hobbyraum (**ihrem** Zimmer).<br>The children are in their hobby room (their room).<br>Wir haben mit **ihrer** Lehrerin gesprochen.<br>We've spoken to their teacher. |
| G | ihres<br>(Ihres) | ihres<br>(Ihres) | ihrer<br>(Ihrer) | Was ist die Meinung **ihres** Lehrers (**ihrer** Lehrerin)?<br>What is their teacher's opinion?<br>Die Zukunft **ihres** Kindes ist wichtig.<br>Their child's future is important. |

| N | ihre<br>(Ihre) | **Ihre** Hobbies (die Hobbies der Kinder) sind Tennis, Ski und Fußball.<br>Their (the children's) hobbies are tennis, skiing and football. |
| A | ihre<br>(Ihre) | Machen sie eigentlich **ihre** Hausaufgaben?<br>Do they do their homework? |
| D | ihren<br>(Ihren) | Unsere Jungen beschäftigen sich nur mit **ihren** Hobbies.<br>Our boys only work at their hobbies. |
| G | ihrer<br>(Ihrer) | Den größten Teil **ihrer** Ferien wollen sie verreisen.<br>They want to spend most of their holiday travelling. |

**334** (1) The formal mode of address has the same forms as the 3rd Pers. Pl.; it is capitalized in all forms.

| | |
|---|---|
| Was macht **Ihr** Sohn, Frau Meier?<br>– Er macht mir viel Ärger, er ist so schlecht in der Schule. | How's your son getting on, Mrs Meier? He is giving me a lot of worry, he's doing so badly at school. |
| Welche Hobbies haben **Ihre** Kinder eigentlich? – Sehr viele, Tennis, Ski, Fußball, usw. | What hobbies do your children have? A lot, tennis, skiing, football, etc. |

Note the difference between the following forms:

| | |
|---|---|
| ihr (personal pronoun): | |
| Seid **ihr** (= Helmut und Marion) morgen zu Hause? | Will you (= Helmut and Marion) be at home tomorrow? |
| Hast du **ihr** (= Frau Braun) geschrieben? | Have you written to her (= Mrs Braun)? |

195

| | |
|---|---|
| ihr (possessive adjective sing.): | |
| Sie sagt, daß **ihr** Beruf ihr Spaß macht. | She says she's enjoying her job. |
| ihr (possessive adjective pl.): | |
| Sie haben erzählt, daß **ihr** Sohn schlecht in der Schule ist. | They told us their son is doing badly at school. |
| Ihr (formal mode of address): | |
| Was macht **Ihr** Sohn, Frau Meier? | How's your son getting on, Mrs Meier? |

**335** (2) In German the stem of the possessive adjective depends on the gender and number of the possessor; the ending depends on the gender, number and case of the thing possessed.

| | |
|---|---|
| Er hat **seine** Brieftasche vergessen. | He has forgotten his wallet. |
| Er braucht **seinen** Wagen heute nicht. | He doesn't need his car today. |

**336** (3) In correspondence, possessives referring to the recipient of the letter are capitalized.

| | |
|---|---|
| Wie geht es **Deinem** Mann? | How's your husband? |
| Habt **Ihr Euer** Wochenendhaus noch? | Do you still have your weekend cottage? |

**337** (4) **The possessive pronouns** (II, 16)

Possessive pronouns end in -*er* or -*es* (cf. *was für einer; irgendeiner; keiner*) in the Nom. Masc. and Nom. and Acc. Neut. This applies to all persons.

196

## Nom. Masc.

| meiner | Ist das dein Autoschlüssel? – Ja, das ist **meiner**.<br>Is this your car key? – Yes, that's mine. |
|---|---|
| deiner | Hier liegt ein Autoschlüssel. Das ist doch **deiner**.<br>Here's a car key. Isn't it yours? |
| seiner, ihrer | Ist das sein (ihr) Regenschirm? – Ja, das ist **seiner** (**ihrer**).<br>Is that his (her) umbrella? – Yes, that's his (hers). |
| uns(e)rer | Ist das euer Wagen? – Ja, das ist **unsrer**.<br>Is that your car? – Yes, it's ours. |
| eurer | Draußen steht ein neuer Wagen. Ist das **eurer**?<br>There's a new car outside. Is it yours? |
| ihrer, Ihrer | Ist das ihr Plattenspieler (. . . der Kinder)? – Ja, das ist **ihrer**.<br>Is that their (the children's) record player? – Yes, it's theirs.<br>Hier hängt noch ein Mantel. Ist das **Ihrer**?<br>There's another coat here. Is it yours? |

## Nom./Acc. Neut.

| meins | Ist das dein Auto? – Ja, das ist **meins**.<br>Is that your car? – Yes, it's mine. |
|---|---|
| deins | Hier liegt ein Ticket. Ist das **deins**?<br>Here's a ticket. Is it yours? |
| seins, ihrs | Ist das sein (ihr) Arbeitszimmer? – Ja, das ist **seins** (**ihrs**).<br>Is this his (her) study? – Yes, it's his (hers). |
| uns(e)res | Ist das euer Haus? – Ja, das ist **unsres**.<br>Is that your house? – Yes, it's ours. |
| eures | Das Wochenendhaus hier auf dem Foto, ist das **eures**?<br>The weekend cottage here in the photo, is it yours? |
| ihrs, Ihrs | Ist das ihr Spielzimmer? – Ja, das ist **ihrs**.<br>Is this their playroom? – Yes, it's theirs.<br>Hier liegt ein Ticket. Ist das **Ihrs**?<br>Here's a ticket. Is it yours? |

Otherwise the possessive pronouns are declined in the same way as the possessive adjectives (see p. 186 ff.).

**338** (5) **Colloquial forms**

The following forms are common in colloquial Germmam:

---

Ist das eure Kamera? – Ja, das ist **unsre**. (instead of unsere)
Ist das euer Haus? – Ja, das ist **unsres** (or **unsers**). (instead of unseres)
Das Haus hier auf dem Foto, ist das eures (or **euers**)?
Welchen Wagen nimmst du? – Ich nehme **unsren** (or **unsern**). (instead of unseren)
Ich habe heute keinen Wagen. Kann ich euren (or **euern**) nehmen?
Fahrt ihr mit eurem Wagen? – Ja, wir fahren mit **unsrem** (or **unserm**). (instead of unserem)
Mein Wagen ist in der Werkstatt. Kann ich heute mit eurem (or **euerm**) fahren?

---

**339** **6. The Reflexive Pronouns** (I, 10, 11, 15) (cf. Reflexive Verbs, p. 76 ff.)

| ich | A | mich | Ich interessiere **mich** sehr für Sport.<br>I'm very interested in sport. |
| | D | mir | Diesen Wagen kann ich **mir** nicht leisten.<br>I can't afford this car. |
| du | A | dich | Freust du **dich** schon auf den Urlaub?<br>Are you looking forward to your holiday? |
| | D | dir | Was wünschst du **dir** zum Geburtstag?<br>What do you want for your birthday? |
| er/sie | A | **sich** | Fräulein Fuchs möchte **sich** verabschieden.<br>Fräulein Fuchs would like to say goodbye. |
| | D | **sich** | Hat er **sich** schon Gedanken um die Zukunft gemacht?<br>Has he given any thought to the future yet? |
| wir | A | uns | Wir haben **uns** lange unterhalten.<br>We had a long chat. |
| | D | | Wir haben **uns** viel Zeit genommen.<br>We allowed plenty of time. |

| ihr | A | euch | Freut ihr **euch** auf Hamburg?<br>Are you looking forward to going to Hamburg? |
| | D | | Was habt ihr **euch** vorgestellt?<br>What did you expect? |
| sie, Sie | A | **sich** | Interessieren **sich** die Kinder noch für Beat?<br>Are the children still interested in beat?<br>Freuen Sie **sich** auf das Konzert?<br>Are you looking forward to the concert? |
| | D | **sich** | Sie (die Kinder) wünschen **sich** einen Plattenspieler.<br>They (the children) are hoping for a record player.<br>Haben Sie (Herr und Frau Müller) **sich** neu eingerichtet?<br>Have you refurnished your home, Mr and Mrs Müller? |

**40** (1) In the 1st and 2nd Pers. Sing. and Pl., reflexive pronouns are identical in form with personal pronouns (see p. 159 ff.). In the 3rd Pers. Sing. and Pl., the reflexive pronoun is *sich*.

**41** (2) The reflexive pronoun is also used after prepositions when it refers to the subject of the verb (III, 13).

| | |
|---|---|
| Er hatte kein Geld **bei sich**.<br>Er fluchte **vor sich** hin. | He had no money on him.<br>He swore to himself. |

Compare:

| | |
|---|---|
| Er denkt nur **an sich**.<br>Er denkt viel **an sie**. | He only thinks of himself.<br>He thinks of her a lot. |

## 42  7. Indefinite Pronouns and Adjectives

Used both as pronouns and determiners: *alle(s), einige, einzelne, jeder, mancher, mehrere, viele, wenige.*
Pronouns only: *einer/keiner, etwas, irgendwer, jemand, man, nichts, niemand.* This group is not fully declined.

## a. all- (II, 20)

**343  alle** (Plural)

| N | alle | **Alle** Maschinen haben Verspätung.<br>All the planes are delayed. |
|---|------|------------------------------------------------|
| A | alle | Wir haben **alle** Bewerbungen geprüft.<br>We have studied all the applications. |
| D | allen | Wir mußten **allen** Bewerbern absagen.<br>We had to turn all the applicants down. |
| G | aller | Der Wunsch **aller** Menschen nach Glück und Zufriedenheit.<br>The wish of all people for happiness and contentment. |

*Alle* is declined in the same way as pronoun and determiner.
(*Alle sind zu spät gekommen.* Everyone arrived too late.)

**344  alles** (Singular)

| N | alles | **Alles** ist in Ordnung.<br>Everything's all right. |
|---|-------|------------------------------------------|
| A | alles | Haben Sie **alles**?<br>Have you got everything? |
| D | allem | Wir sind mit **allem** einverstanden.<br>We agree to everything. |
| G | – | |

**345**  (1) *Alle* stands for people and things, *alles* only for things (except when it refers to an entire group of people).

| **Alles** hörte zu, als er von seiner Reise berichtete. | Everybody listened when he told about his trip. |
|---|---|
| **Alles** war begeistert, als das Ergebnis bekanntgegeben wurde. | Everyone was thrilled when the result was announced. |
| **Alles** aussteigen! | All change! |

200

**346** (2) When *alle* appears before an article or pronoun, the ending is often dropped.

| | |
|---|---|
| Wir waren bei **all** unseren Freunden eingeladen. | We were invited to go and see all of our friends. |
| **All** diese Leute wollen zum Skifahren. | All these people want to go skiing. |

**b. ein-/kein-** (II, 1)

**ein-**

**347 Singular**

| | Masc. | Neut. | Fem. | |
|---|---|---|---|---|
| N | einer | eins | eine | Ist Thomas ein moderner Mann? – Ja, er ist **einer**. <br> Is Thomas a modern man? – Yes, he is. <br> Ist das ein Düsenflugzeug? – Ja, das ist **eins**. <br> Is that a jet plane? – Yes, it is. <br> Ist das eine Automobilfabrik? – Ja, das ist **eine**. <br> Is that a car factory? – Yes, it is. |
| A | einen | eins | eine | Haben Sie einen Wagen (ein Haus, eine Garage)? – Ja, ich habe **einen** (**eins**, **eine**). <br> Have you got a car (a house, a garage)? – Yes, I have. |
| D | einem | einem | einer | Was sagst du zu meinem neuen Plattenspieler? – Toll, mit so **einem** wäre ich auch zufrieden. <br> What do you say to my new record player? – Terrific, I'd be quite happy with one like that too. |

| | Masc. | Neut. | Fem. | |
|---|---|---|---|---|
| | | | | Wie findest du das Hotel? – Sehr schön. In so **einem** habe ich noch nie gewohnt.<br>What do you think of the hotel? – Very nice. I've never stayed in one like this.<br>Wie gefällt dir meine neue Wohnung? – Gut. In so **einer** würde ich auch gern wohnen.<br>How do you like my new flat? – Very much. I'd like to live in one like this too. |
| G | – | – | – | |

## 348 Plural

| N | (welche) | Haben wir noch ein paar Flaschen Bier? – Ja, im Kühlschrank sind noch **welche**.<br>Have we still got a few bottles of beer? – Yes, there are still some in the fridge. |
|---|---|---|
| A | (welche) | Wir brauchen noch Zigaretten. – Gut, ich hole **welche**.<br>We still need cigarettes. – Good, I'll go and get some. |
| D | (welchen) | Die neue Bahn wird von drei Firmen gebaut. – Wissen Sie, von **welchen**?<br>The new railway is being built by three firms. – Do you know which ones? |
| G | – | |

**kein-**

**Singular**

| | Masc. | Neut. | Fem. | |
|---|---|---|---|---|
| N | keiner | keines | keine | Ist Thomas ein moderner Mann? – Nein, er ist **keiner**. Is Thomas a modern man? – No, he isn't. Ist das ein Düsenflugzeug? – Nein, das ist **keins**. Is that a jet plane? – No, it isn't. Ist das eine Automobilfabrik? – Nein, das ist **keine**. Is that a car factory? – No, it isn't. |
| A | keinen | keins | keine | Haben Sie einen Wagen? – Nein, ich habe **keinen**. Have you got a car? – No, I haven't. Haben Sie ein Haus? – Nein, ich habe **keins**. Have you got a house? – No, I haven't. Haben Sie eine Garage? – Nein, ich habe **keine**. Have you got a garage? – No, I haven't. |
| D | keinem | keinem | keiner | Was sagt ihr zu unseren Vorschlägen? – Wir sind mit **keinem** einverstanden. What do you say to our suggestions? – We don't agree to any of them. Wie sind die neuen Geräte? – Wir sind mit **keinem** besonders zufrieden. What are the new gadgets like? – We're not very satisfied with any of them. |

| | Masc. | Neut. | Fem. | |
|---|---|---|---|---|
| G | – | – | – | Kennen Sie die neuen Mitarbeiterinnen? – Nein, ich habe mit **keiner** bisher gesprochen.<br>Do you know the new colleagues? – No, I haven't spoken to any of them yet. |

**350 Plural**

| | | | | |
|---|---|---|---|---|
| N | | keine | | Sind da noch Zigaretten? – Nein, da sind **keine** mehr.<br>Are there any cigarettes left? – No, there aren't. |
| A | | keine | | Haben Sie noch Karten bekommen? – Nein, ich habe **keine** mehr bekommen.<br>Did you get any tickets? – No, there weren't any left. |

*Einer/keiner* refers to a previously mentioned noun with an indefinite article.

| | |
|---|---|
| Ist Thomas **ein moderner Mann?** | Is Thomas a modern man? |
| – Ja, ich glaube er ist **einer**. | – Yes, I think he is. |
| – Nein, ich glaube er ist **keiner**. | – No, I don't think so. |

Cf. indefinite article, p. 119 ff.

## c. einig- (II, 20)[1]

**351 einige (pl.)**

| | | |
|---|---|---|
| N | einige | **Einige** Politiker schlugen vor, das Ladenschlußgesetz zu ändern.<br>Some politicians suggested changing the closing-time law. |
| A | einige | Hören Sie **einige** Ausschnitte aus dem Programm.<br>Listen to some extracts from the programme. |
| D | einigen | In **einigen** Ländern ist das Rauchen in öffentlichen Verkehrsmitteln verboten.<br>In some countries smoking is prohibited in public transport. |
| G | einiger | Nach Auffassung **einiger** Politiker sollte das Ladenschlußgesetz geändert werden.<br>In the opinion of some politicians the closing-time law should be changed. |

In some set phrases *einig-* appears in the singular. It then means about the same as *geraum-*.

| | |
|---|---|
| Er hat schon **vor einiger Zeit** sein Examen gemacht.<br>(= Er hat schon **vor geraumer Zeit** . . . = Er hat schon vor längerer Zeit . . .) | He took his exams some time ago. |
| Er befand sich **in einiger Entfernung** von der Unfallstelle. | He was some distance from the site of the accident. |

**352 einiges (sing.)**

| | | |
|---|---|---|
| N | einiges | **Einiges** hat uns an dem Stück nicht gefallen.<br>There were some things about the play we didn't like. |
| A | einiges | Ich habe Ihnen **einiges** mitzuteilen.<br>I have one or two things to tell you. |
| D | einigem | Mit **einigem** bin ich nicht einverstanden.<br>There are some things I don't agree to. |
| G | – | |

---

[1] *Einzeln-* (II, 15) and *mehrer-* (II, 17) follow the same pattern.

**353**  **d. einzeln-** (II, 15), see *einig-*, p. 205.

**e. etwas; nichts**

**354**  (1) *Etwas* and *nichts* are always in the singular and cannot be declined.

| | |
|---|---|
| **Etwas** ist nicht berücksichtigt worden, nämlich . . . | One thing has not been considered, and that is . . . |
| Ihm ist **nichts** passiert. | Nothing happened to him. |
| Wir haben **etwas** gefunden. | We have found something. |
| Hast du schon **etwas** gegessen? | Have you had anything to eat? |
| Wir haben noch **nichts** gegessen. | We haven't had anything to eat yet. |
| Er hat **nichts** zugegeben. | He admitted nothing. |

**355**  (2) The short form of *etwas* is *was*.

| | |
|---|---|
| Ist euch **was** (davon) bekannt? | Do you know anything (about it)? |
| Da ist **was** passiert. | Something happened there. |

**356**  (3) If *etwas* or *nichts* is followed by an adjective, the adjective is declined and capitalized.

| | |
|---|---|
| Gibt's **(et)was Neues**? – Nein, **nichts Besonderes**. | Is there any news? – No, nothing special. |

**357**  (4) *Etwas* and *nichts* can have a dependent infinitive.

| | |
|---|---|
| Gibt es hier **(et)was zu lesen**? | Is there anything to read here? |
| Haben Sie **nichts zu schreiben**? | Have you nothing to write? |

**358**  (5) Examples of *etwas* used in conjunction with a noun or adjective:

| | |
|---|---|
| Haben Sie **etwas Zeit**? (= Haben Sie noch ein bißchen Zeit?) | Do you have a little time? |
| Ist noch **etwas Brot** da? | Is there a little bread left? |

206

| | |
|---|---|
| Das Haus müßte **etwas größer** sein. | The house should be a little larger. |
| Das Kleid ist **etwas zu lang**. | The dress is a bit too long. |

## f. irgendwer (III, 7)

**59** (1) Words combined with *irgend-* acquire a vague, indefinite sense. (For declension of *wer*, see p. 184 ff.)

| | |
|---|---|
| **Irgendwer** hat nach dir gefragt. (i. e. Jemand hat nach dir gefragt, aber ich weiß nicht wer.) | Someone was asking about you (but I don't know who). |
| **Irgendwen** wirst du schon treffen. | You'll meet somebody, don't worry. |

*Irgend jemand* (for declension of *jemand* see p. 209) and *irgendwer* have the same meaning.

| | |
|---|---|
| **Irgend jemand** (= **Irgendwer**) hat gesagt, daß Herr Baumann erst morgen kommt. | Somebody said Mr Baumann wasn't coming till tomorrow. |

**60** (2) Other combinations with *irgend-* (cf. also *irgendwann, -wo, -woher, -wohin*):

| | |
|---|---|
| **Irgend etwas** ist hier los. (short form: **irgendwas**) | Something is going on here. |
| Woher wissen Sie das? – Das hat mir **irgendein** Bekannter erzählt. | How do you know that? Some acquaintance or other told me. |
| **Irgendeiner** hat mir das erzählt. | Someone or other told me that. |
| **Irgendwelche** Leute sind immer dagegen. | Some people are always against it. |

**361 g. jed-** (II, 3)

| | Masc. | Neut. | Fem. | |
|---|---|---|---|---|
| N | jeder | jedes | jede | **Jeder** Einkauf kostet viel Zeit. <br> Every purchase takes a lot of time. <br> **Jedes** Projekt kostet drei Millionen. <br> Each project costs three million. <br> **Jede** Fahrt in die Innenstadt dauert zwei Stunden. <br> Every trip into town takes 2 hours. |
| A | jeden | jedes | jede | Er geht **jeden** Abend schwimmen. <br> He goes swimming every evening. <br> **Jedes** Wochenende fährt er weg. <br> He goes away every weekend. <br> Er muß **jede** Minute kommen. <br> He should be here any minute now. |
| D | jedem | jedem | jeder | Sie soll sich in **jedem** Fall um die Stelle bewerben. <br> She should in any case apply for the position. <br> Sein Sohn hat in **jedem** Fach gute Noten. <br> His son got good marks in every subject. <br> Er beschäftigt sich mit Musik in **jeder** freien Minute. <br> He devotes every spare moment to music. |
| G | jedes | jedes | jeder | Das Recht **jedes** Menschen auf Freizeit. <br> Everyone's right to leisure time. |

| Masc. | Neut. | Fem. | |
|-------|-------|------|---|
| | | | Die Pflicht **jedes** Kindes, im Haushalt zu helfen.<br>Every child's duty to help with the housework.<br>Die Auswirkung **jeder** Arbeitszeitverkürzung ist zu überprüfen.<br>The effect must be investigated of every reduction in working time. |

*Jed-* has no plural.
*Einzel-* is used to emphasize *jed-* (III, 8).

| | |
|---|---|
| **Jedem einzelnen** Bürger sollte man einen interessanten Arbeitsplatz schaffen. | Every single citizen should be provided with an interesting job. |
| **Jeder einzelne** ist verantwortlich. | Every single person is responsible. |

## 362  h. jemand/niemand (I, 8)

| N | jemand | **Jemand** wollte dich sprechen.<br>Someone wanted to speak to you. |
|---|--------|---|
| A | jemand(en)[1] | Kennen Sie **jemand**, der sich für dieses Buch interessiert?<br>Do you know anyone who is interested in this book? |
| D | jemand(em)[1] | Er ist mit **jemand** in der Stadt verabredet.<br>He has an appointment with someone in town. |
| G | jemandes | Kann es in **jemandes** Interesse liegen, daß er den Betrieb verläßt?<br>Can it be in anyone's interest that he leaves the firm? |

---

[1] In the accusative and dative the endings are often dropped.

*Niemand* is declined like *jemand*.

| | |
|---|---|
| Ich habe angerufen, aber es ist **niemand** zu Hause. | I rang up but there's nobody at home. |
| Ist morgen **jemand** im Büro? – Nein, morgen ist **niemand** da. | Will there be anyone in the office tomorrow? – No, nobody will be there tomorrow. |

**363   i. man** (I, 6; III, 5)

| Nom. | man | Wie kommt **man** zum Bahnhof, bitte?<br>How do you get to the station, please? |
|---|---|---|
| Acc. | einen | So enttäuscht **einen** das Leben.<br>That's how life can disappoint one. |
| Dat. | einem | Jeden Abend Besuch, das wird **einem** bald zuviel.<br>Visitors every evening – that soon gets too much (for one). |
| Gen. | – | |

*Man* is a common pronoun (the German equivalent to the French *on*), rendering *one, people, you, they* etc. according to context. It frequently replaces the passive (see p. 48).

*Man* has this form only in the nominative; in the accusative and dative, the forms of *ein-* are used (cf. p. 201 ff.). The possessive adjective corresponding to *man* is *sein*, the reflexive pronoun is *sich*.

| | |
|---|---|
| **Man** sollte mehr Sport treiben.<br>**Man** tut eben **sein** Bestes. | We should go in more for sport.<br>One does one's best, after all. |

**364   j. manch-** (III, 6, 15)

| | |
|---|---|
| **Manche** Fabrik wird in wenigen Jahren vollautomatisiert sein. | Some factories will be fully automated in a few years. |
| **Manchen** Menschen gefallen die modernen Hochhäuser nicht. | Some people don't like the modern skyscrapers. |

210

| Mancher wäre froh, wenn er sich das leisten könnte. | Many a man would be happy if he could afford that. |
|---|---|
| Was sich **manche** so vorstellen! | What ideas some people get! |

Before the indefinite article, *manch-* has no ending (III, 15).

| **Manch einer** (= **Mancher**) wäre froh, wenn er noch einmal zur Schule gehen dürfte. | Many a person would be glad if he were able to go back to school again. |
|---|---|
| **Manch einen** hat das Geld schon unglücklich gemacht. | Many a man has been made unhappy by money. |

**365   k. mehrer-** (II, 17) (see *einig-*, p. 205)

**l. viel-; wenig-**

**366   Plural**

| N | viele | **Viele** Studenten müssen nebenbei arbeiten.<br>Many students have to take a job on the side. |
|---|---|---|
| A | viele | Es gibt **viele** Gründe, weshalb wir gegen das Gesetz sind.<br>There are many reasons why we are against the law. |
| D | vielen | Er hat schon **vielen** Menschen geholfen.<br>He has already helped many people. |
| G | vieler | Nach Meinung **vieler** Kritiker müßten in modernen Siedlungen mehr Spielplätze gebaut werden.<br>In the opinion of many critics, more playgrounds should be built into modern housing estates. |

**367   (1)** *Wenig-* is declined like *viel-*.

| Es haben sich nur **wenige** Interessenten gemeldet. | Only a few people wrote expressing interest. |
|---|---|
| Wir haben nur **wenige** Bekannte in dieser Stadt. | We have only got a few friends in this town. |

**368** (2) In the plural, *viel-* and *wenig-* are declined like adjectives. See also the forms in conjunction with the definite article.

| | |
|---|---|
| Was wollen **die vielen Leute** hier? | What are all these people doing here? |
| **Die wenigen Parties**, die wir bisher gegeben haben . . . | The few parties we have given up to now . . . |

**369 Singular**

| N | viel | Es wurde **viel** Geld investiert.<br>A lot of money was invested. |
|---|---|---|
| A | viel | Ich wünsche Ihnen **viel** Glück.<br>I wish you every happiness. |
| D | viel | Sie kam mit **viel** Gepäck.<br>She came with a lot of luggage. |
| G | – | |

**370** (1) Similarly *wenig*:

| | |
|---|---|
| Er hat nur **wenig** Geld zur Verfügung. | He only has a little money available. |
| Sie kam mit **wenig** Gepäck. | She came with little luggage. |

**371** (2) *Viel-* and *wenig-* take no endings in the singular, except after the definite article, after a possessive or a demonstrative pronoun.

| | |
|---|---|
| **Das wenige Geld**, das uns zur Verfügung stand, haben wir schnell ausgegeben. | We soon spent the little money we had at our disposal. |
| **Die viele Zeit**, die du hast, könntest du besser nutzen. | You could put all that time you have to better use. |
| Was machst du nur mit **deiner vielen Freizeit**? | Whatever do you do with all your free time? |
| **Diese viele Arbeit** macht ihm nichts aus. | All this work doesn't bother him. |

212

**2** (3) If an adjective follows, it is declined and capitalized.

| | |
|---|---|
| Er hat **viel Interessantes** erlebt. | He has experienced many interesting things. |
| Sie hat **wenig Neues** geschrieben. | She wrote little that was new. |

**3** (4) **As a pronoun**

Singular

| N | vieles | Hier hat sich **vieles** in den letzten Jahren geändert. |
|---|---|---|
| | | A lot has changed here in the last few years. |
| A | vieles | Wie fandest du den Vortrag? – Ich habe **vieles** leider nicht verstanden. |
| | | What did you think of the lecture? – I'm afraid there was a lot I didn't understand. |
| D | vielem | Wir sind mit **vielem** unzufrieden. |
| | | There's a lot we're not satisfied with. |
| G | – | |

# The Prepositions

German prepositions present the English-speaking student with two main problems. The first is the correct choice of preposition, particularly after verbs (see p. 87 ff.). The second difficulty is the correct case to use with that preposition.

There are five groups of prepositions in German:

**374** (1) prepositions that always take the accusative,

| | |
|---|---|
| Dieses Buch ist **für meinen Bruder**. | This book is for my brother. |

**375** (2) prepositions that always take the dative,

| | |
|---|---|
| Hol bitte das Bier **aus dem Kühlschrank**. | Please get the beer from the fridge. |

**376** (3) prepositions that always take the genitive,

| | |
|---|---|
| **Während der Ferien** regnete es pausenlos. | During the holidays it rained non-stop. |

**377** (4) prepositions that take either the accusative or the dative. The accusative appears in phrases denoting motion towards something (question: *wohin?*), otherwise (question: *wo?*) the dative is used.

| | |
|---|---|
| Lege das Bier bitte **in den Kühlschrank**. (Question: *wohin?* = accusative) | Please put the beer in the fridge. |
| Der Kühlschrank steht **in der Küche**. (Question: *wo?* = dative) | The fridge is in the kitchen. |

(5) prepositions that are used without an article.

> **Ab sofort** rauche ich nicht mehr.
>
> From now on I'm not going to smoke any more.
>
> Sie arbeitet **als Lehrerin**.
>
> She is working as a teacher.

## 1. Prepositions taking the accusative

**379**  **bis** (I, 18)
(see also *von . . . bis*, p. 220)

---

(1) Question: *bis wohin?*

Wir fahren morgen **bis Hamburg** und übermorgen dann weiter nach Dänemark.

Tomorrow we are driving as far as Hamburg, and then the next day we're going on to Denmark.

Der Zug fährt **bis Freiburg** (und nicht weiter).

The train goes to Freiburg (and no further).

(2) Question: *bis wann?*

Wir können den Wagen **bis morgen** reparieren.

We can repair the car by tomorrow.

Man sollte am Freitag **bis 21 Uhr** einkaufen können.

On Friday one should be able to shop till 9 p. m.

(3) *Bis* is often combined with another preposition.

**Bis zum Bodensee** werdet ihr zwei bis drei Stunden brauchen.

To reach Lake Constance you'll need two to three hours.

**Bis vor kurzer Zeit** hatte er noch keinen Führerschein.

Until just recently he still didn't have a driving licence.

Sie haben **bis in die Nacht** diskutiert.

They discussed right into the night.

Der Schaden wird **bis zu 2000 Mark** ausmachen.

The damage will amount to 2000 marks.

---

**380 durch** (I, 17)

| | |
|---|---|
| Die beiden sind **durch ganz Europa** gefahren. | The two of them drove through the whole of Europe. |
| Nehmen Sie den kürzesten Weg direkt **durch die Innenstadt**. | Take the shortest way straight through the centre of town. |

**381 für** (I, 4; III, 10)

Question: *für wen?*

| | |
|---|---|
| Dieses Geschenk ist **für meinen Bruder**. | This present is for my brother. |

Question: *für wie lange? für wann?*

| | |
|---|---|
| Er ist **für einen Tag** nach Aachen gefahren. | He has gone to Aachen for one day. |
| Sie hat **für eine Woche** Urlaub genommen. | She took leave for one week. |
| Brauchen wir noch Wein **für heute abend**? | Do we need any more wine for this evening? |

**382 gegen** (I, 13)

Question: *wogegen? gegen wen?*

| | |
|---|---|
| Der Wagen ist **gegen einen Baum** gefahren. | The car hit a tree. |
| Heute spielt Bayern München **gegen Schalke 04.** | Today Bayern München is playing Schalke 04. |

Question: *wann?*

| | |
|---|---|
| Wir kommen **gegen drei Uhr**. (= ungefähr um drei Uhr) | We're coming around three o'clock. |
| **Gegen Ende des Jahres** wird die neue Straße fertig sein. (= ungefähr Ende des Jahres) | The new street will be finished about the end of the year. |

216

**83**  ohne (II, 16) (opposite: see *mit*)

| | |
|---|---|
| In vielen Neubausiedlungen kann man **ohne Auto** nicht mehr einkaufen. | In many new housing areas you can't go shopping without a car. |
| Ist sie **ohne ihren Freund** gekommen? | Did she come without her boyfriend? |

**84**  um (I, 5)

(1) Question: *wo? worum?*

| | |
|---|---|
| **Um seinen Garten** hat er eine Hecke gepflanzt. | He planted a hedge round his garden. |
| Das Raumschiff kreist seit drei Tagen **um die Erde**. | The spaceship has been circling the earth for three days. |

(2) Question: *wann?*

| | |
|---|---|
| Wir sind **um 7 Uhr** vor dem Kino verabredet. | We are to meet at 7 o'clock in front of the cinema. |
| Diese Gebäude wurden **um 1900** gebaut. (= etwa, ungefähr 1900) | These buildings were built around 1900. |

But for the question: *wie spät ist es?*

| | |
|---|---|
| Es ist **sieben Uhr**. | It's seven o'clock. |

**2. Prepositions taking the dative**

**85**  aus (I, 2, 11)

Question: *woher?*

| | |
|---|---|
| Kommen Sie **aus Hamburg**? | Do you come from Hamburg? |
| Hol bitte das Bier **aus dem Kühlschrank**. | Please get the beer from the fridge. |
| Ich hole jetzt das Abendessen **aus der Küche**. | I'll go and get supper from the kitchen now. |

217

**386 außer** (II, 19; III, 13)

| | |
|---|---|
| **Außer der Lehrzeit** hat sie noch in keiner Firma gearbeitet. (Nur während der Lehrzeit . . .) | Except for her apprenticeship, she has never worked in a firm. |
| Haben Sie **außer uns** noch andere Bekannte in der Stadt? (Kennen Sie noch andere Leute in der Stadt?) | Do you know anyone else in the town apart from us? |

**387 bei** (I, 13, 14; III, 13)

| | |
|---|---|
| Question: *wo? bei wem?* | |
| Hoechst liegt **bei Frankfurt**. | The Hoechst concern is near Frankfurt. |
| Es ist schon spät. Ihr könnt **bei uns** übernachten. | It's late. You can stay the night with us. |
| Die Programme können Sie **bei Frau Weber** bestellen. | You can order the programmes from Mrs Weber. |
| Bestellen Sie die Getränke **beim Ober**. | Order the drinks from the waiter. |
| Sie wohnt noch **bei ihren Eltern**. | She is still living with her parents. |

**388 gegenüber** (III, 10)

| | |
|---|---|
| (1) Question: *wo?* | |
| Die Apotheke liegt **gegenüber der Post**. | The pharmacy is opposite the post office. |
| Er saß **mir gegenüber**. | He sat opposite me. |
| (2) Question: *wem gegenüber?* | |
| Jeder Bürger hat Verpflichtungen **gegenüber dem Staat und der Gesellschaft**. | Every citizen has obligations towards the state and society. |

**89 gemäß** (II, 18)

*gemäß* can appear either before or after the noun.

| | |
|---|---|
| Gisela Schüler hat **gemäß den bestehenden Vorschriften** der Industrie- und Handelskammer die Prüfung bestanden. | Gisela Schüler has passed the examination in accordance with the existing regulations of the Chamber of Trade and Commerce. |
| Er handelte **den Vorschriften gemäß**. | He acted in accordance with the regulations. |

**90 mit** (I, 13, 15) (opposite: see *ohne*, p. 217)

| | |
|---|---|
| Question: *womit? mit wem?* | |
| Er ist **mit dem Wagen** in Urlaub gefahren. | He went on holiday by car. |
| Meine Eltern haben **mit uns** einen Ausflug an den Bodensee gemacht. | My parents went on an outing to Lake Constance with us. |

**91 nach** (I, 3, 5)

| | |
|---|---|
| (1) Question: *wohin?* | |
| Er fährt morgen **nach Hamburg**. | He's going to Hamburg tomorrow. |
| Er will im Sommer **nach Schweden**. | He wants to go to Sweden in the summer. |
| But: **in die Schweiz, in die Türkei** etc. (cf. p. 124 ff.). | |
| Ich gehe jetzt **nach Hause**. | I'm going home now. |
| (2) Question: *wann?* | |
| **Nach dem Einkaufen** gehen wir immer essen. | After shopping we always go for a meal. |
| (3) Question: *wie spät ist es?* | |
| Es ist **10 nach 7**. | It's ten past seven. |

**392  seit** (I, 9; II, 2)

| | |
|---|---|
| Seit wann studiert er in Deutschland? – Ich glaube **seit zwei Jahren**. | How long has he been studying in Germany? Two years, I believe. |
| Er ist **seit Jahren** in diesem Betrieb beschäftigt. | He has been working in this business for years. |

**393  von** (I, 14; II, 2; III, 9)

(1) Question: *von wo . . . bis wo? von wem?*

| | |
|---|---|
| **Vom Fernsehturm** hatten wir einen herrlichen Blick über die Stadt. | From the television tower we had a splendid view of the city. |
| Die Strecke der Schnellbahn reicht **von Hamburg bis München**. | The high-speed express route runs from Hamburg to Munich. |
| Holen Sie bitte die Karten **vom Reisebüro**. | Please get the tickets from the travel agent. |

(2) Question: *wann? ab wann? von wann bis wann?*

| | |
|---|---|
| Die Geschäfte sind **von 8 bis 18 Uhr** geöffnet. | The shops are open from 8 to 6. |
| **Vom 5. August ab** bin ich in Urlaub. (= Ab 5. August . . .) | I'll be on holiday from 5th August. |
| Diese Regelung gilt **vom 21. Januar 1975 an**. | This regulation will be in force from 21st January 1975. |

**394  zu** (I, 14, 18)

(1) Question: *wohin?*

| | |
|---|---|
| Wie komme ich **zum Bahnhof**, bitte? | How do I get to the station, please? |
| Ich fahre am Wochenende **zu meinen Eltern**. | I'm going to see my parents over the weekend. |

220

(2) Question: *wann?*

| | |
|---|---|
| **Zum Abendessen** bin ich wieder zurück. | I'll be back again for supper. |
| **Bis zum Ende der Woche** muß die Arbeit fertig sein. | The work must be finished by the end of the week. |
| **Zu Weihnachten (Zu Ostern)** haben wir Besuch eingeladen. | We'll be having some guests for Christmas (for Easter). |

### 3. Prepositions taking the genitive

**395**  **außerhalb** (III, 5) (opposite: see *innerhalb*)

| | |
|---|---|
| Wir wohnen **außerhalb der Stadt**. | We live outside the town. |
| Sie möchte nicht nur Hausfrau sein, sondern auch **außerhalb des Haushalts** arbeiten. | She doesn't want to be just a housewife, but also work outside the house. |

**396**  **innerhalb** (II, 6)

| | |
|---|---|
| Die Verkehrsbestimmung gilt **innerhalb des Stadtgebietes.** | The traffic regulation applies within the city area. |
| Die Rechnung ist **innerhalb von drei Wochen** zu bezahlen. | The bill is to be paid within three weeks. |

**397**  **statt** (II, 2)

| | |
|---|---|
| **Statt des Plastikbeutels** sollte man eine Tasche zum Einkaufen nehmen. | Instead of a plastic bag, one should take a shopping bag when going shopping. |
| **Statt der Arbeiter** werden bald Roboter an den Fließbändern stehen. | Soon robots will be standing at the assembly line instead of workers. |

221

**398 trotz** (III, 6)

| | |
|---|---|
| **Trotz des Regens** geht er zu Fuß zur Arbeit. (= Obwohl es regnet, . . .) | He's walking to work despite the rain. |
| Ich kaufe das Buch **trotz des hohen Preises**. (= . . ., obwohl der Preis hoch ist.) | I'll buy the book in spite of its high price. |

**399 während** (II, 18)

| | |
|---|---|
| **Während des Studiums** mußte er Geld verdienen. | He had to earn money while he studied. |
| **Während der Ferien** regnete es pausenlos. (= Die Ferien über . . .) | During the holidays it rained non-stop. |

**400 wegen** (II, 13; III, 5)

| | |
|---|---|
| **Wegen des schlechten Wetters** mußte die Kundgebung verschoben werden. | Because of the bad weather, the rally had to be postponed. |
| Er ist **wegen Geschwindigkeitsüberschreitung** vorbestraft. | He was previously ticketed for speeding. |

*Wegen* can also follow the noun, as long as this is used with an article.

| | |
|---|---|
| Sie hat **der Kinder wegen** aufgehört zu arbeiten. | She stopped working for the sake of the children. |

## 4. Prepositions taking the accusative or dative

**01  an** (I, 9, 12)

---

(1) Question: *wo?* (dat.)

**Wart ihr an der Adria**?
Sie wollten per Anhalter nach Österreich und haben **an der Autobahn** zwei Stunden warten müssen.

Were you at the Adriatic Sea?
They wanted to hitchhike to Austria and had to wait by the motorway for two hours.

(2) Question: *wohin?* (acc.)

**Wir fahren morgen an den Tegernsee.**
Hilfst du mir, die Wohnung für den Faschingsball zu dekorieren?
Du brauchst nur ein bißchen buntes Papier **an die Wände** zu hängen und ein paar Luftschlangen **an die Decke**.

We are going to the Tegernsee tomorrow.
Will you help me decorate the flat for the carnival party?
You only need hang a little coloured paper on the walls and a few paper streamers from the ceiling.

(3) Question: *wann?*

**An dem Wochenende,** wo wir einen Ausflug gemacht haben, war das Wetter überall sehr schlecht.
**Am Abend** ist er nie zu Hause.
(Cf. am Anfang, am Ende, am Wochenende, am Tage, am Morgen; but: in der Nacht)
**An Feiertagen** sind die Geschäfte geschlossen.

Sie ist **am 20. Mai** in Wolfsburg geboren.

The weather was very bad everywhere the weekend we went on our trip.

He is never at home in the evening.

On public holidays the shops are closed.

She was born in Wolfsburg on 20th May.

But when no exact date is given:

**Im Juni** dieses Jahres zogen wir nach Braunschweig um.

We moved to Brunswick in June this year.

---

**402  auf** (I, 11)

(1) Question: *wo?* (dat.)

| | |
|---|---|
| Der Wein steht **auf dem Balkon**. | The wine is on the balcony. |
| Ein Reporter interviewte die Leute **auf der Straße**. | A reporter interviewed the people on the street. |
| **Auf Landstraßen** darf man 100 Stundenkilometer fahren. | On the motorways you can often only drive 130 kilometers an hour. |

(2) Question: *wohin?* (acc.)

| | |
|---|---|
| Stell bitte den Wein **auf den Balkon**. | Please put the wine on the balcony. |
| Die Kinder rannten **auf die Straße**, ohne auf die Autos zu achten. | The children ran into the street without heeding the traffic. |

**403  hinter** (II, 4)

(1) Question: *wo?* (dat.)

| | |
|---|---|
| Die Polizeikontrolle war gleich **hinter der großen Kurve**. | The police check was just behind the big curve. |
| Das Gepäck hat **hinter dem Rücksitz** Platz. | There is room for the luggage behind the back seat. |

(2) Question: *wohin?* (acc.)

| | |
|---|---|
| Leg bitte das Gepäck **hinter den Rücksitz**. | Please put the luggage behind the back seat. |

**404  in** (I, 1, 3, 11, 16)

(1) Question: *wo?* (dat.)

| | |
|---|---|
| Was machst du so lange **in der Küche?** | What are you doing all this time in the kitchen? |
| Das Bier liegt **im Kühlschrank**. | The beer is in the fridge. |

224

| Klaus ist schon zwei Jahre **im Ausland**. | Klaus has already been abroad two years. |
|---|---|
| **In der Bundesrepublik** leben 62 Millionen Menschen. | 62 million people live in West Germany. |

**(2) Question: *wohin?* (acc.)**

| Hast du das Bier **in den Kühlschrank** gelegt? | Have you put the beer in the fridge? |
|---|---|
| Er ging **in ein Kaufhaus** und kaufte ein. | He went into a department store and did some shopping. |
| Brigitte geht bald **ins Ausland**. | Brigitte's going abroad soon. |

**(3) Question: *wann? in welcher Zeit?***

| Die Kinder fahren **im Winter** oft Ski. | The children often go skiing in winter. |
|---|---|
| **Im Jahre 1969** wurde mit der Planung der neuen Autobahn begonnen. | In 1969 planning was begun on the new motorway. |
| **In Zeiten des Wohlstands** sind Antiquitäten das große Geschäft. | In times of prosperity, antiques are the great line of business. |
| **In einer Woche** bin ich wieder zurück. | I'll be back again in a week. |
| **In 14 Tagen** beginnen die großen Ferien. | In a fortnight the summer holidays begin. |
| Diese Arbeit muß **in 3 bis 4 Tagen** geschafft werden. (= innerhalb von 3 bis 4 Tagen) | This work must be finished in 3 or 4 days. |

**405  neben** (I, 19; III, 3)

**(1) Question: *wo?* (dat.)**

| **Rechts neben dem Museum** liegt die Staatsbibliothek. | Next to the museum on the right is the state library. |
|---|---|
| Er saß direkt **neben mir**. | He sat right next to me. |

(2) Question: *wohin?* (acc.)

Er setzte sich **neben mich**.

He sat down next to me.

(3) **Neben den Ausstellungen** in Brüssel und Genf gibt es auch in Nürnberg eine Messe, auf der Erfindungen vorgestellt werden können.

Apart from the exhibitions in Brussels and Geneva, there is also a fair in Nuremberg where inventions can be presented.

**406  über** (I, 10)

(1) Question: *wo?* (dat.)

Das Restaurant auf dem Fernsehturm befindet sich 250 Meter **über der Stadt**.

The restaurant on the television tower is 250 meters above the town.

(2) Question: *wohin?* (acc.)

Die Kinder rannten **über die Straße,** ohne auf den Verkehr zu achten.

The children ran across the street without heeding the traffic.

Vom Fernsehturm hat man einen schönen Blick **über die Stadt.**

From the television tower there is a lovely view over the town.

(3) Wir fahren **über Wien** nach Jugoslawien.

We are driving to Yugoslavia via Vienna.

Sie mußte beim Arzt **über eine Stunde** warten. (= mehr als eine Stunde)

At the doctor's she had to wait for over an hour.

Seine Schulden betragen **über 5000 Mark.** (= mehr als 5000 Mark)

His debts amount to over 5000 marks.

(opposite: **unter** or **weniger als** 5000 Mark)

Im Mittelmeer kann man **das ganze Jahr über** baden. (= während des ganzen Jahres)

In the Mediterranean you can swim all the year round.

**07  unter** (I, 18)

(1) Question: *wo?* (dat.)

| | |
|---|---|
| Sie wartete **unter einem Baum**, bis der Regen aufhörte. | She waited under a tree until the rain stopped. |

(2) Question: *wohin?* (acc.)

| | |
|---|---|
| Er setzte sich **unter den Sonnenschirm**. | He sat down under the sunshade. |
| (3) Die Tagung stand **unter dem Motto** . . . | The conference had the motto . . . |
| Zuschriften **unter AZ 14** an den Weser-Kurier. | Answer Box AZ 14, Weser-Kurier. |
| Das Zimmer kostet bestimmt **unter 200 Mark**. (= weniger als 200 Mark) | The room is sure to cost less than 200 marks. |
| (opposite: **mehr als** 200 Mark) | |
| Junge Leute **unter zwanzig** sagen in dieser Zeitschrift ihre Meinung zu aktuellen Problemen. | In this magazine young people under 20 give their views on current problems. |

**08  vor** (I, 5)

(1) Question: *wo?* (dat.)

| | |
|---|---|
| Wir treffen uns **vor der Tür** des Restaurants. | We're meeting in front of the restaurant door. |

(2) Question: *wohin?* (acc.)

| | |
|---|---|
| Stell doch die Blumen **vors Fenster**. | Please put the flowers by the window. |

(3) Question: *wann?*

| | |
|---|---|
| **Vor wenigen Jahren** ist das Rauchen in der Schule erlaubt worden. | A few years ago smoking was allowed in schools. |

| | |
|---|---|
| Das Geschäft wurde **vor drei Wochen** geschlossen. (opposite: **In drei Wochen** wird das Geschäft geschlossen.) | The shop was closed three weeks ago. |
| Wir gehen noch **vor dem 20. August** in Urlaub. (opposite: Wir gehen **erst nach dem 20. August** in Urlaub.) | We're going on holiday before August 20th. |
| (4) Question: *wie spät ist es?* | |
| Es ist 20 **vor drei**. (opposite: 20 **nach drei**) | It's twenty to three. |

## 409 zwischen (II, 4)

| | |
|---|---|
| (1) Question: *wo?* (dat.) | |
| Die Polizeikontrolle war **zwischen dem Krankenhaus und der großen Kurve**. | The police check was between the hospital and the big curve. |
| (2) Question: *wohin?* (acc.) | |
| Sie setzte sich **zwischen Klaus und seinen Freund**. | She sat down between Klaus and his friend. |
| (3) Question: *wann?* | |
| Ich komme **zwischen 2 und 3 Uhr**. | I'm coming between 2 and 3 o'clock. |
| (4) Die Arbeitszeit liegt **zwischen 40 und 48 Stunden**. | Working hours amount to between 40 and 48 (per week). |
| Er verdient **zwischen 2000 und 3000 Mark**. | He earns between 2000 and 3000 marks. |
| Das Abkommen wurde **zwischen der Gewerkschaft und den Unternehmern** getroffen. | The agreement was made between the union and management. |

## 5. Prepositions used without an article

**410** **ab** (II, 2; III, 5)

---

(1) Question: *ab wann?*

**Ab sofort** rauche ich nicht mehr.

From now on I'm not going to smoke any more.

**Ab 1985** fährt die neue Fernschnellbahn.

The new super-speed railway will be running from 1985.

**Ab nächsten Monat** ist das Geschäft geschlossen.

From next month on the shop will closed.

(2) Question: *von wo ab?*

Der Zug fährt **ab Hauptbahnhof**.

The train starts at the main station.

(3) Dieser Film ist erst **ab 18 Jahre** zugelassen.

Only those over 18 are admitted to this film.

Sämtliche Pullover **ab DM 20,–**.

All pullovers from 20 marks.

---

**411** **als** (III, 17)

---

Sie arbeitet **als Lehrerin**.

She is working as a teacher.

**Als Kind** armer Eltern hatte sie keine Berufsausbildung.

As the child of poor parents, she had no vocational training.

---

# The Conjunctions

In German one must distinguish between two groups of conjunctions:

**412**  (1) *coordinating conjunctions* – these link clauses of the same rank and do not affect the structure of the sentence: *aber, bzw. (beziehungsweise), denn, oder, sondern, und.*

| | | |
|---|---|---|
| Ich arbeite in München. | | Ich **wohne** in Augsburg. |
| Ich arbeite in München, | **aber** | ich **wohne** in Augsburg. |

Connected with these are the *correlative conjunctions*; these consist of two parts, the second being necessary to complete the first, e. g. *entweder . . . oder, zwar . . . aber, nicht nur . . . sondern auch.*

| | |
|---|---|
| **Entweder** du beeilst dich, **oder** du **mußt** zu Hause bleiben. | Either you hurry up or you must stay at home. |

**413**  (2) *subordinating conjunctions* – these connect a subordinate clause with a main clause or with another subordinate clause, and in German the verb must go to the end of the clause they introduce.

| | | | |
|---|---|---|---|
| Ich bleibe zu Hause. | | Das Wetter **ist** schlecht. | |
| Ich bleibe zu Hause, | **weil** | das Wetter schlecht | **ist**. |

**414**  Note: Any subordinate clause, whether introduced by a conjunction or another type of word, takes the verb at the end and is set off by commas. There are the following types of subordinate clause:
the *relative clause,* introduced by a relative pronoun (see p. 181ff.),

| | |
|---|---|
| Die Frau, **die** ich gerade gesprochen **habe,** ist meine Nachbarin. | The woman I just spoke to is my neighbour. |
| **Wer** viel **raucht**, gefährdet seine Gesundheit. | Anyone who smokes a lot endangers his health. |

the *conjunctional clause,* introduced by a subordinating conjunction,

| Er ging spazieren. | | Der Regen **hatte** aufge-hört. | |
|---|---|---|---|
| Er ging spazieren, | **nachdem** | der Regen aufgehört | **hatte.** |
| Er hat keine Zeit zum Skilaufen. | | Er **muß** arbeiten. | |
| Er hat keine Zeit zum Skilaufen, | **weil** | er arbeiten | **muß.** |

and the *indirect question* (introduced by an interrogative pronoun, see p. 182ff., an interrogative adverb, see p. 158, or *ob.*)

| | Was **sind** seine Eltern? | |
|---|---|---|
| Ich weiß nicht, | **was** sie | **sind.** |
| | Wann **kommt** Brigitte | **an?** |
| Ich weiß nicht, | **wann** sie | **ankommt.** |
| | **Läuft** der neue Film schon? | |
| Ich weiß nicht, | **ob** er schon | **läuft.** |

Exceptions:

indirect statements without *daß* (see p. 237),

| Sie sagte, sie **wäre** gern ge-kommen. (= Sie sagte, **daß** sie gern ge-kommen **wäre.**) | She said she would like to have come. |
|---|---|

unreal clauses of comparison with *als* (see p. 235).

| Sie macht den Eindruck, **als wäre** sie krank. | She gives the impression of being sick. |
|---|---|

Note the word order when the dependent clause stands at the beginning of the sentence.

**Er ging** spazieren, nachdem der Regen aufgehört hatte.
Nachdem der Regen aufgehört hatte, **ging er** spazieren.

### 1. Coordinating (and correlative) conjunctions

**415   aber, zwar ... aber (I, 2; III, 1)**

| | |
|---|---|
| Der Ausflug war schön, **aber** anstrengend. | The outing was fun, but tiring. |
| Ich arbeite in München, **aber** ich wohne in Augsburg. | I work in Munich, but I live in Augsburg. |
| Wir hätten die Einladung gerne angenommen, **aber** wir haben leider keine Zeit. | We would have been happy to accept the invitation, but unfortunately we haven't got the time. |
| **Zwar** gefällt mir diese Musik nicht, **aber** die Platte kaufe ich doch. | I don't like this music, but I'm still buying the record. |
| Dieses Gesetz gibt es **zwar** noch nicht, **aber** es wird vorbereitet. | It's true that this law doesn't yet exist, but it's being prepared. |

**416   beziehungsweise (bzw.) (II, 21)**

| | |
|---|---|
| Sagen Sie das Herrn Baumann **bzw.** seiner Sekretärin. | Tell that to Mr Baumann or his secretary. |
| Sie müssen sich um die Stelle sofort bewerben **bzw.** anrufen und sich vorstellen. | You must apply for the post at once – or call and have an interview. |

232

**417  denn** (II, 13)

| | |
|---|---|
| Ich kann nicht länger bleiben, **denn** ich bin verabredet. (= Ich kann nicht länger bleiben, **weil** ich verabredet **bin**.) | I can't stay any longer as I've got an appointment. |
| Er hat es sehr eilig, **denn** sein Zug fährt in einer halben Stunde. (= Er hat es sehr eilig, **weil** sein Zug in einer halben Stunde **fährt**.) | He's in a tremendous hurry because his train's leaving in half an hour. |

**418  entweder . . . oder** (III, 18)

| | |
|---|---|
| **Entweder** du beeilst dich, **oder** du mußt zu Hause bleiben. | Either you hurry up or you must stay at home. |
| Die Menschen werden eines Tages vor der Wahl stehen, **entweder** sich zu vereinigen **oder** aber ihre Zivilisation wieder zu zerstören. | One day mankind will be confronted with the choice of either uniting or else destroying its civilization. |

**419  oder** (I, 13)

| | |
|---|---|
| Möchten Sie Bier **oder** Wein? | Would you like beer or wine? |
| Könnt ihr heute zu uns kommen, **oder** habt ihr etwas anderes vor? | Can you come over today or are you doing something else? |

**420  sondern** (II, 8)

| | |
|---|---|
| Er will nicht studieren, **sondern** sofort in den Beruf gehen. | He doesn't want to go to University, he wants to get a job right away. |
| Sie möchte nicht nur Hausfrau sein, **sondern** (sie) will weiter in ihrem Beruf arbeiten. | She doesn't want to be just a housewife but to go on working at her job. |

| | |
|---|---|
| Berufstätige Frauen geben ihre Kinder **nicht deshalb** in ein Heim, **weil** sie schlechte Mütter sind, **sondern weil** sie arbeiten müssen. | Women who go out to work put their children in a home, not because they are bad mothers, but because they have to work. |

Note:

| | |
|---|---|
| Meine Wohnung ist **nicht** billig, **sondern** ziemlich teuer. | My flat's not cheap, it's quite expensive. |
| Der Ausflug war schön, **aber** anstrengend. | The outing was fun, but tiring. |

**421 nicht nur . . ., sondern auch** (III, 9)

| | |
|---|---|
| Das Essen war **nicht nur** teuer, **sondern auch** noch schlecht. | The food was not only expensive, it was also bad. |
| Er hat **nicht nur** Rechte, **sondern auch** Pflichten. | He has not only rights, but obligations too. |
| **Nicht nur** die Preise sind gestiegen, **sondern auch** die Löhne sind gewachsen. | Not only have prices risen, salaries have increased too. |

**422 und** (I, 1)

| | |
|---|---|
| Er ist Student **und** arbeitet in München. | He is a student and works in Munich. |
| Er ist Journalist, **und** sie ist Lehrerin. | He is a journalist, and she is a teacher. |

## 2. Subordinating conjunctions

**423**  **als** (I, 19; II, 21)

---

*Comparisons*:

| | |
|---|---|
| Der Fernsehturm in München ist höher **als** die Frauenkirche. | The television tower in Munich is taller than the Frauenkirche. |
| Er ist zwei Jahre älter **als** sein Bruder. | He is two years older than his brother. |
| Er spricht besser deutsch, **als** ich gedacht habe. | He speaks better German than I thought. |

*Unreal comparisons*:

Note: the verb follows directly after *als*.

| | |
|---|---|
| Sie macht den Eindruck, **als wäre** sie krank. | She gives the impression of being sick. |
| Er tat so, **als wüßte** er nichts. | He pretended not to know anything. |

*Conjunction of time*:

| | |
|---|---|
| **Als** ich im Zug saß, fiel mir ein, daß ich meinen Paß vergessen hatte. | When I was sitting in the train, it occurred to me that I had forgotten my passport. |
| Er war erst 35 Jahre alt, **als** er starb. | He was only 35 years old when he died. |
| **Als** der Regen aufgehört hatte, machte er einen Spaziergang. (= **Nachdem** der Regen aufgehört hatte, machte er einen Spaziergang.) | When the rain had stopped, he went for a walk. |

Note (III, 3): *Als* is used to express the temporal meaning of *when* in the past.

| | |
|---|---|
| **Wenn** meine Frau **verreist, muß** ich den Haushalt versorgen. | When my wife goes away, I must see to the housework. |
| **Als** meine Frau **verreist war, mußte** ich den Haushalt versorgen. | When my wife was away, I had to see to the housework. |

---

## 424 als ob (III, 20)

| | |
|---|---|
| Er tat so, **als ob** er nichts wüßte. | He pretended not to know anything. |
| Sie machte den Eindruck, **als ob** sie krank wäre. | She gave the impression of being sick. |

## 425 (an)statt daß/(an)statt . . . zu

| | |
|---|---|
| **Anstatt daß** er uns half (**Anstatt** uns **zu** helfen), sah er fern. | Instead of helping us, he watched television. |
| Er fuhr zum Skifahren, **anstatt zu** arbeiten. | Instead of working, he went skiing. |

## 426 bevor (III, 12)

| | |
|---|---|
| Er hat mich angerufen, **bevor** er verreist ist. | He rang me up before he went away. |
| Sie muß eine Aufnahmeprüfung machen, **bevor** sie anfangen kann. | She must take an entrance exam before she can start. |

## 427 bis

| | |
|---|---|
| Du mußt warten, **bis** du an der Reihe bist. | You must wait your turn. |
| **Bis** du zurückkommst, bin ich fertig. | By the time you come back, I'll be finished. |

## 428 da (III, 10)

| | |
|---|---|
| **Da** es keine Studienplätze mehr gab, mußte er ein anderes Fach studieren. | Since no more students were being admitted (to the department), he had to take another subject. |
| In conversation *weil* is preferred. | |
| Warum studiert er jetzt ein anderes Fach? – **Weil** es keine Studienplätze mehr gibt. | Why is he studying another subject now? – Because no more students are being admitted. |

**129 damit** (I, 24)

| | |
|---|---|
| Ich gebe meiner Tochter Geld, **damit** sie sich ein Kleid kaufen kann. | I'm giving my daughter some money so that she can buy herself a new dress. |
| Setzen Sie sich bitte, **damit** wir anfangen können. | Please take a seat so we can start. |
| Herr Schwarz gibt seinen Beruf auf, **damit** er in die Politik gehen kann. | Mr Schwarz is giving up his job so that he can go into politics. |
| (= Herr Schwarz gibt seinen Beruf auf, **um** in die Politik **zu** gehen.) | |

**130 daß** (I, 18)

| | |
|---|---|
| Wir teilen Ihnen mit, **daß** die Miete DM 89,– monatlich beträgt. | This is to inform you that the rent is DM 89,– per month. |
| Jochen schreibt aus England, **daß** es ihm gut geht. | Jochen writes from England that he's getting on fine. |
| **Daß** er nicht besonders fleißig ist, ist bekannt. | It's well-known that he's not particularly hard-working. |
| (= Es ist bekannt, **daß** er nicht besonders fleißig ist.) | |
| Man rechnet **damit, daß** Arbeiter entlassen werden könnten. | It is expected that workers might be dismissed. |
| Wir haben uns (**darum**) bemüht, **daß** er sich bei uns wohl fühlt. | We went out of our way to make him feel at home with us. |
| Ich habe (es) gewußt, **daß** er nicht kommen würde. | I knew he wouldn't come. |

**131 ehe**

| | |
|---|---|
| **Ehe** du ins Büro fährst, bring bitte die Kinder zur Schule. | Before you go to the office, please take the children to school. |
| (= **Bevor** du ins Büro fährst, ...) | |

## 432 je ... desto (III, 5)

| | |
|---|---|
| Je größer das Haus, **desto** höher ist die Miete. | The larger the house, the higher the rent. |
| Je mehr Geld sie verdient, **desto** höher werden ihre Ansprüche. | The more money she earns, the higher her standards get. |

## 433 je nachdem (III, 12)

| | |
|---|---|
| Ich nehme die Wohnung vielleicht, **je nachdem** wie hoch die Miete ist. | I'll possibly take the flat, depending on how high the rent is. |
| **Je nachdem** wie das Wetter ist, fahren wir weg oder bleiben zu Hause. | Depending on what the weather is like, we'll either go away or stay at home. |

## 434 nachdem (II, 9)

| | |
|---|---|
| **Nachdem** alle Redner gesprochen hatten, begann die Diskussion. | When all the speakers had had their say, the discussion was thrown open to the floor. |
| **Nachdem** er gegessen hatte, ging er spazieren. | After he had eaten, he went for a walk. |

## 435 ob (I, 20)

| | |
|---|---|
| Wissen Sie, **ob** die Maschine nach Köln schon gestartet ist? | Do you know if the plane to Cologne has already taken off? |
| Er fragt, **ob** ich ihm helfen kann. | He asks if I can help him. |
| **Ob** er heute noch anruft, ist nicht sicher. | It's not certain whether he'll still phone today. |
| (= Es ist nicht sicher, **ob** er heute noch anruft.) | |

## 36 obwohl (III, 6)

| | |
|---|---|
| **Obwohl** das Spiel schon angefangen hatte, waren nur wenige Zuschauer da. | Although the game had already started, only a few spectators were there. |
| Ich erkannte ihn sofort, **obwohl** ich ihn nur einmal gesehen hatte. | I recognized him immediately, although I had only seen him once. |
| Note: | |
| **Obwohl** es regnet, geht Hans zu Fuß nach Hause. | Although it's raining, Hans is walking home. |
| = Es regnet. **Trotzdem** geht Hans zu Fuß nach Hause. | |
| =Es regnet. Hans geht **trotzdem** zu Fuß nach Hause. | |

## 37 ohne . . . zu (III, 2)

| | |
|---|---|
| Sie ging nach Hause, **ohne** ein Wort **zu** sagen. ( = Sie ging nach Hause, **ohne daß** sie ein Wort sagte.) | She went home without saying a word. |
| **Ohne zu** bezahlen, verließ er das Restaurant. | He left the restaurant without paying. |

## 38 seit(dem) (II, 13)

| | |
|---|---|
| **Seit(dem)** er in Hamburg wohnt, habe ich ihn nicht mehr gesehen. | Since he has been living in Hamburg, I haven't seen him any more. |
| Wir waren erst einmal im Theater, **seit(dem)** wir aus dem Urlaub zurückgekommen sind. | We've only been to the theatre once since we came back from our holiday. |

**439 so daß** (II, 24)

| | |
|---|---|
| Er bekam Geld, **so daß** das Projekt realisiert werden konnte. | He was given money so that the project could be carried out. |
| Er lernte die Sprache schnell, **so daß** er sich nach wenigen Wochen gut verständigen konnte. | He learnt the language fast, so he could communicate well after only a few weeks. |

*So* appears in the main clause when it refers to an adjective or adverb.

| | |
|---|---|
| Es war schon **so** spät, **daß** kein Zug mehr fuhr. | It was already so late that no more trains were running. |
| Das Orchester spielte **so** perfekt, **daß** alle begeistert waren. | The orchestra played so perfectly that everybody was enraptured. |

**440 sobald** (III, 17)

| | |
|---|---|
| **Sobald** du fertig bist, fahren wir in die Stadt. (= **Wenn** du fertig bist, fahren wir in die Stadt.) | As soon as you're ready, we'll drive to town. |
| **Sobald** er seinen neuen Posten angetreten hatte, verschaffte er seinen Mitarbeitern höhere Gehälter. (= **Nachdem** er seinen neuen Posten angetreten hatte . . .; **Als erstes, nachdem** er seinen neuen Posten angetreten hatte . . .) | As soon as he had taken over his new post, he procured higher wages for his co-workers. |

**441 solange** (III, 4)

| | |
|---|---|
| Er möchte in seinem Haus wohnen bleiben, **solange** er lebt. | He wants to go on living in his house as long as he lives. |
| **Solange** er Student ist, wird er sich keine eigene Wohnung leisten können. | As long as he's a student, he won't be able to afford a flat of his own. |

## 42 sowohl ... als auch (III, 9)

| | |
|---|---|
| Die Datenbank in Hoechst kann von allen benutzt werden, **sowohl** von Mitarbeitern **als auch** von Ärzten aus der ganzen Welt. | Hoechst's data bank can be used by everyone, both by members of their staff and by doctors from all over the world. |
| **Sowohl** in der Bundesrepublik **als auch** im Ausland besteht großes Interesse an einer Zusammenarbeit. | There is great interest in cooperation, both in the Federal Republic and abroad. |

## 43 um ... zu (II, 10)

| | |
|---|---|
| Sie trafen sich, **um zu** diskutieren. | They got together to have a discussion. |
| Sie gab ihren Beruf auf, **um** sich den Kindern **zu** widmen. | She gave up her work in order to devote herself to the children. |

## 44 während (I, 21; III, 16)

| | |
|---|---|
| **Während** er las, sah sie fern. | While he was reading, she watched television. |
| Dieser Brief ist gekommen, während du verreist warst. (= Dieser Brief kam **während** deiner Reise.) | This letter came when you were away. (= This letter came while you were on your travels.) |
| **Während** das Gesetz breite Unterstützung bei der Bevölkerung fand, stieß es bei der Opposition auf Bedenken. (= Bei der Bevölkerung fand das Gesetz breite Unterstützung, aber bei der Opposition stieß es auf Bedenken.) | Whereas the law found wide support among the people, it met with misgivings from the Opposition. |

**445  weil** (I, 9)

| | |
|---|---|
| Warum gehen sie so selten aus? – **Weil** sie sparen müssen. | Why do they go out so seldom? – Because they must save money. |
| Sie darf nicht heiraten, **weil** sie noch nicht volljährig ist. (Sie darf nicht heiraten, **da** sie noch nicht volljährig ist.) (= Sie darf nicht heiraten; **denn** sie ist noch nicht volljährig.) | She's not allowed to marry because she's not yet of age. |

**446  wenn** (I, 22; II, 8, 12)

| | |
|---|---|
| **Wenn** es regnet, bleiben wir zu Hause. (Either: Wenn es regnen sollte, bleiben wir zu Hause. Or: Immer wenn es regnet, bleiben wir zu Hause.) | If it rains, we'll stay at home. (Or: When it rains we stay at home.) |
| **Wenn** ich den ganzen Tag gearbeitet habe, bin ich müde. | When I have been working the whole day, I'm tired. |

Note: When speaking of an event in the past, use *als*.

| | |
|---|---|
| **Als** es **anfing** zu regnen, **gingen** wir nach Hause. (Preterite) | When it started to rain, we went home. |
| **Wenn** Sie sich für Fußball **interessieren, gehen** Sie doch mit uns ins Stadion. (Present) | If you're interested in soccer, come with us to the stadium. |
| **Wenn** Sie zum Flughafen **wollen**, müssen Sie jetzt ein Taxi bestellen. (Indicative) | If you want to go to the airport, you must call a taxi now. |
| **Wenn** ich Geld **hätte**, würde ich dir ein großes Geschenk machen. (Subjunctive) | If I were rich, I would buy you a big present. |

> *Wie* is used in comparisons to express similarity. Adjectives and adverbs are preceded by *so* or *ebenso*.
>
> | | |
> |---|---|
> | Er ist beschäftigt **wie** nie zuvor. | He is busy as never before. |
> | Er ist **so** alt **wie** du. | He's as old as you are. |
> | Spielt er **so** gut Klavier, **wie** er gesagt hat? | Does he play the piano as well as he said he does? |
> | Die Mode ist mir **ebenso** (= **genauso**) gleichgültig **wie** die moderne Musik. | I am just as indifferent to fashion as I am to modern music. |
> | Ich bleibe nur **so lange** im Ausland, **wie** es nötig ist. | I am only staying abroad as long as it's necessary. |
> | Eine Stadt **wie** Bremen braucht keine U-Bahn. | A town like Bremen doesn't need an underground. |
> | In einer Stadt **wie** München möchte ich auch leben. | I'd like to live in a place like Munich, too. |
>
> Note:
>
> | | |
> |---|---|
> | Ich bleibe **so** lange, **wie** es nötig ist. | I'll stay as long as necessary. |
> | Ich bleibe **nicht länger, als** nötig ist.[1] | I'll not stay any longer than necessary. |

### 3. Adverbs as coordinating conjunctions

**448** Some adverbs can function as coordinating conjunctions. They differ from other conjunctions as follows:

(1) the verb follows immediately after the conjunction (cf. main clauses like: *Heute habe ich keine Zeit.*)
(2) they can also stand in the middle of the clause.

---

[1] In colloquial language *wie* and *als* are frequently confused. One can also hear and read: *Ich bleibe so lange als nötig. Ich bleibe nicht länger wie nötig.*

| | | |
|---|---|---|
| Der Vortrag interessiert mich nicht. | | Ich **habe** keine Zeit. |
| Der Vortag interessiert mich nicht; | **außerdem** | **habe** ich keine Zeit. |
| Der Vortrag interessiert mich nicht; | | ich **habe außerdem** keine Zeit. |

## 449 also

| | |
|---|---|
| Ich möchte eine Reise machen; **also** muß ich sparen. (. . . , ich muß **also** sparen.) | I want to go on a big trip, so I must save. |

## 450 außerdem

| | |
|---|---|
| Ich gehe jetzt nach Hause. Es ist schon spät; **außerdem** darf ich nichts mehr trinken. (. . . ; ich darf **außerdem** nichts mehr trinken.) | I'm going home now. It's late, and besides that, I shouldn't drink any more. |

## 451 dadurch (II, 9)

| | |
|---|---|
| Der Skiflieger berührte mit den Händen den Boden; **dadurch** wurde sein Sprung ungültig. (. . . ; sein Sprung wurde **dadurch** ungültig.) | The skijumper touched the ground with his hands, which invalidated his leap. |

## 452 daher

| | |
|---|---|
| Er hat in Deutschland studiert; **daher** spricht er so gut Deutsch. | He studied in Germany; that's why he speaks such good German. |

## deshalb/deswegen[1] (II, 13)

| | |
|---|---|
| Sein Zug fährt in 20 Minuten; **deshalb** hat er es so eilig. (...; er hat es **deshalb** so eilig.) | His train is leaving in 20 minutes – that's why he's in such a hurry. |
| Sie war schlecht in Englisch; **deswegen** ist sie nach England gegangen. (...; sie ist **deswegen** nach England gegangen.) | She was bad at English – that's why she went to England. |

## 53 inzwischen

| | |
|---|---|
| Ich mache jetzt das Abendessen; **inzwischen** kannst du deine Mutter anrufen. (...; du kannst **inzwischen** deine Mutter anrufen.) | I'll make supper now – meanwhile you can phone your mother. |

## 54 nämlich

*nämlich* always stands in the middle of the clause.

| | |
|---|---|
| Er hatte einen Unfall; er ist **nämlich** zu schnell gefahren. | He had an accident – he was driving too fast, you see. |

## 56 sonst

| | |
|---|---|
| Wir müssen uns beeilen, **sonst** kommen wir zu spät. (...; wir kommen **sonst** zu spät.) | We must hurry, otherwise we'll be too late. |

---

[1] In colloquial language *deshalb* and *deswegen* are used indiscriminately.

Er hat schon viele Bewerbungen geschrieben; **trotzdem** hat er noch keine neue Stelle.

(. . .; er hat **trotzdem** noch keine neue Stelle.)

He has already written many applications, but he still hasn't got a new job yet.

# Appendix

## List of Strong and Irregular Verbs

| Infinitive (Present) | | Preterite | Present Perfect |
|---|---|---|---|
| abbringen von | to dissuade from | brachte . . . ab | hat abgebracht |
| abhängen von | to depend on | hing . . . ab | hat abgehangen |
| abheben | to lift, withdraw | hob . . . ab | hat abgehoben |
| abnehmen (nimmt . . . ab) | to take off | nahm . . . ab | hat abgenommen |
| abreißen | to tear off | riß . . . ab | hat abgerissen |
| abrufen | to recall | rief . . . ab | hat abgerufen |
| abspringen | to jump off | sprang . . . ab | ist abgesprungen |
| anbieten | to offer | bot . . . an | hat angeboten |
| anbringen | to fix, place | brachte . . . an | hat angebracht |
| anerkennen | to recognize | erkannte . . . an | hat anerkannt |
| anfangen (fängt . . . an) | to begin | fing . . . an | hat angefangen |
| angeben (gibt . . . an) | to give, specify | gab . . . an | hat angegeben |
| anhalten (hält . . . an) | to stop | hielt . . . an | hat angehalten |
| ankommen (auf) | to arrive, depend on | kam . . . an | ist angekommen |
| annehmen (nimmt . . . an) | to assume | nahm . . . an | hat angenommen |
| anrufen | to ring up, phone | rief . . . an | hat angerufen |
| ansehen (als) (sieht . . . an) | to look at, consider | sah . . . an | hat angesehen |
| (sich) ansehen (sieht . . . an) | to look at oneself | sah . . . an | hat angesehen |
| antreiben | to push, urge | trieb . . . an | hat angetrieben |

| Infinitive (Present) | | Preterite | Present Perfect |
|---|---|---|---|
| antreten (tritt . . . an) | to take up, begin | trat . . . an | hat angetreten |
| anwenden | to use | wandte . . . an | hat angewandt |
| anziehen | to put on | zog . . . an | hat angezogen |
| aufgeben (gibt . . . auf) | to give up | gab . . . auf | hat aufgegeben |
| aufkommen | to appear, show up | kam . . . auf | ist aufgekommen |
| aufnehmen (nimmt . . . auf) | to take a picture | nahm . . . auf | hat aufgenommen |
| aufrechterhalten (erhält . . . aufrecht) | to maintain, keep up | erhielt . . . aufrecht | hat aufrechterhalten |
| aufrufen zu | to call (s. o.) to | rief . . . auf | hat aufgerufen |
| aufschlagen (schlägt . . . auf) | to open, to hit | schlug . . . auf | ist/hat aufgeschlagen |
| aufschreiben | to write down | schrieb . . . auf | hat aufgeschrieben |
| aufstehen | to stand up | stand . . . auf | ist aufgestanden |
| aufwachsen (wächst . . . auf) | to grow up | wuchs . . . auf | ist aufgewachsen |
| ausgeben (gibt . . . aus) | to spend | gab . . . aus | hat ausgegeben |
| ausgehen | to go out | ging . . . aus | ist ausgegangen |
| sich aushelfen | to help out | halfen sich . . . aus | haben sich ausgeholfen |
| ausschließen | to rule out | schloß . . . aus | hat ausgeschlossen |
| aussehen (sieht . . . aus) | to look, appear | sah . . . aus | hat ausgesehen |
| aussprechen (spricht . . . aus) | to pronounce | sprach . . . aus | hat ausgesprochen |
| aussteigen | to get out, disembark | stieg . . . aus | ist ausgestiegen |
| ausziehen | to take off | zog . . . aus | ist/hat ausgezogen |
| bedenken | to consider | bedachte | hat bedacht |
| bedürfen (bedarf) | to need, require | bedurfte | hat bedurft |
| befehlen (befiehlt) | to order, command | befahl | hat befohlen |

| Infinitive (Present) | | Preterite | Present Perfect |
|---|---|---|---|
| beginnen | to begin | begann | hat begonnen |
| begraben (begräbt) | to bury | begrub | hat begraben |
| behalten (behält) | to keep, remember | behielt | hat behalten |
| beibehalten (behält . . . bei) | to keep, continue | behielt . . . bei | hat beibehalten |
| beitragen (zu) (trägt . . . bei) | to contribute | trug . . . bei | hat beigetragen |
| beitreten (tritt . . . bei) | to join (a club) | trat . . . bei | ist beigetreten |
| bekanntgeben (gibt . . . bekannt) | to announce | gab . . . bekannt | hat bekanntgegeben |
| bekanntwerden (wird . . . bekannt) | to become known | wurde bekannt | ist bekanntgeworden |
| bekommen | to receive | bekam | hat bekommen |
| benennen | to name, appoint | benannte | hat benannt |
| beraten (berät) | to advise | beriet | hat beraten |
| beschreiben | to describe | beschrieb | hat beschrieben |
| besitzen | to own | besaß | hat besessen |
| besprechen (bespricht) | to discuss | besprach | hat besprochen |
| bestehen (aus) | to pass (an exam), consist of | bestand | hat bestanden |
| betragen (beträgt) | to be, amount to | betrug | hat betragen |
| betreffen (betrifft) | to concern | betraf | hat betroffen |
| betreiben | to practise, pursue | betrieb | hat betrieben |
| betreten (betritt) | to step on | betrat | hat betreten |
| beweisen | to prove | bewies | hat bewiesen |
| sich bewerben (um) (bewirbt sich) | to apply (for) | bewarb sich | hat sich beworben |
| (sich) beziehen (auf) | to refer (to) | bezog | hat bezogen |
| bieten | to offer | bot | hat geboten |

249

| Infinitive (Present) | | Preterite | Present Perfect |
|---|---|---|---|
| bitten | to ask, request | bat | hat gebeten |
| bleiben | to stay | blieb | ist geblieben |
| braten (brät) | to fry, roast | briet | hat gebraten |
| (sich) brechen (bricht sich) | to break | brach (sich) | hat (sich) gebrochen |
| bringen | to bring | brachte | hat gebracht |
| | | | |
| dürfen (darf) | to be allowed | durfte | hat gedurft |
| durchlesen (liest . . . durch) | to read through | las . . . durch | hat durchgelesen |
| | | | |
| sich einfinden | to come, to appear | fand sich . . . ein | hat sich eingefunden |
| eingehen | to come in | ging . . . ein | ist eingegangen |
| einladen (lädt . . . ein) | to invite | lud . . . ein | hat eingeladen |
| einschlafen (schläft . . . ein) | to fall asleep | schlief . . . ein | ist eingeschlafen |
| einsteigen | to get in, embark | stieg . . . ein | ist eingestiegen |
| eintreten (tritt . . . ein) | to enter | trat . . . ein | ist eingetreten |
| einwenden | to object | wandte . . . ein | hat eingewandt |
| einziehen | to move in | zog . . . ein | ist eingezogen |
| empfangen (empfängt) | to receive, greet | empfing | hat empfangen |
| empfinden als | to consider | empfand | hat empfunden |
| enthalten (enthält) | to contain | enthielt | hat enthalten |
| entlassen (entläßt) | to release, dismiss | entließ | hat entlassen |
| (sich) entscheiden (für) | to decide | entschied | hat entschieden |
| sich entschließen | to decide | entschloß | hat sich entschlossen |
| entsprechen (entspricht) | to correspond to | entsprach | hat entsprochen |
| entstehen | to come about, emerge | entstand | ist entstanden |

| Infinitive (Present) | | Preterite | Present·Perfect |
|---|---|---|---|
| erfahren (erfährt) | to experience, learn | erfuhr | hat erfahren |
| erfinden | to discover | erfand | hat erfunden |
| (sich) ergeben (für) (ergibt) | to result | ergab | hat ergeben |
| erhalten (erhält) | to receive | erhielt | hat erhalten |
| erkennen | to recognize | erkannte | hat erkannt |
| erlassen (erläßt) | to issue | erließ | hat erlassen |
| erscheinen | to seem, appear | erschien | ist erschienen |
| erschrecken (erschrickt) | to frighten | erschrak | ist erschrocken |
| ertrinken | to drown | ertrank | ist ertrunken |
| erwerben (erwirbt) | to acquire | erwarb | hat erworben |
| erziehen | to educate | erzog | hat erzogen |
| essen (ißt) | to eat | aß | hat gegessen |
| | | | |
| fahren (fährt) | to drive, go, ride | fuhr | ist gefahren |
| fallen (fällt) | to fall | fiel | ist gefallen |
| fernsehen (sieht . . . fern) | to watch television | sah . . . fern | hat ferngesehen |
| feststehen | to be certain | stand . . . fest | hat festgestanden |
| finden | to find | fand | hat gefunden |
| fliegen | to fly | flog | ist geflogen |
| frieren | to freeze | fror | hat gefroren |
| | | | |
| geben (gibt) | to give | gab | hat gegeben |
| gefallen (gefällt) | to please | gefiel | hat gefallen |
| gehen | to go | ging | ist gegangen |
| gelingen | to succeed | gelang | ist gelungen |

| Infinitive (Present) | | Preterite | Present Perfect |
|---|---|---|---|
| gelten (als, für) (gilt) | to be considered, apply | galt | hat gegolten |
| genießen | to appreciate, enjoy | genoß | hat genossen |
| geraten (gerät) | to come (upon) | geriet | ist geraten |
| gewinnen | to win, gain | gewann | hat gewonnen |
| gießen | to pour | goß | hat gegossen |
| sich gleichen | to be similar | glichen sich | haben sich geglichen |
| greifen zu | to grasp, reach for | griff | hat gegriffen |
| | | | |
| hängen | to hold, consider | hielt | hat gehalten |
| halten (für) (hielt) | to hang | hing | hat gehangen |
| heben | to lift | hob | hat gehoben |
| heißen | to be named, mean | hieß | hat geheißen |
| helfen (hilft) | to help | half | hat geholfen |
| hinterlassen (hinterläßt) | to leave (behind) | hinterließ | hat hinterlassen |
| hinweisen auf | to mention, indicate | wies . . . hin | hat hingewiesen |
| | | | |
| kennen | to know | kannte | hat gekannt |
| können (kann) | to be able | konnte | hat gekonnt |
| kommen | to come | kam | ist gekommen |
| | | | |
| lassen (läßt) | to leave | ließ | hat gelassen |
| laufen (läuft) | to walk, run | lief | ist gelaufen |
| leiden (an, unter) | to suffer (from) | litt | hat gelitten |
| lesen (liest) | to read | las | hat gelesen |
| liegen | to lie | lag | hat gelegen |
| liegenlassen (läßt . . . liegen) | to leave (lying) | ließ . . . liegen | hat liegenlassen |

| Infinitive (Present) | | Preterite | Present Perfect |
|---|---|---|---|
| messen (mißt) | to measure | maß | hat gemessen |
| mißraten (mißrät) | to fail, turn out badly | mißriet | ist mißraten |
| sich mißverstehen | to misunderstand (each other) | mißverstanden sich | haben sich mißverstanden |
| mögen (mag) | to like | mochte | hat gemocht |
| müssen (muß) | to have to | mußte | hat gemußt |
| nachdenken (über) | to ponder, consider | dachte . . . nach | hat nachgedacht |
| nachsehen (sieht . . . nach) | to check, find out | sah . . . nach | hat nachgesehen |
| nehmen (nimmt) | to take | nahm | hat genommen |
| nennen | to call | nannte | hat genannt |
| pfeifen | to whistle, blow | pfiff | hat gepfiffen |
| radfahren (fährt Rad) | to (ride a) bicycle | fuhr Rad | ist radgefahren |
| raten (rät) | to advise | riet | hat geraten |
| rennen | to run | rannte | ist gerannt |
| rufen | to call | rief | hat gerufen |
| saufen (säuft) | to drink, booze | soff | hat gesoffen |
| schaffen | to create | schuf | hat geschaffen |
| scheinen | to shine, seem | schien | hat geschienen |
| schießen | to shoot | schoß | hat geschossen |
| schlafen (schläft) | to sleep | schlief | hat geschlafen |
| schließen | to close | schloß | hat geschlossen |
| schneiden | to cut | schnitt | hat geschnitten |

253

| Infinitive (Present) | | Preterite | Present Perfect |
|---|---|---|---|
| schreiben | to write | schrieb | hat geschrieben |
| schwimmen | to swim | schwamm | ist geschwommen. |
| sehen (sieht) | to see | sah | hat gesehen |
| sein (ist) | to be | war | ist gewesen |
| singen | to sing | sang | hat gesungen |
| sitzen | to sit | saß | hat gesessen |
| skifahren (fährt ... ski) | to ski | fuhr ... ski | ist skigefahren |
| spazierengehen | to take a walk, stroll | ging ... spazieren | ist spazierengegangen |
| sprechen (spricht) | to speak | sprach | hat gesprochen |
| springen | to jump | sprang | ist gesprungen |
| standhalten (hält ... stand) | to withstand | hielt ... stand | hat standgehalten |
| stattfinden | to take place | fand ... statt | hat stattgefunden |
| stehen | to stand | stand | hat gestanden |
| stehenlassen (läßt stehen) | to leave (standing) | ließ ... stehen | hat stehenlassen |
| stehlen (stiehlt) | to steal | stahl | hat gestohlen |
| steigen | to climb | stieg | ist gestiegen |
| sterben (an) (stirbt) | to die (of) | starb | ist gestorben |
| stoßen (auf) (stößt) | to bump, discover | stieß | ist gestoßen |
| streichen | to paint | strich | hat gestrichen |
| teilnehmen an (nimmt ... teil) | to participate, take part | nahm ... teil | hat teilgenommen |
| tragen (trägt) | to carry, wear | trug | hat getragen |
| treffen (trifft) | to meet | traf | hat getroffen |
| treiben | to drive, float | trieb | hat getrieben |
| treten (tritt) | to step | trat | ist getreten |

| Infinitive (Present) | | Preterite | Present Perfect |
|---|---|---|---|
| trinken | to drink | trank | hat getrunken |
| tun | to do | tat | hat getan |
| | | | |
| überfahren (überfährt) | to drive over, run over | überfuhr | hat überfahren |
| überfallen (überfällt) | to raid, attack | überfiel | hat überfallen |
| übernehmen (übernimmt) | to take over | übernahm | hat übernommen |
| sich überschlagen | | | |
|   (überschlägt sich) | to tumble, roll over | überschlug sich | hat sich überschlagen |
| überschreiten | to step over, surpass | überschritt | hat überschritten |
| übertreiben | to exaggerate | übertrieb | hat übertrieben |
| übertreffen (übertrifft) | to exceed | übertraf | hat übertroffen |
| überwiegen | to predominate | überwog | hat überwogen |
| (sich) umsehen (sieht . . . um) | to look around | sah . . . um | hat umgesehen |
| umziehen | to move | zog . . . um | ist umgezogen |
| unterbrechen (unterbricht) | to interrupt | unterbrach | hat unterbrochen |
| untergehen | to sink | ging . . . unter | ist untergegangen |
| (sich) unterhalten (über) | to talk (about) | unterhielt | hat unterhalten |
|   (unterhält) | | | |
| unterschreiben | to sign | unterschrieb | hat unterschrieben |
| sich unterziehen | to take (a test) | unterzog sich | hat sich unterzogen |
| | | | |
| verbieten | to forbid | verbot | hat verboten |
| verbinden (mit) | to connect, link | verband | hat verbunden |
| verbringen | to spend (time) | verbrachte | hat verbracht |
| verfallen (verfällt) | to disintegrate, decay | verfiel | ist verfallen |

255

| Infinitive (Present) | Preterite | Present Perfect |
|---|---|---|
| vergehen | verging | ist vergangen |
| vergessen (vergißt) | vergaß | hat vergessen |
| vergleichen (mit) | verglich | hat verglichen |
| sich verhalten (verhält sich) | verhielt sich | hat sich verhalten |
| verlassen (verläßt) | verließ | hat verlassen |
| verlieren | verlor | hat verloren |
| vermeiden | vermied | hat vermieden |
| verschieben | verschob | hat verschoben |
| verschlafen (verschläft) | verschlief | hat verschlafen |
| verschlingen | verschlang | hat verschlungen |
| verschwinden | verschwand | ist verschwunden |
| versprechen (verspricht) | versprach | hat versprochen |
| verstehen | verstand | hat verstanden ' |
| vertreten (vertritt) | vertrat | hat vertreten |
| vorbringen | brachte . . . vor | hat vorgebracht |
| vorgehen | ging . . . vor | ist vorgegangen |
| vorkommen | kam . . . vor | ist vorgekommen |
| sich vorkommen | kam sich . . . vor | ist sich vorgekommen |
| vorlesen (liest . . . vor) | las . . . vor | hat vorgelesen |
| vorschlagen (schlägt . . . vor) | schlug . . . vor | hat vorgeschlagen |
| vorschreiben | schrieb . . . vor | hat vorgeschrieben |
| | | |
| wachsen (wächst) | wuchs | ist gewachsen |
| wegwerfen (wirft . . . weg) | warf . . . weg | hat weggeworfen |
| sich wenden an | wandte sich | hat sich gewandt |

to pass
to forget
to compare (with)
to behave
to leave
to lose
to avoid
to postpone
to oversleep
to devour
to disappear
to promise
to understand
to represent
to present
to precede
to occur
to feel
to lecture
to suggest
to prescribe

to grow
to throw away
to ask, turn to

| Infinitive (Present) | | Preterite | Present Perfect |
|---|---|---|---|
| sich widersprechen (widerspricht sich) | to contradict ( o. s.) | widersprach sich | hat sich widersprochen |
| wiedererkennen | to recognize | erkannte . . . wieder | hat wiedererkannt |
| wiedergeben (gibt . . . wieder) | to reproduce | gab . . . wieder | hat wiedergegeben |
| wiegen | to weigh | wog | hat gewogen |
| wissen (weiß) | to know | wußte | hat gewußt |
| wollen (will) | to want to | wollte | hat gewollt |
| | | | |
| zulassen (läßt . . . zu) | to admit | ließ . . . zu | hat zugelassen |
| zunehmen (nimmt . . . zu) | to gain | nahm . . . zu | hat zugenommen |
| sich zurückziehen | to withdraw | zog sich zurück | hat sich zurückgezogen |
| zusammensitzen | to sit together | saß . . . zusammen | hat zusammengesessen |
| zusehen (sieht . . . zu) | to watch | sah . . . zu | hat zugesehen |
| zusprechen (spricht zu) | to award | sprach . . . zu | hat zugesprochen |
| sich zuwenden | to turn (to) | wandte sich . . . zu | hat sich zugewandt |
| zwingen | to force | zwang | hat gezwungen |

# Index

Numbers refer to pages. The strong and irregular verbs listed on pp. 247–257 are not included.

Abbreviations; A = accusative; adj. = adjective; adv. = adverb; conj. = conjugation; D = dative; decl. = declension; f. = and the following page; ff. = and the following pages; inf. = infinitive; part. = participle; perf. = perfect; pl. = plural; prep. = preposition; pres. = present; pret. = preterite; pron. = pronoun; refl. = reflexive; sing. = singular.

The swung dash (~) represents the word or part of word quoted.

261

262

# Deutsch 2000

## An Introduction to Modern Everyday German

> „In the hands of a good teacher this course could be an inspiration to many students." *Babel*

> ... *Deutsch 2000* can be thoroughly recommended for any group of adults and is well suited to the requirements of say, a further education group or an evening institute class.
> *Modern Languages in Scotland*

The aim of the three-volume basic course *Deutsch 2000* is proficiency in speaking and writing modern everyday German: the student should be able to express himself fluently in all situations of everyday life, to understand news articles and, with the aid of reference books, to start reading technical or literary texts.

The course itself is monolingual and contains no grammatical terminology. The terms most commonly used in the student's own language appear in this grammar.

Each level of the course includes, apart from the basic student's book, a full range of optional materials, such as slides, tapes, cassettes, and workbooks.

---

### Erste Unterrichtsstufe

**Lehrbuch Band 1**
168 pages, illustrated throughout with line drawings, with 8 pages of colour plates, paperback (Hueber-No. 1180)
**Lehrerheft** (32.1180)
**Glossar Deutsch-Englisch** (62.1180)
**Arbeitsbuch** (22.1180)
**Graded German Reader 1** (23.1180)
**Tests** (52.–54.1180; 31.1180)

A complete recording of the texts of the student's book:
**Tonband** (55.1180) or **Cassette** (83.1180) or **Schallplatten** (26.1180)
Slides or filmstrips reproducing the illustrations from the first eight lessons of the student's book:
**Diapositive** (51.1180) or **Filmstreifen** (57.1180)

**Sprechübungen**:

**Tonbänder** (56.1180) or **Cassetten** (84.1180)

**Textheft** (59.1180)

## Zweite Unterrichtsstufe

### Lehrbuch Band 2
168 pages, illustrated throughout with line drawings and black-and-white photos, with 8 pages of colour plates, paperback (Hueber-No. 1181)
**Lehrerheft** (32.1181)
**Glossar Deutsch-Englisch** (62.1181)
**Arbeitsbuch** (22.1181)
**Graded German Reader 2** (24.1181)

A complete recording of the texts of the student's book:
**Tonband** (55.1181) or **Cassette** (27.1181) or **Schallplatten** (26.1181)

**Sprechübungen**:

**Tonbänder** (56.1181) or **Cassetten** (84.1181)

**Textheft** (59.1181)

## Dritte Unterrichtsstufe

### Lehrbuch Band 3
144 pages, illustrated throughout with black-and-white photographs and drawings and with an 8-page supplement of colour plates, paperback (Hueber-No. 1182)
**Lehrerheft** (32.1182)
**Glossar Deutsch-Englisch** (62.1182)

A recording of all the reading and additional texts from Volume 3:
**Tonband** (55.1182) or **Cassette** (27.1182) or **Schallplatten** (26.1182)

**Musical cassette:**
Stereo cassette of selections of German music from Bach to Brahms (83.1182)